VISIONS

of

LIBERTY

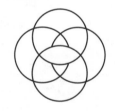

VISIONS
of
LIBERTY

Edited by // AARON ROSS POWELL & PAUL MATZKO

Copyright © 2020 by the Cato Institute.
All rights reserved.

Print ISBN: 978-1-948647-25-0
eBook ISBN: 978-1-948647-26-7

Library of Congress Cataloging-in-Publication Data available.

Cover design: Lindy Martin, Faceout Studio
Cover imagery: Shutterstock

Printed in Canada.

CATO INSTITUTE
1000 Massachusetts Avenue NW
Washington, DC 20001
www.cato.org

CONTENTS

Foreword

David Boaz

Libertarians are often criticized for their "ivory tower" mindset, spinning out abstract theories that don't account for real-world problems. It is a charge familiar to visionary thinkers from across the political spectrum.

But sometimes libertarian policy experts display the opposite tendency. They can become so immersed in the details of policy, or so focused on short-term improvements, that the inspiring vision is lost. From school choice to health savings accounts to needle exchanges, libertarian policy proposals are designed to lessen the negative effects of existing government policies. That is a valuable goal, to be sure, but it is insufficiently inspiring to people looking for a fundamental alternative to the status quo.

One of the great modern thinkers in the classical liberal/libertarian community, F. A. Hayek, warned us not to be timid about proposing sweeping change:

> Socialist thought owes its appeal to the young largely
> to its visionary character; the very courage to indulge in

Utopian thought is in this respect a source of strength to the socialists which traditional liberalism sadly lacks. . . .

We must make the building of a free society once more an intellectual adventure, a deed of courage. What we lack is a liberal Utopia, a program which seems neither a mere defense of things as they are nor a diluted kind of socialism, but a truly liberal radicalism which does not spare the susceptibilities of the mighty . . . which is not too severely practical, and which does not confine itself to what appears today as politically possible.[1]

In this book, Cato Institute policy analysts take a step back from current debates and ask instead what a full libertarian transformation of their field would accomplish. What would education, health care, or money and banking look like in a libertarian utopia?

Unlike some utopias—remember, etymologically the word means "no place"—this libertarian utopia is intended to be possible and achievable, fully in accord with the laws of physics and economics and the reality of human nature. Peace, freedom, and abundance, brought about by the rule of law, the protection of individual rights, property rights, and free markets—that utopian vision is attainable.

If I were to choose one word to underlie the following prescriptions for a libertarian utopia, it might be "separation." We've already recognized the benefits of the separation of church and state. How about the separation of education and state, family and state, money and state, art and state? Some ideologies promise to take control of state power and wield it in different ways. Libertarians propose to radically reduce, limit, and constrain state power so as to allow society to develop spontaneously.

One intellectual problem in describing a libertarian utopia is our ignorance of the future. *We don't know* what will happen when people are free to create, invent, innovate, and trade. What will the schools look like in your libertarian world? What will happen to the poor? And, always, who will build the roads? Since I'm not assigned here to describe a future policy outcome, I can just say that I don't know. I don't know what the schools will look like or if there will even be schools. No one really knows how society will evolve. Predictions about the future have often been wildly off. Bill Gates published a book in 1995 that was dismissive of this new thing called the internet. A year later, he had to publish a new edition that devoted much more attention to the web. And Google.com was registered a year after that.

It's hard to predict inventions because it's hard to predict the ways people will find to achieve their goals. One of my favorite stories about this comes from a Cato paper published in 1987 by logistics expert Robert V. Delaney. He pointed out that by 1977, a number of economists had concluded that regulation had raised trucking rates by 40 percent or more; the Congressional Budget Office estimated that deregulation would lead to annual savings of $5 billion to $8 billion. But in 1987, after about seven years of deregulation, Delaney estimated that the annual savings had been $56 billion to $90 billion. Why the huge discrepancy? Delaney found that improved trucking practices had allowed companies to make massive reductions in their logistics and inventory costs. Economists had not anticipated the efficiencies that businesses would find once reliable and inexpensive trucking existed.

This intellectual humility—libertarians' willingness to admit that they don't know exactly what will happen if their advice is implemented—has obvious political problems. People aren't keen on voting for candidates who won't promise specific results. Members of Congress hesitate to deregulate or privatize without a guarantee that no one will be unhappy. All I can say is that, when we get beyond immediate incremental reforms, my study of economics, sociology, and history convinces me that freedom works better than coercion, markets work better than monopoly, and competition works better than control. When countries stop trying to enforce a single religion, they become more peaceful and harmonious. When barriers to the legal equality of women, racial minorities, gay people, or other marginalized people are eliminated, those individuals are free to flourish in ways that benefit not only themselves but also others. When markets were liberated in northwestern Europe around 1800, we got a 30-fold increase in living standards. When Maoist communism was replaced by a partially open, market economy in China, a billion people rose out of poverty. The more freedom countries have, as measured by the Economic Freedom of the World survey and the Human Freedom Index, the more prosperous their citizens are.

The authors in this book draw on those understandings to present their visions of how a libertarian society would work in various areas. Let it open our minds to the possibilities of freedom, even as we remember that the future is unknowable and that we have many past examples of freed people creating vastly more interesting products, services, and institutions than were dreamed of before the controls were lifted.

Introduction

Aaron Ross Powell and Paul Matzko

All of us, no matter what our political affiliations, want the world to be better. We want people everywhere to be healthier, happier, safer, and more prosperous than ever before. What distinguishes libertarianism from other political perspectives is the belief that increased individual liberty—the freedom to live our lives as we want while affording others the right to do the same—is the best way to achieve that goal.

Rather than seeing the world's problems as justification for government action—as both the left and right commonly do—we see many of those problems as rooted in prior, ill-advised government action. Even well-intentioned government intervention can create a miserable downward spiral of unintended consequences, inflicting unnecessary suffering and loss on humanity. The solution to these intractable problems isn't more laws, regulations, and political programs, but fewer.

When it comes to political change, libertarians aren't content to tinker around the margins, offering policies to make the state slightly more effective or efficient. Rather, we want to see liberty given primacy in political considerations, which means doing things rather differently from what most of us are used to in the political sphere. And the most significant political changes happen when movements transform the public imagination.

Yet this view sometimes creates a problem when attempting to persuade others that libertarianism offers the best way to achieve a better world. If you listen to our Cato Institute colleagues on cable news or read their analyses on our blog or in our policy papers, you'll hear a lot of negatives. *No*, don't expand that government program. *Stop* doing this ineffective thing. *End* regulations that limit the reach of markets. *Leave people be*, both in this country and overseas. You might get the impression that libertarians are *against* a whole lot, but not actually *for* much of anything—except for liberty, of course.

But "liberty," by itself, can be rather abstract. We know what it means in our own lives: the ability to choose for ourselves, instead of having others choose for us. But what does a world where everyone has more liberty—a *lot* more liberty—look like?

Even if we're unhappy with the status quo, it's at least a known quantity. We grasp what the public school in our district looks like even if it's failing to educate our kids effectively. We know how Social Security works even if we worry about its running out of money. We have a decent sense of the kinds of things America's military does with its global presence, even if we wish the country weren't fighting so many wars. We're used to getting health insurance from our employers and are wary of changes that might mean paying more out of pocket, even if that increase were offset by a smaller deduction from our paychecks. We see the fruits of government's expansive funding of science and don't much want to rock the boat by exploring alternatives. In short, we know how things work now and fear the uncertainty of change, though we also gripe about things not being quite as good as we'd like or as good as they were in an imagined past.

Libertarians come into this conversation asking to make big changes to the way government works and to the range of things it does. Yes, we say that the institutions you are familiar with could be drastically improved if they were made to be radically different. But often we don't do a good job of describing the kind of world those changes aim toward or exactly how these libertarian alternatives would work. It will be a freer world, to be sure, but what would it look like? Is it a place where we'd want to live?

Visions of Liberty seeks to answer those questions. It's a book about libertarianism and public policy and serves as a good introduction to both. But the book aims to do more than that. We want it to leave you with a strong sense—a clear vision—of what the application of genuine libertarian policies would look like in practice. So while policy change is central to the discussions in these chapters, the goal is not just to articulate what reforms need to be made, but also to explore the kind of world we believe those changes will bring about.

All of us at Cato and at Libertarianism.org do the work we do because we know the world can be better, and we're convinced that political liberty is how we all will get there. Our hope is that by answering questions you're likely to have asked when you've heard libertarians discuss their policy ideas, *Visions of Liberty* will help you better understand why libertarians are so passionate about greater social and economic freedom. Consider what would happen if we abandoned restrictions on the flow of goods between nations? What would happen if we let people move freely across national borders to find work? How would the world change if education came from the creativity of entrepreneurs instead of the control of governments? How might technologies, freed from burdensome regulations, enable new ways of communicating or engaging in economic activity? How would the needs of the poor be met if welfare shifted from public and centralized provision to private and decentralized?

Our contributors take different approaches. Some look to the past, pointing out how things worked before government got involved. Others look forward, offering future histories that describe how things could play out if we make certain choices. But each of them shares our firm belief that when freed from the meddlesome and coercive hand of the state, people can do amazing things and that radically greater liberty will enable them to unleash their ingenuity, drive, compassion, and vision, and so create a world truly worth striving for.

Let's explore what that will look like.

1

Poverty and Welfare

Michael D. Tanner

The stereotypes of libertarian attitudes toward the poor range from indifference to outright hostility. Yet a libertarian world would offer the poor a greater opportunity to escape poverty, become self-sufficient, and attain their full potential than does our current government-run social welfare system.

A libertarian approach to fighting poverty would be very different from our current one, which primarily consists of throwing money at the problem. This year, federal, state, and local governments will spend more than $1 trillion to fund more than 100 separate anti-poverty programs.[1] In fact, since Lyndon Johnson declared war on poverty 52 years ago, anti-poverty programs have cost us more than $23 trillion.[2] That's a huge sum of money by any measure.

Although far from conclusive, the evidence suggests that this spending has successfully reduced many of the deprivations of material poverty. That shouldn't be a big surprise. As George Mason University economist Tyler Cowen notes, under most classical economic theories, "a gift of cash always makes individuals better off."[3] Regardless of how dim a view one takes of government competence in general, it would be virtually impossible for the government to spend $23 trillion without benefiting at least some poor people.

Yet it is impossible to walk through many poor neighborhoods, from inner cities to isolated rural communities, and think that our welfare system is working the way it should. These are areas where the government has spent heavily to reduce poverty. A high percentage of residents are receiving some form of government assistance. And as a result, the poor may well be better off financially than they would be in the absence of government aid. Yet no one could honestly describe those communities or the people living in them as thriving or flourishing in any sense of the word.

Perhaps *The Economist* put it best:

> If reducing poverty just amounts to ushering Americans to a somewhat less meagre existence, it may be a worthwhile endeavor but is hardly satisfying. The objective, of course, should be a system of benefits that encourages people to work their way out of penury, and an economy that does not result in so many people needing welfare in the first place. Any praise for the efficacy of safety nets must be tempered by the realization that, for one reason or another, these folks could not make it on their own.[4]

And therein lies the real failure of government anti-poverty efforts. Our efforts have been focused on the mere alleviation of poverty, making sure that the poor have food, shelter, and the like. That may be a necessary part of an anti-poverty policy, but it is far from sufficient. A truly effective anti-poverty program should seek not just to alleviate poverty's symptoms but to eradicate the disease itself. We should seek to make sure not only that people are fed and housed, but also that they are able to rise as far as their talents can take them. In a sense, we focus too much on poverty and not enough on prosperity.

Attacking the Root Causes of Poverty

A libertarian approach to poverty would instead attack the underlying causes of poverty, including structural barriers to economic success.

Consider the criminal justice system, for example. Ample evidence indicates that overcriminalization and the abuses inherent in the U.S. criminal justice system contribute significantly to poverty. As President Barack Obama's Council of Economic Advisers pointed out in 2016:

> Having a criminal record or history of incarceration is a barrier to success in the labor market, and limited employment or depressed wages can stifle an individual's ability to become self-sufficient. Beyond earnings, criminal sanctions can have negative consequences for individual health, debt, transportation, housing, and food security. Further, criminal sanctions create financial and emotional stresses that destabilize marriages and have adverse consequences for children.[5]

Harvard's William Julius Wilson—taking note of the nearly 1.5 million young African American men who have been rendered largely unmarriageable because of their involvement with the criminal justice system—has written extensively about the effect of criminal justice on nonmarital birthrates in poor communities. Conservatives are often quick to lecture poor women on the need to delay pregnancy until after marriage—and the evidence suggests that nonmarital childbearing can make it more difficult to escape poverty—but that begs the question of who poor women are supposed to marry. If large numbers of men in their communities cannot find work because of a criminal record or are simply not present because they are incarcerated, the likelihood of having children outside marriage increases dramatically.

Scholars at Villanova University found that our criminal justice policies have increased poverty by an estimated 20 percent. And another study found that a family's probability of being poor is 40 percent greater if the father is imprisoned. Given that 5 million children have an imprisoned parent, that factor is an enormous contributor to poverty in America.[6]

But a more libertarian society would end overcriminalization and dramatically reduce overincarceration. Ending the war on drugs, and legalizing other victimless activities from prostitution to gambling, would remove this enormous barrier to economic participation and self-sufficiency.

Education provides another example. Numerous studies show that educational success is a key determinant of poverty.[7] The days in which a person could drop out of school, head down to the local factory, and find a job that enabled him to support a family are long gone. Someone who drops out of school is five times more likely to be persistently in poverty before age 30 than someone who completes high school.[8]

At the same time, government-run schools are doing an increasingly poor job of educating children, especially children who grow up in poverty. Studies have consistently shown that schools attended mostly by poor children have poorer records of educational achievement than schools attended by more affluent students.[9]

Libertarian policies will break up the government education monopoly. Whether we are talking about taking incremental steps, such as charter schools, vouchers, and tuition tax credits, or more fully separating school and state, a libertarian approach to education would lead to more competition and innovation in educational alternatives and would give parents the ability to escape poorly performing schools.

Libertarian policies would also reduce the cost of living, especially for those with low incomes. For instance, trade barriers significantly raise the cost of many basic goods that make up a large portion of the poor's budget. Tariffs levied on shoes and clothing alone cost the average household in the poorest quintile $92 a year, and those with children often pay far more.[10]

Zoning and land-use policies can add as much as 40 percent to the cost of housing in some cities.[11] In neighborhoods like New York's Manhattan, the zoning tax is even higher, at 50 percent or more. And these regulations are thought to affect far more than just housing prices: geographic mobility, economic and racial integration, and economic growth are all affected negatively.

Libertarians would eliminate these costly regulations that make it difficult for the poor to afford basic goods and services.

Most important, libertarian policies would lead to more rapid economic growth and would ensure that the benefits of that growth were spread more inclusively. As President Obama once pointed out, "The free market is the greatest producer of wealth in history—it has lifted billions of people out of poverty."[12] By reducing taxes and regulations, libertarians would spur economic growth, increasing the overall wealth in society.

But to really raise the poor out of poverty, we must ensure that they can fully participate in the opportunities that a growing economy provides. Here again, libertarian policies would benefit the poor by removing barriers to economic participation. For example, an estimated 40 percent of professions in the United States currently require some form of government license to practice. That includes more than 1,100 different professions requiring a license in at least one state—from florists to funeral attendants, from tree trimmers to makeup artists.[13] Removing licensure barriers not only unlocks employment and entrepreneurial opportunities for the poor in low-skill occupations, but also lowers prices in industries such as health care where occupational licensure restricts competition.

Effective Charity

Of course, even if all the reforms discussed above were completely successful, some people would still be unable to become fully self-sufficient. A libertarian world would support a vigorous network of private charity to assist them.

Charity works where government does not for a variety of reasons. For one thing, private charities can better individualize their approach to the circumstances of the poor in ways that a government program can never do. For reasons both legal and bureaucratic, government regulations must be designed in ways that treat all similarly situated recipients alike. As a result, most government programs rely on the simple provision of cash or in-kind goods and services without any attempt to differentiate the specific needs or circumstances of individual recipients.

Do individuals have family problems or mental health issues? Do they lack job skills or have a criminal record? What prevents them from becoming self-supporting? Administrators of government programs seldom know or care. And even if they did, they must still respond with a one-size-fits-all answer.

Private charities are also much better at directing assistance to those who need it most. That ability is not just a question of efficiency, although relatively few successful charities have the burdensome bureaucratic infrastructure of government programs. Rather, private charities have the discretion necessary to focus their assistance where it will do the most good. Private charity is also more likely to target short-term emergency relief, rather than long-term support. Consequently, it can both better address a crisis and avoid problems of dependency.

To the degree that poverty results from individual choices and behavior, private charities can demand a change in behavior in exchange for aid. For example, a private charity may withhold funds if a recipient doesn't stop using alcohol or drugs, doesn't get a job, or gets pregnant. For any number of reasons, we don't want the government to adopt such paternalistic measures, but private charities have proven effective when they do so.[14]

Governments lack the knowledge of individual circumstances that would enable them to intervene in matters of individual behavior. Moreover, paternalistic interventions inevitably run headlong into divisive cultural issues. Allowing government to enforce particular points of view on such issues is questionable on ethical grounds and a certain recipe for political conflict. And charities are better at scaling up or down in response to particular needs or issues, whereas government bureaucracies inevitably seek to continue or expand their mission.

Finally, private charity builds an important bond between giver and receiver. For recipients, private charity is not an entitlement, but a gift carrying reciprocal obligations. But more important, private charity demands that donors become directly involved. It is easy to be charitable with someone else's money. As Robert Thompson of the University of Pennsylvania noted a century ago, using government money for charitable purposes is a "rough contrivance to lift from the social conscience a burden that should not be either lifted or lightened in any way."[15]

Can Charity Be Provided Voluntarily?

Americans are an amazingly generous people. In 2015, we donated $373 billion to charity. Roughly $265 billion of that, or fully 71 percent, was given by individuals (the rest came from corporations, foundations, and other organizations).[16] More than

83 percent of adult Americans make some charitable contribution each year.[17] True, a substantial portion of that giving went to entities like universities, hospitals, and the arts, rather than to direct human services to the poor. But even so, Americans voluntarily gave tens of billions of dollars to help the poor.

And it wasn't just money. We also donated more than 3.2 million hours of our time. Roughly 65 percent of Americans perform some form of volunteer work. And that doesn't include the countless hours given to help friends, family members, neighbors, and others outside the formal charity system.

Still, if we reduced or eliminated government welfare spending, would there be enough charity to meet the needs of the poor? The numbers provide a reason for concern: as much as Americans give, that amount currently falls well short of the nearly $1 trillion that federal, state, and local governments spend on anti-poverty programs.[18]

But that fact ignores evidence suggesting that, in the absence of government welfare programs, private charitable giving will almost certainly increase. Numerous studies have documented a "displacement effect," whereby government programs crowd out private giving.[19]

For example, a comparison of charitable giving across countries confirms the finding that government welfare spending reduces private charitable efforts. Among rich countries, those with lower social expenditures as a share of the economy see a higher portion of their population donate to charity. Moreover, people in countries with a smaller welfare state are also more likely to volunteer (see Figure 1.1).

Figure 1.1

Public expenditures, donations, and volunteering

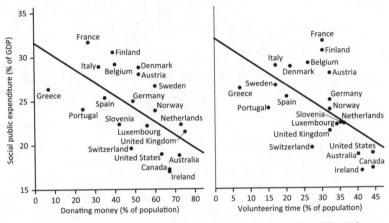

Sources: Format from Julia Bredtmann, "Does Government Spending Crowd Out Voluntary Labor and Donations?" IZA World of Labor, 2016, https://wol.iza.org/articles/does-government-spending-crowd-out-voluntary-labor-and-donations/long. Data from "CAF World Giving Index 2015," https://www.cafonline.org/docs/default-source/about-us-publications/caf_world givingindex2015_report.pdf?sfvrsn=2; and OECD Social Expenditure Database 2015, https://stats.oecd.org/Index.aspx?datasetcode=SOCX_AGG#.

History suggests that people intuitively respond to greater levels of need with higher levels of giving. Charitable giving, which had risen steadily from the end of World War II until the mid-1960s, declined dramatically in the wake of the Great Society. In the 1980s, when the rise in welfare spending began to flatten out (and, not coincidentally, the public was deluged with media stories warning of cutbacks to social welfare programs), the public responded with increased private giving.[20]

Economists Jonathan Meer, David Miller, and Elisa Wulfsberg find that levels of giving fell after the most recent recession even after considering the giver's individual economic situation. Moreover, Meer and his colleagues point out that this shift could portend a broader change in attitude toward charitable giving.[21] Of course, this effect might be a one-time response to the unusual circumstances surrounding this recession. But since charitable habits are hard to break once formed, it is something to keep an eye on.[22]

Giving and Civil Society

True charity is ennobling of everyone involved, both those who give and those who receive. A government grant is ennobling of no one. Alexis de Tocqueville recognized this point more than 150 years ago when he called for the abolition of public relief, citing the fact that private charity established a "moral tie" between giver and receiver. That tie is destroyed when the money comes from an impersonal government grant. The donors (taxpayers) resent their involuntary contribution, while the recipients feel no real gratitude for what they receive.

As a matter of policy, therefore, it would be preferable to shift as much of the burden of caring for the poor as possible to private charities. Doing so would avoid the pitfalls of coercive redistribution and the bureaucratic failures of traditional welfare.

The total dollar amount spent on charity, both private and public, is secondary to the effectiveness of each dollar spent. Well-functioning institutions of civil society like churches and other associational organizations may have significantly greater bang for their buck than government spending.

Utah provides an instructive example here. The state government spends relatively little on social welfare compared with other states, yet Utah has one of the lowest poverty rates and the highest rate of upward mobility among the states.[23] Behind Utah's success in caring for its least well off is the Church of Jesus Christ of Latter-Day Saints (LDS).

In response to the failures of New Deal relief during the Great Depression, the LDS church established a well-coordinated yet highly decentralized network for the purpose of delivering aid to LDS adherents. Heber Grant, an LDS leader, described the aim of this effort: "To set up insofar as it might be possible, a system under which the curse of idleness would be done away with, the evils of a dole abolished and independence, industry, thrift and self-respect be once more established among our people. The aim of the Church is to help the people to help themselves. Work is to be re-enthroned as the ruling principle of the lives of our Church membership."[24]

To remain in good standing within the church, Mormons must contribute at least 10 percent of their income to the church, a portion of which goes to supporting a safety net for Mormons who fall on hard times. Mormons are also strongly encouraged to volunteer and provide a "fast offering," which is the dollar equivalent of two meals per month.

And although funds and labor are no doubt important, the true strength of the Mormon safety net lies in the cultivation of deep interpersonal bonds among LDS members. For instance, the ministering program requires every Mormon to offer regular counseling and support to sometimes as many five families. Such personal connections are the greatest advantage that private charitable efforts have over those run by the state. This approach allows assistance to be tailored specifically to an individual's needs and to deliver the emotional support government welfare can't buy.

Charity premised on voluntary associations rather than government coercion has not been solely the domain of religious institutions. During the first part of the 20th century, African Americans were generally excluded from government social welfare programs. Black lodges, such as the Prince Hall Masons, and other institutions established a wide-ranging and highly successful charitable network. They built orphanages and old-age homes, provided food to the hungry and shelter to the homeless, and helped the unemployed find work. Black lodges also provided medical care, hiring physicians to treat members and their families. Known as "lodge-practice medicine," the networks were so extensive that African Americans were more likely than whites to have some form of health insurance than were whites during the early years of the 20th century.[25] (Unfortunately, those private African American charitable networks were squeezed simultaneously by racism on one side and by the growing welfare state on the other. Today, they have largely faded away.)

Emerging technologies offer additional opportunities to restore the civil society bonds that are a precondition to effective charity. In particular, blockchain technology enables individuals to give directly to the needy without relying on any third party. At its most basic, a blockchain is a decentralized platform that can be used to transfer money electronically. Because all blockchain transactions are verified on a transparent ledger via a decentralized network of computers, users can be confident that their transfers are secure. Yet the possibilities that blockchain technology creates for charitable innovation are enormous. For instance, donors may choose to write conditions to blockchain transactions to ensure that charitable funds are well spent. Such preconditions might include requiring that individuals purchase only healthy foods or attend religious services. For donors, such requirements restore the basic sense of accountability that is necessary to prompt voluntary generosity. At the same time, recipients benefit from being nudged to integrate with civil society institutions and build productive interpersonal relationships.

Of course, even with increased charitable giving, we may never completely eliminate the need for a government safety net. But we should recognize the important role that private charity fulfills, and we should lean, whenever possible, in that direction.

Freeing Charity

Libertarians would also remove government-imposed barriers to private charity. For example, Wilmington, North Carolina, passed an ordinance that prohibits sharing food on city streets and sidewalks. And Las Vegas bans "the providing of food or meals to the indigent for free or for a nominal fee" in city parks. Similarly, Orlando, Florida, prohibits sharing food with more than 25 people in city parks without a permit and limits groups to doing so twice a year. Atlanta mandates that all aid to the homeless must pass through one of eight municipally approved organizations. Baltimore requires organizations to obtain a food service license before feeding the homeless. And so on.[26]

Moreover, numerous states have prevented doctors from providing free medical care to the poor because those physicians are not licensed in the state. For example, in the aftermath of tornadoes that devastated Joplin, Missouri, the Tennessee-based organization Remote Area Medical, which provides free medical care, was blocked from providing free eyeglasses to the victims.[27] And New York State blocked Remote Area Medical from providing free health care services to the poor because the group uses mobile rather than fixed facilities.[28]

Other municipalities have used zoning ordinances to block homeless shelters. For instance, in several cities, zoning laws prohibit churches from operating homeless shelters on their property.[29]

When charities and the needs of the poor run into entrenched special interests that can use government power to achieve their desires, the charities are all too often the losers. In a more libertarian world, private charity would have much more latitude.

Less Poverty in a Libertarian World

We can expect libertarian policies to significantly reduce poverty and increase the ability of the poor to become self-sufficient, full participants in a growing economy. Even if libertarian reforms have only a small immediate effect, we should expect an altered landscape to affect future generations substantially. Thus, what would begin as a small wedge of increased self-sufficiency would steadily widen as the children of the poor have an opportunity to grow up under very different circumstances. Ideally, intergenerational mobility would also increase. The curve may start to bend today, but the biggest effect will be in the future. The number of people in need of government assistance will, it is hoped, be much smaller than it is today.

At the same time, a libertarian world would unleash the full potential of private charity. Those charitable efforts not only would be more effective, but would be focused on a much smaller population. Can we guarantee that libertarian policies will eliminate poverty? Of course not. Utopia is not an option. But we can provide for the poor effectively—more effectively than current policies. Shifting from government welfare to private action should not—and does not—mean turning our backs on the poor. It *does* mean finding a *better* way to help them.

2

Education

Neal P. McCluskey

Nothing, perhaps, captures what the basis of an education system in a free society should be better than the Declaration of Independence's explanation of what government is instituted to do: secure the rights of the people, especially to "Life, Liberty, and the Pursuit of Happiness." It should be a system grounded in free decisions about what to teach and learn, when and how to pursue education, and how to preserve and protect diverse people, ideas, and ways of life. It should, frankly, be undergirded by intentions directly opposite those explicitly offered by many who have advanced public—that is, government—schooling: to homogenize minds. Government involvement should be restricted to dealing with proven neglect of children, and education should otherwise be left to the free decisions of all involved.

Must ... Manufacture ... Citizens!

How did a country founded on the ideals enumerated in the Declaration end up with a system in which almost 90 percent of elementary and secondary students are in government schools, are taught largely state-formed curricula, and are under the overall increasing direction of the federal government? Numerous factors have been at play, but arguably the most potent has been fear: fear that some people might not be strongly attached to the state, or sufficiently moral, or economically competitive, or that they might just be too *different*. It has often been fear harbored by political elites—but sometimes by large swaths of the population—that has brought us to this very unlibertarian of places.

Some members of the Founding generation were among the earliest advocates of government-run schooling. And the fear many seemed to have was not totally irrational, though it caused them to propose schooling at odds with the liberty at the heart of their new nation. Creating a country in which the people would be sovereign was a bold leap, and many of the Founders had serious worries about letting "the people" control the levers of government. The new country was also composed of states that were often more likely to elicit popular allegiance than the federation they created. That some would want an education system geared toward enlightening the people to inoculate against bad government, and to foster attachment to the new country, was understandable.

Benjamin Rush—a signatory of the Declaration of Independence, the surgeon general of the Continental army, and a very prominent Pennsylvanian—was perhaps the most direct in stating his desire to use public schooling to manage freedom. As he wrote in his "Thoughts upon the Mode of Education Proper in a Republic," "Our schools of learning, by producing one general and uniform system of education, will render the mass of the people more homogeneous and thereby fit them more easily for uniform and peaceable government."[1] He went on, "Our country includes family, friends, and property, and should be preferred to them all. . . . Let our pupil be taught that he does not belong to himself, but that he is public property."[2]

Noah Webster—of speller and dictionary fame—called for public schooling that would inculcate attachment to the new nation, right down to teaching distinctly American—and phonetically more logical—spellings for English words: no *u* in "color" or *k* in "music." He wrote: "Americans, unshackle your minds and act like independent beings. You have been children long enough, subject to the control and subservient to the interest of a haughty parent. You have now an interest of your own to augment and defend: you have an empire to raise and support by your exertions and a national character to establish and extend by your wisdom and virtues."[3] Webster was very successful in spreading his American spellings, but not primarily through the public schooling that he desired. No, he was successful through millions of people independently buying his wildly popular spellers.

The fear of difference—especially moral difference—even more than of weak attachment to the country, fueled public schooling. Almost all well-known early advocates for public schooling emphasized a need for a virtuous citizenry in a country in which the people ruled, and such virtue was roughly defined as holding elite, broadly Protestant values. Rush, Webster, George Washington, and many others emphasized the necessity of virtue. It was also a major theme for Horace Mann, the first secretary of the Massachusetts Board of Education and the "Father of the Common School."

Mann was a member of the Boston elite who in the 1830s and 1840s became the nation's leading crusader for free, uniform, government schools. Reading his voluminous writings advocating for common schools, one clearly sees that Mann thought that far too many parents were dangerously ignorant of proper child rearing and were morally ungrounded. Some of the impetus for that thinking was the arrival of many rural New Englanders into cities as industrialization burgeoned in the region. Mann seemed to perceive them as bumpkins and critiqued everything from their plugging up what he thought were valuable drafts in children's bed chambers to their ignorance of phrenology, the belief that the bumps of one's skull revealed crucial information about one's mental condition.[4] He also saw base desires running rampant that perpetuated such evils as the lottery, which he said "cankers the morals of entire classes of the people."[5] Lotteries, he declared, "await the dawning of that general enlightenment which common schools could so rapidly give, to be banished from the country forever." (Today, of course, many states justify lotteries in part by directing some proceeds to public schools.) Mann asserted that by teaching a sort of pan-Protestant morality and overriding the foolishness of parents, the common schools would create "more far-seeing intelligence, and a purer morality, than has ever existed among communities of men."[6]

As time went on, fear of disunity and dissimilarity became even more powerful as waves of people not of the Anglo-Saxon,

Protestant mold arrived, including Germans, Irish Catholics, immigrants from eastern and southern Europe, and Mexicans and Asians. Confronted by such demographic upheaval, public schooling's reach was expanded and control increasingly centralized.

Part of that response was driven by rural sensibilities and "middle America," where the conviction developed that public schooling inculcating Christian morals and a strong attachment to the country would usher in the 1,000-year period of enlightenment that would precede the return of Christ. "Educate the rising generation mentally, morally, physically, just as it should be done," a Republican senator pronounced, "and this nation and this world would reach the millennium within one hundred years."[7]

In more urban areas, the greater impetus was fear of insular ethnic and linguistic communities running their own schools and perpetuating "un-American" ways of life, plus a powerful desire to ensure that constantly growing factories would have compliant workers. Urban elites consolidated power through increasingly large school districts, eliminating often ethnically homogenous neighborhood control and creating bureaucracies staffed by "experts" who would apply science to schooling by organizing it along industrial lines and deciding through such measures as IQ tests what students' futures would hold. It rendered schools often callous factories designed to churn out Americanized widgets. Indeed, historian David Tyack reports that urban children often preferred factory work to school. Explained one 13-year-old boy as he cried over being ordered to school, "They hits ye if yer don't learn, and they hits ye if ye whisper, and they hits ye if ye have string in your pocket, and they hits ye if yer seat squeaks, and they hits ye if ye don't stan' up in time, and they hits ye if yer late, and they hits ye if ye ferget the page."[8]

For some, the homogenizing goal of public schooling was explicit. Wrote Ellwood Cubberley—a leading Progressive Era education thinker—of non-"Anglo-Teutonic" immigrants:

> Everywhere these people tend to settle in groups of set-tlements, and to set up their national manners, customs, and observances. Our task is to break up these groups of settlements, to assimilate and amalgamate these people as a part of our American race, and to implant in their chil-dren, as far as can be done, the Anglo-Saxon conception of righteousness, law and order, and to awaken in them a reverence for our democratic institutions and for those things in our national life which we as a people hold to be of abiding worth.[9]

Today, outright assimilation goals do not weigh as heavily as they did when the modern system was cemented in the industrial era, but the goal of creating uniformity remains. Democracy and education theorists, such as University of Pennsylvania president Amy Gutmann, argue that government should control education because society as a whole—as if we all shared one mind—must be able to perpetuate itself. Similarly, enabling people to choose schools without sacrificing their tax dollars raises the specter of "Balkanization"—the splintering of the country, and presum-ably subsequent warring. As Justice John Paul Stevens wrote in his dissent in *Zelman v. Simmons-Harris*, which found school vouchers acceptable under the U.S. Constitution as long as parents freely choose:

> I have been influenced by my understanding of the impact of religious strife on the decisions of our forbears to migrate to this continent, and on the decisions of neighbors in the Balkans, Northern Ireland, and the Middle East to mistrust one another. Whenever we remove a brick from the wall that was designed to separate religion and government, we increase the risk of religious strife and weaken the foundation of our democracy.[10]

Beyond fear of difference and disunity is worry that absent public schooling, children will not be educated at all, or will be educated poorly, and the country will suffer scientifically and economically. Cubberley wrote early in the 20th century that public schooling must prepare people for their essentially preordained places in the economy. "We should give up the exceedingly democratic idea that all are equal and that our society is devoid of classes," he wrote.[11] "The employee tends to remain an employee; the wage earner tends to remain a wage earner."[12]

In the 1950s, following the psyche-shattering Soviet launch of Sputnik 1, reforming the education system was thought to be key to catching up with our archnemesis. In the 1980s, the fear of economic death from the poison of bad education was crystalized in the federal report "A Nation at Risk," which led off with: "Our Nation is at risk. Our once unchallenged preeminence in commerce, industry, science, and technological innovation is being overtaken by competitors throughout the world."[13] It then declared, "If an unfriendly foreign power had attempted to impose on America the mediocre educational performance that exists today, we might well have viewed it as an act of war." The report was seminal in doubling down on command-and-control public schooling, helping inspire the creation of the National Education Goals and eventually the federal No Child Left Behind Act, which required all states to have centralized standards, tests, and punishments for poorly performing schools. The impotence of that law then drove efforts to have Washington coerce state adoption of nationally uniform curriculum standards known as the Common Core.

The Libertarian Edu-Vision

A libertarian vision of education is not shackled by fear, not just because libertarians cherish freedom and loathe government coercion—coercion backed by a legal monopoly on force—but because of the powerful evidence that freedom *works*. It is a vision in which families and students choose education in the amounts and time frames they want, and educators freely decide what to teach, how, and for what price. It is a vision in which education isn't privileged over the countless other goods competing for our finite resources—housing, vacation, transportation, video games, the latest fashions, annual physicals, cotton candy, and on and on—and a vision in which a political majority, or powerful minority, doesn't get to tell everyone what learning they will pay for. This vision contains only one government role: to intervene if children do not receive the literacy and numeracy necessary to become free adults.

Education in a libertarian world would, for all intents and purposes, work like a free market, which is just another way of saying like a free society. Educators would establish schools—or tutoring services, or online academies, or would invent machines that instantly fill minds with knowledge—and would decide what they will teach, when, and how. They would face no government curriculum or testing mandates. They would decide whether to teach whole language or phonics, if calculus would be necessary to earn a diploma from their school, and whether history was taught from a "great man" paradigm or as endless class struggle. They could test students every day, administer only nationally standardized tests once a year, or not test at all. And they would charge on the basis of individual needs, what they think the education they are providing is worth, whether they want to be charitable, and myriad other considerations that millions of individual human beings may have. They would need little if any regulation—maybe just basic health and fire inspections for brick-and-mortar institutions—because real, immediate accountability would come through customers, using their own money or money voluntarily given to them by others, deciding whether the service being rendered was worth their hard-earned cash.

This approach would be especially empowering for those to be educated. Parents, representing the interests of their children, would choose schools on the basis of whatever criteria they deemed important, and in the order they prioritized everything encompassed in education—from the time of day school starts to whether an institution has a core curriculum covering Aesop or Zarathustra. Price would also be a consideration, and it should be: prices are how we tell how much everyone collectively values any one thing versus any other—we value a $20,000 car 200,000 times more than a 10-cent piece of candy—while also letting individuals weigh education against countless competing demands for their resources.

But wouldn't the cost be too high for many families? The average price for a private school is about $11,000 a year, which certainly feels pretty daunting.[14] But schools and charitable organizations often help people pay, and charitable giving would likely grow substantially if we didn't assign government the job of supplying "free" education.

That said, the cost of education would almost certainly drop. In the current system, the schools that the vast majority of people attend do not compete with one another on price or anything else. The closest we get is towns competing, to some extent, for residents, and schools are only part of that blunt competition, lumped in with public services, such as police and parks, on property tax bills that people have no choice but to pay. And what any district can do to differentiate itself has been severely curtailed as states and the federal government have centralized decisions over everything from academic standards to teacher qualifications.

Freely charging educators—and having families pay with their own money or money they receive voluntarily from others, be they Grandma or church parishioners—would put steady downward pressure on prices. Families would be much more directly invested in, and aware of, education costs, and providers would compete on, among other things, price. And all that pressure would catalyze something else minimized in public schooling: innovation. In the current system, the need for single schools to deal with large, highly diverse student bodies—and to comply with state and federal dictates—chokes off numerous potential avenues for specialization and innovation, innovation that could greatly reduce the cost of an education.

It is easy to imagine many cost-subduing innovations. Start with mastery versus seat time; if some students can learn to read in a few months, maybe aided by a computer, they can move on to the next thing rather than having to wait weeks or months for other students to catch up. And all students could potentially move much more quickly to completion if not locked in to schooling that must run six hours per day, 180 days a year. Schools could save money with larger class sizes but more effective teachers—maybe even teachers paid through subscriptions, who teach hundreds of thousands of kids each year, as seen in South Korean "cram schools."[15] Maybe some people would decide that art, home economics, or trigonometry are unnecessary, not to mention study hall requiring paid monitors. And those are just possibilities we can easily imagine; the really great thing about unleashing innovation is that we have a hard time foreseeing the game-changers that someone, somewhere, may just be playing with in their heads right now.

A Legitimate Government Role

Would government have any role in a libertarian edu-world? Yes, but it would be reduced to the relative size of a pin. The fundamental difference between how libertarians approach education and many other issues—drugs, employment regulations, religious rights—is that education, at least at the K–12 level, is about children, not adults. And a basic libertarian tenet is that government should not intervene in the voluntary exchanges of *adults* capable of self-government; by definition, *not* children.

Since children are not generally considered capable of self-government, someone has to act on their behalf, which could be parents, government, or both. There should be powerful resistance to government exercising any meaningful control over children, especially over what goes into their minds. Give government that authority, and it will too often lay the groundwork for those with power to indoctrinate children to perpetuate that power. Of course, parents will also try to instill their own beliefs and values, but it is far better that such decisions be decentralized so that in society a thousand flowers can bloom—liberals and conservatives, atheists and born-again Christians, Yankees and Red Sox fans—and so that when children become adults, they will have countless ways of life from which to choose.

But there's still the matter of enabling children to become self-governing adults. Here, it seems parents have a duty to supply at least basic skills so that when children become adults they are equipped to choose their own paths. We might say that children have a right to education, but the corresponding duty falls only on parents. Say that it falls on society through government, and all people are compelled to provide education to children they had no role in bringing into the world, and freedom-stifling collective decisions about what will be taught must be made. Members of society may absolutely of their own volition help educate children not their own—that is *true* community and *true* charity—but a legal obligation must not be imposed.

How would this work? Government would require all parents to get their children the basic skills they need to continue learning on their own. That means basic literacy and numeracy—the ability to read, write, and do math—which are necessary to eventually tackle history, science, art, and numerous other subjects in which most people will want to become educated. Such skills would enable students to tackle countless issues—evolution, the New Deal, sex education—that are too controversial to allow government to decide what is taught and how. It is unclear where the line of basic literacy and numeracy should be drawn—maybe an ability to read at an eighth-grade level and handle algebra—but the important thing is that government be concerned only with basic skills.

Of course, the vast majority of parents care about their children and will probably want them to learn far more than that. Indeed, human biology compels parents to care about their children.[16] They may also have the selfish motivation of wanting their children to care for them in their old age. Their kids will need the economic wherewithal, which is heavily influenced by educational attainment, to do that.

That basic literacy and numeracy would not be enforced through compelled school attendance, or by sending inspectors to all children's homes, or anything so intrusive. Instead, withholding education would be treated as any other sort of neglect. Suspicion of failure to educate would be reported to authorities—perhaps by a neighbor who asked a child to read something and found that the child could not, or by the parent of a friend—and police would investigate. If the authorities found enough evidence of neglect, they would press charges, and the accused parents, assumed innocent until proven guilty, would get their day in court. Only if they were found guilty would government intervene by requiring—and if necessary, forcibly providing—education. Of course, such a situation would almost certainly be preceded by worse neglect; parents who would totally ignore their children's education would likely be neglectful in more dangerous and earlier ways in their children's lives, such as by failing to adequately feed or clothe them.

The Evidence

Unfortunately, the entire world has adopted the same basic education structure as the United States, so finding current real-world examples of education systems that are closely akin to the libertarian vision is impossible. We can, though, see some pale shades of the vision to have some evidence that it would work. Many developed countries—for instance, Belgium, Canada, and the Netherlands—have systems that offer a lot more choice than the American education system, and they all surpassed the United States on the most recent Program for International Student Assessment scores.[17] Of course, many factors affect test scores, and different tests get different results, so take that with a grain of salt. Experts on those other systems also generally report no negative association between choice and social cohesion—the big things that early public school proponents were so worried about.[18] Indeed, the Netherlands has long had a very liberal system of choice, with almost anyone able to choose among myriad schools. And despite the high popularity of religious schools, the population has become extremely secular.

We could also look at our own higher education system to see the superiority of more freedom in education. American higher education is heavily subsidized by government, but attendance is voluntary, institutions have significant autonomy, and much of the subsidy is attached to students who freely decide which schools to attend. The result is a system offering a great variety of institutions, including community colleges, private liberal arts schools, for-profit institutions, massive public research institutions like the University of Michigan, and the Ivy League. That system promotes specialization and competition, and as a result, American institutions regularly vie with one another to attract the best scholars in the world.

Meanwhile, most countries run their higher ed systems like we provide K–12 education: schooling is largely free to the students and is provided at government institutions. As a result, American colleges regularly dominate international rankings, and the country is by far the most popular destination for students studying outside their homelands.[19] Our biggest problem is the price—sticker prices typically rise well in excess of inflation almost every year—but that problem is fueled by government, not freedom: student aid programs such as Pell Grants and federal loans enable students to pay high prices, and colleges raise their prices to bring in always-desired cash.

We can also look at some of the poorest places in the world to see the importance of people paying with their own money and of educators working for profit. Researcher James Tooley has documented widespread for-profit schooling industries in many of the poorest slums of the world, such as Hyderabad, India, and Lagos, Nigeria.[20] These schools work with the world's most destitute families and typically outperform the better-funded public schools. Why? Because their paying customers will leave if unsatisfied. In government schools, money arrives regardless of customer satisfaction.

History, too, can show us that freedom works in education. The British tradition during the time of American colonization was essentially one of no government involvement in education, and that is what Americans tended to adopt. A few colonies required parents to provide basic skills, akin to the libertarian vision. But a seemingly big break occurred in 1647, when Massachusetts passed the Old Deluder Satan Act requiring all towns of 50 to 99 families to retain someone to teach children and of 100 or more families to maintain a grammar school. The schooling, however, wasn't expected to be free, attendance wasn't compulsory, and adherence to the law eventually crumbled in Massachusetts and wasn't replicated in most other colonies.

The absence of public schooling did not appear to have a negative effect on learning, with more than 90 percent of white adults literate by 1840.[21] On the flip side, governments often prohibited African Americans from being taught to read. Public schooling's absence also did not appear to have a negative political effect. Before public schooling, the nation pronounced its independence, did so with a declaration laying out its Founding principles, won a revolution, and enacted the Constitution we still use; so much for public schooling being necessary to a free nation.

What about assimilating newcomers? Public schools often grabbed that mission, but the evidence suggests that immigrants assimilated despite the schools' often heavy-handed efforts.[22] While coercive efforts often belittled immigrants and inspired resistance, newcomers had a natural incentive to blend in with broader society, preferably without having to sacrifice aspects of their cherished identities. Life is simply more comfortable when you share things in common with greater society—maybe an interest in baseball, popular music, or hamburgers—and it is easier to advance economically if you can work with people from other communities.

The evidence is also compelling that private schools tend to be better than public schools at inculcating core civic and social values like voting or volunteering in one's community.[23] Perhaps the reason is that private schools, rather than having to offer lowest-common-denominator instruction to avoid conflict among diverse constituencies, can furnish rigorous, clear civics curricula that all involved accept because all are there voluntarily.

Of course, we have much better examples of how free markets work if we look outside education. Whether it is the constant improvement of ubiquitous consumer electronics or ridesharing services like Uber and Lyft, we can see that freedom provides the things we need and constantly improves them. Nothing is inherent in education that puts it beyond the same forces.

Skip the Vouchers—Freedom Now!

If the libertarian vision for education is so wonderful, why bother with half measures like vouchers, or tax credits for people who use private schools or who donate to groups that provide scholarships? Why not separate school and state immediately, ending compulsory attendance laws and public funding for education? Why not go right to the promised land?

First, it is going to take a while for large swaths of the public to let go of government schooling. No one alive today remembers when the norm was not compulsory education and attending public school. Many people simply assume that education equals public schooling, and the idea of choosing a school—much less having a full free market—is almost incomprehensible. And even if the concept were widely embraced, relatively few people have actual experience with choosing schools, at least other than buying a home in a "good district." A transition period—during which people change their mindsets from passive recipients of schooling to active seekers of it—is inevitable.

Second, practical matters need to be addressed. Unless a move to full freedom sends most people to online options—and even those would need some time to scale up—private schools do not have enough seats to suddenly accommodate tens of millions of new students. Many public schools would convert to private, but that too would require adapting to autonomy over curriculum, hiring, and myriad other functions. Moreover, district and state education employees would no longer be needed in the much leaner private system and would need to be transitioned out.

Conclusion

Public schooling is inconsistent with a free society. Like so much in opposition to liberty, the system is undergirded largely by fear—fear of difference, fear of economic failure. The libertarian realizes that those fears are unfounded and that only educational freedom is consistent with a harmonious, prosperous nation grounded in liberty.

3

Health Care

Michael F. Cannon

Futurists, investors, and health law programs all try to catch a glimpse of the future of health care. Lucky for you, you've got . . . me. I'm *from* the future. I've traveled back in time from the year 2050. And I am here to tell you, the future of health care reform is awesome.[1]

When I presented these observations at a Willamette University College of Law symposium in 2015,[2] I was tickled by how many people I saw using iPhones. I mean, *iPhones*! How quaint. Don't get me wrong. We have iPhones in the future. Mostly they're on display in museums as historical relics or used as a medium for artists. Hipsters—yes, we still have hipsters—wouldn't even know how to use an iPhone and will sometimes wear them as fashion accessories. Other than that, iPhones can be found propping up wobbly restaurant tables. I also noticed you're still operating general hospitals—in *2020*! Again, how quaint.[3]

Here are answers to a few questions people always ask me about the year 2050:

- Justin Bieber crashed pretty hard. He is bald, broke, overweight, and has gone home to Canada where taxpayers must now pay for his diabetes care.[4]

- Skynet is not self-aware. At least, not yet. (Fingers crossed!)[5]

- The arc of history is long, but it continues to bend toward justice, equality, freedom, peace, and progress.[6]

- Mortality from war and disease has continued the erratic but substantial long-term decline that you have already begun to see in your lifetimes.[7]

- Billions of people across the globe have been lifted out of poverty and saved from hunger and disease because we continue to find new, better, and cheaper ways of meeting basic human needs.[8]

- Finally—and I cannot overemphasize this fact—we have more excellent water slides than any other planet we communicate with.[9]

Nowhere has this progress been more astounding and rapid than in health care.

Health Care Is Easier

In the future, medicine is still complex. But health care is simpler.

Just about every health plan and provider network offers each patient a personal concierge who is equal parts counselor, clinician, and financial adviser. Your concierge helps you communicate with your medical team, helps you understand your treatment options, and even acts as a cost-sharing consultant. As a patient, you understand how much you're going to pay *before* you choose a treatment plan.

Patients can communicate with their concierges—or, if they want, with their doctors, health coaches, dieticians, geneticists, and health plans—in a variety of electronic ways. Alternatively, patients can consult diagnostic software on their own—human attention when you want it, technology when you don't.

It's easier to see the doctor, or even to get your teeth cleaned. Often, you don't have to leave home. Telemedicine is a huge part of health care delivery.[10] We keep people out of waiting rooms and hospitals thanks to a revolution that began with, of all things, a car service. I think you called its first generation "Uber."[11] If you need a doctor, even a specialist, your concierge can schedule a house call, or you can summon one yourself, at a time convenient for *you*. Your specialist not only comes prepared with your entire, accurate medical history but can perform an increasing number of diagnostic tests and even procedures in your own home.[12]

Not everyone uses a concierge or health apps or the other cool stuff that we have and you don't. Just as some people like to homeschool their kids, brew their own beer, raise their own chickens, and build their own log cabins, others still prefer the complexity of pure indemnity insurance, finding their own specialists, and researching their own treatment options. That choice is still there.

But generally speaking, grandparents frighten—okay, bore— their kids and grandkids with horror stories about when they had to carry *all* their medical records and *all* their prescriptions to *all* their doctors' offices, trying to remember *all* the often-conflicting things each doctor told them. That's what everyone expected. That was normal.

The kids and grandkids just shake their heads. They have health care providers who know their names, their needs, and their values. They have a single point of contact who coordinates all that complexity, so they can focus on what is important to them. That's the *new* normal.

Health Care Is Better

Simplifying the patient experience and coordinating care has led to greater treatment compliance, fewer medical errors, and even fewer misdiagnoses.[13]

Initially, there was a lot of resistance to letting nonphysician clinicians, assisted by diagnostic software, make diagnoses that government regulation previously allowed only physicians to make. But that resistance—which came exclusively from physician groups, which benefited financially—became farcical when the software reached the point where the nurse practitioners, physician assistants, and registered nurses started getting the diagnoses right more often (and at a lower cost) than the MDs. People with less education, aided by technology, started outperforming people with more education.[14] Health care prices plummeted, and thank God they did.

In the future, we also have more new treatments and total cures. I hate to depress you, dear readers, but some of you are going to die from diseases that no longer cause death in the future. Some of those diseases have cures. Other once-fatal illnesses are now managed as chronic conditions. Many once-difficult chronic conditions are now as easy to manage as clipping your fingernails.

Health Insurance Is Better, Especially If You're Sick

People have an easier time believing humanity mastered time travel than believing what I tell them about the future of health insurance.

So-called young invincibles voluntarily purchase health insurance in droves. We don't force them to buy it or force employers to offer it. We simply removed the barriers government had put in the way of insurers offering cash back to people who don't file claims. That made buying coverage look like a better deal to people who thought traditional health insurance was a lousy deal.[15]

Insurance against preexisting conditions is easy to obtain. It costs less than powering up your self-driving car, and a *lot* less than buying a health insurance policy. You don't even have to buy health insurance to get it. Once you buy low-cost "pre-ex" insurance, you can wait until you get sick to buy health insurance, and you will still pay the same premium as if you were healthy:

> "For these economically uncertain times, the United-Health Group has a 'first of its kind' product: the right to buy an individual health policy at some point in the future even if you become sick. . . . Those who do pass a medical review, will pay 20 percent each month of the current premium on an individual policy to reserve the right to be insured under the plan at some point in the future. . . .

But if changes to the health insurance system do occur under the Obama administration, they say, United-Health's new product may become obsolete. . . . It is initially available in 25 of the 40 states where UnitedHealth currently sells individual insurance, which do not include [states that have enacted community-rating price controls like] New York and New Jersey. The company is applying to sell it in the other 15 states, including Connecticut, where it now sells to individuals. . . . A 50-year-old male in Columbus, Ohio, who planned to eventually take an individual policy in which he would be obliged to pay the first $3,500 in medical bills would pay $32 a month for the right to eventually get that coverage—or 20 percent of a policy that now costs $159 a month."[16]

Governments used to try to achieve the same thing by imposing "community-rating" price controls on health insurance premiums. But pre-ex insurance protects patients without the problems government price controls inevitably create. Community rating creates adverse selection, which has destroyed health insurance markets.[17] Even where markets didn't collapse, community rating still drove average premiums higher and created a race to the bottom by forcing insurance companies to compete on the basis of who could provide the worst care to the sick.[18] And supporters of the Affordable Care Act called that consumer protection!

If you find pre-ex insurance hard to believe, you're going to want to sit down for this next part. *In the future, health insurance comes with a total-satisfaction guarantee.* If you don't think your health plan is managing your diabetes or cancer care well, if you think its network is too narrow, or if you are unsatisfied with your health plan for any reason, you can fire your health plan, and other health plans will *compete* to cover you, rather than avoid you.[19]

Even Death Is Better

Some things haven't changed. Mortality is still with us. We haven't cured all diseases. And when people do get a fatal disease, they can fight it to the very end. They can participate in a clinical trial to help find cures that continue to elude us. It is their choice.

What might strike you the most about dying in the future is how often it happens at home. People more often choose not to die in hospitals hooked up to multiple machines, but at home, surrounded by their families. Death, dying, and bereavement are more often an intentional process.[20]

How that happened was simple: we just ended government subsidies for heroic end-of-life measures. The government leaves that choice to the patient, without creating financial incentives to encourage patients to choose one path over another. The social and professional norms surrounding end-of-life care changed dramatically. Every health plan has a "life panel" to help patients make their choice by providing them with information about the cost-effectiveness of all their treatment options.[21]

Health Care Is More Universal

In the future, health care is more affordable for the poor, and they are getting better care.

Lower-skilled clinicians like nurse practitioners, physician assistants, registered nurses, and dental hygienists are providing an ever-increasing range of services, and at lower prices than physicians and dentists did. It is not just diagnostics. Lower-cost clinicians are writing prescriptions and performing procedures that used to be the sole province of high-cost clinicians.[22] The quality is higher, with fewer medication errors and complications.

Health care is also more universal in the future because, as I mentioned at the outset, the future has *less poverty*—in part because we stopped forcing the poor to surrender so much of their income to an unconscionably wasteful health care system.[23]

How Did It Happen?

The health care revolution occurred when we realized that whenever we tried to *legislate* better, more affordable, and more secure health care, it never happened. We could never legislate or regulate our way to higher-quality, lower-cost care. And we figured out why.

Better, more affordable health care represents a threat to the revenue streams of existing high-cost and low-quality providers. That is true whether you are trying to get them to change their business model directly[24] or trying to change legal rules to enable competitors to offer better and lower-cost services.[25] The dinosaurs *do not like it* when you disrupt their revenue streams. But imagine where humanity would be if government had made it illegal to introduce lower-cost ways of producing food unless high-cost farmers were held harmless. We'd all still be doing backbreaking physical labor on farms, if not starving. (Actually, that's not a bad analogy for health care in 2020.)

Whenever we tried to legislate our way to better health care, the dinosaurs thwarted us at every turn. The political process responds to whoever has the resources and the incentive to organize and engage in politics, especially legislative and administrative lobbying. In those contests, consumers and innovators cannot compete with incumbent providers. Those providers can therefore bend any new legislation or regulation to protect themselves from competition.[26] As a result, the political process *protects* the very providers of high-cost and low-quality care we hoped to *reform*. We realized we had to get those decisions out of the political process and reassign them to the market process, where the dinosaurs have no choice but to compete.

Another impetus to change occurred when we stopped trying to pretend health insurance is the solution to every problem. We learned that beyond a certain point, more health insurance actually makes access *worse*. A couple of decades ago, we had a president who is now hailed as our greatest health care reformer. One of her most quoted slogans was, "I would rather have $50 MRIs and no health insurance than $1,000 MRIs and universal coverage."[27] Of course, that was back when people still used MRIs.

Change was set in motion when Congress and the president repealed a law that was *supposed* to protect patients and make health care affordable.[28] That one step jettisoned the preexisting condition regulations that were preventing innovators from protecting people against preexisting conditions. It made coverage more affordable by restoring people's freedom to purchase or not purchase coverage. It led to a rethinking of the entire enterprise and a flood of reform.[29]

States began to recognize that beyond a certain point, consumer protection regulation makes health insurance and health care so expensive that it actually hurts consumers rather than helps them. So states let consumers decide where that point is by letting them choose the consumer protections offered by regulators in other states.

Around the same time we noticed that the mid-level clinicians were beating the doctors on diagnoses, we noticed that medical licensing doesn't improve quality at all.[30] On top of being just an income transfer from patients and lower-skilled clinicians (e.g., dental hygienists) to higher-skilled clinicians (e.g., dentists),[31] licensing increased prices, reduced the availability of services,[32] blocked new delivery models, and reduced quality.

What really crystallized the licensing issue for policymakers was how each state's physician lobby used licensing laws to prevent out-of-state clinicians from treating the poor for free.[33] Starting around 2010, states started fixing that problem.[34] After that, the floodgates opened. The more states liberalized their health care markets, the more innovation we saw and the more access to quality health care surged. Support for medical licensing plummeted, and states repealed it. The poor benefited most of all.

The single most transformative thing we did was to change who controls the money. We took all the health care dollars that government controls and spends on behalf of patients and gave it to the patients.[35] We took all the health care dollars employers control and spend on behalf of workers, and we gave it to the workers who earned it.[36] Patients now control that money and spend it on their own behalf. We let them choose which, and how much, coverage to purchase.

That change was also the single most powerful thing we did to improve access for the poor. We did so not so much because the poor get to control more of their own money—although that certainly matters a lot to them—but because those changes turned the *other* 300 million Americans into more cost-conscious and demanding consumers.

When those 330 million consumers got control of the $4 trillion this nation spends on medical care,[37] they changed their behavior, which in turn transformed health care. All 330 million of them became more careful and demanding consumers. They demanded lower prices and higher quality in a way they never had before. Competition forced prices down, aided by the elimination of regulations that had been protecting high-cost and low-quality providers. Political support from hundreds of millions of newly cost-conscious "health care voters" helped us eliminate even more cost-increasing regulation. That's when we really saw an innovation explosion in both health insurance and health care delivery.

Once we eliminated the price controls that were supposed to protect against preexisting conditions and gave consumers the freedom to choose their own health plans, consumers demanded protection from the risks of high premiums and uninsurability. Insurers responded with innovations like pre-ex insurance, total-satisfaction guarantees, and more. It all began with a seemingly small change that created a free, parallel market in health insurance to compete with the government-run market.[38]

We saw an explosion in integrated delivery systems and prepaid group plans like Kaiser Permanente, which delivered innovations in coordinated care, concierge care, medical teams, e-health, and life panels.[39]

We're even solving public-goods problems like those surrounding effectiveness research.[40] We have more information on the effectiveness, comparative effectiveness, and cost-effectiveness of medical treatments than ever before.

Integrated prepaid group plans were doing so much effectiveness research and quality certification of medical technologies, one day we woke up and realized we were sitting on a private-sector alternative to the Food and Drug Administration (FDA). So we got rid of the FDA. We don't even miss it. In its place, private, integrated health plans are evaluating the safety and efficacy of drugs, medical devices, nutritional supplements, and health claims faster—and in a way that doesn't deny patients the right to make their own health decisions.[41] Health plans attract enrollees by competing to have the most reliable quality seal of approval.

Conclusion

In the future, we are making health care better, more affordable, and more secure every day. We have given consumers greater protections against illness and financial insecurity than when we tried to legislate our way to better health care. And the progress never ends.

We still have gaps in our health care sector. We still have to worry about quality. We still have to worry about effectiveness. We still have to worry about insurance carriers' solvency.

Not everyone has health insurance. Then again, health insurance is a lot less necessary.

Yet all of these challenges are smaller than they were in 2020. No one wants to go back to the bad old days of the so-called Affordable Care Act, when an obsession with health *insurance* got in the way of providing everyone with health *care*. Access to care is now more universal than when we tried to legislate our way to universal coverage. The future of health care is so bright, I prescribe sunglasses.[42]

Now, forgive me, before I can return to the year 2050, I need to pop down to the corner drugstore for a little plutonium.[43] If you happen to run into my past self, do me a favor and distract him. Otherwise, well . . . things could get ugly.[44]

4

The War on Drugs

Trevor Burrus

AUTHOR'S NOTE: This fictionalized account imagines how drugs could be legalized in America and what would happen after 15 years. The setting is the mid-21st century, but the account incorporates facts about the present-day situation.

It's been 15 years since all drugs were legalized in America. In the throes of an overdose crisis that claimed, at its peak, more than 100,000 lives per year, an increasingly angry public forced American policymakers to look for a solution.[1] Analyses of various drug policy regimes around the world clearly showed that the situation was markedly better in the few European countries that had responded to their own overdose crises by decriminalizing all drug use.

Portugal had been first to try it, and for many decades, the country has had one of the lowest overdose rates in all of Europe.[2] Before decriminalization, Portugal had one of the highest overdose death rates in Europe, nearly 80 deaths per million inhabitants.[3] After decriminalization, it had about three deaths per million inhabitants, far below the European average.[4]

And decriminalization did more than just save lives. To the surprise of many, drug use rates declined or remained steady in Portugal and other countries that decriminalized.[5] Many predicted that if potential drug users weren't dissuaded by the possibility of criminal sanctions, then drug decriminalization would lead to an epidemic of drug use. That didn't happen.[6] It seemed that the threat of criminal punishment was not the primary reason people stayed away from drugs, or even a significant factor.

For decades, America was gripped by an opioid crisis in which more and more people died every year.[7] In response, the government cracked down on how many opioid pills could be produced, monitored doctors' prescribing practices, surveilled opioid producers and distributors to ensure that drugs weren't being diverted to illicit users, and intensified efforts to disrupt the illegal trade in heroin and fentanyl.[8] Yet nothing seemed to stem the tide of opioid overdoses.

Opioid users began dying in ever-larger numbers from fentanyl overdoses, a medical opioid that can be 50–100 times more potent than typical black-market heroin. In response, lawmakers focused on intercepting fentanyl coming from China or Mexico.[9] The drug is so potent, however, that thousands of doses could be easily hidden in envelopes, in small shipping boxes, or in hiding spots in larger shipping containers. A lethal dose of fentanyl is about two to three milligrams, so one gram of fentanyl is enough to kill 300–500 people.[10] In some situations, people can even die from a lower dose of about 500 micrograms, or half a milligram.[11] In fact, fentanyl is significantly more lethal than traditional poisons like arsenic, which typically has a lethal dose of 70–180 milligrams.[12]

You might wonder why the opioid users were willing to take something so dangerous. Often, they didn't know they were taking it. Users of both heroin and cocaine would purchase their regular drugs from their regular dealer, unaware that perhaps 10 percent or more of the drug was fentanyl.[13] After injecting or snorting their usual amount, they'd overdose.[14] Overdoses began to resemble point-source outbreaks, with hospitals treating 15 to 20 users from the same neighborhood who had presumably received tainted drugs from the same supplier.[15]

Other users didn't have a choice if they wanted to avoid withdrawal. Fentanyl, with its high potency and small size, was increasingly crowding heroin out of the market. And with the government cracking down on how many prescription opioids could be produced, many addicts were left with fentanyl-tainted heroin as the only way to get their fix. When asked whether he was willing to use fentanyl-tainted heroin, one user said it would depend on "the availability of other batches and how sick I am. If I'm sick, I gotta do it, you know?" But he knew he had to be cautious: "I won't do half a gram. You know, I'll do a little pinch and I'll figure it out from there, but I won't start big."[16]

Many users were afraid of fentanyl, especially of taking fentanyl unwittingly, and strongly disliked the drug's effects. They tried to alter their drug use accordingly, whether that meant snorting heroin rather than shooting it, sticking to trusted dealers, or trying to find increasingly rare prescription opioids. But they were beholden to an unpredictable illicit market. Said one user: "I used to take just the pills, and then I started doing dope, the heroin, only when I could get it, when it was cheaper. But I don't prefer it because you never know what you're getting. It's scary, so I'm more into pills."[17]

After years of increasing overdose deaths, it seemed that almost nothing could be done to stop them. Overdose deaths broke 140,000 during a presidential election year, and it became the most crucial issue of the campaign. By that point, almost everyone had been directly or indirectly affected by the opioid crisis in some way. Although America's gun-violence issues had long received substantial political attention, the opioid crisis claimed more than 10 times the number of victims annually as did gun homicides.[18]

* * * * *

Drugs have now been legal for about 15 years, but how did such a shocking change happen? During the presidential campaign 16 years ago, a charismatic young senator emerged as the clear front-runner. His easygoing, charming nature endeared him to voters of both sides. During a debate among the party nominees, the question of how to deal with the opioid crisis was raised. To everyone's shock, the candidate revealed that, up until eight years before, he had been an opioid user for more than a decade. He had overdosed once and was clinically dead for a few minutes before being resuscitated. In his opinion, opioids—and in fact all drugs—should be legalized. It was the only effective way to save lives. "In case you haven't realized," he said, "drugs won the drug war, and they're not going away."

An audible gasp went through the audience. During the ensuing press coverage, the senator gave extended interviews, describing how he became a user, how he had overdosed from fentanyl-tainted heroin, and how he had quit using before entering politics. "I grew out of it; that tends to happen," he said.

The revelation had the opposite effect from what many expected: it humanized heroin users. If someone who had gone to Harvard Law School, had been attorney general of Ohio, and had become a senator could be a heroin user, then anyone could be a user. It also showed that drugs, even heroin, didn't necessarily ruin your life, as everyone had been taught. The senator was clear on that point: he gave up heroin because he grew out of it, and it wasn't fun anymore as his life became filled with more responsibilities. Yes, it was a little hard to quit, but quitting cigarettes can be even harder.[19] No, drugs didn't almost ruin his life, prohibition did. In fact, it almost killed him.

For years, the prevailing narrative had been that heroin and other "hard" drugs—methamphetamine, PCP, crack, cocaine, and the like—were so dangerous that people could become addicted if they tried them even once. That perception has always been wrong, but relatively few people would come out and say it. Some ardent prohibitionists had admitted that most drug use is casual, but they regarded casual users as particularly pernicious. William J. Bennett, the drug czar under President George H. W. Bush, understood that nonaddicted users "still comprise the vast bulk of our drug-involved population," but such users were more dangerous because each represented "a potential agent of infection for the non-users in his personal ambit."[20]

The Drug Enforcement Administration had also pushed hard against the idea that drug users could be "normal": "one of the basic contentions of advocates of legalization is that drug users are essentially normal people," said a manual published by the DEA that was originally entitled "How to Hold Your Own in a Drug Legalization Debate."[21] But that's not true, it argued, because drugs "undo the bounds that keep many seemingly normal people on an even keel."

The senator's story helped demonstrate that the prohibitionists had been overselling their case. Science confirmed it too. As Columbia University neuroscientist Carl Hart wrote, "Most people who use any drug do so without problems."[22] People began to wonder, if alcohol wasn't banned because of the relatively small percentage of users who cause problems, why were other drugs banned? The narrative slowly changed.

Then, drug users began outing themselves. The hashtag #OpiumDin began circulating, and famous actors, writers, television personalities, and venerated musicians came "out of the closet," so to speak, as casual users of heroin, meth, or crack. The comparison to the gay rights movement is apt.

When gays were "in the closet," the most visible type of homosexual activity was the least mainstream: ostentatious gay bars, bathhouses, and flamboyant gay-rights parades. Conservative Americans could believe that homosexuals were a uniquely strange and promiscuous subculture that was confined to small communities in coastal cities. But when your suburban neighbor comes out—the nice guy who snowblows your driveway and is a raging Dallas Cowboys fan—or your daughter does, suddenly you're forced to reevaluate your image of homosexuals.

The image of drug users, especially heroin users, had long been dominated by the "junkie": an emaciated, Sid Vicious–type character with visible track marks and a thousand-yard stare, who is so consumed by addiction that it destroys his life and personal relations. That certainly happens, far too often. Yet judging heroin users by this image is like judging alcohol users by binge-drinking college students. According to one study, only 23.1 percent of heroin users ever experience dependence.[23] Although that amounts to nearly one in four users, it still paints a different picture of a drug many believed to be so seductive that anyone who tries it once will become an addict. Another study found that 4.4 percent of young adults had tried crack; however, only 1.1 percent had used it in the previous year, and only 0.3 percent had used it in the previous month.[24] That means that 93 percent of those who had tried a supposedly dangerous and highly addictive drug hadn't even used it once a month.

When the image of the drug user became familiar rather than foreign—your boss doing a shot at a workplace happy hour, a lawyer relaxing with a joint after a long day in the office—then a cornerstone for legalization had been laid. Marijuana legalization spread across the country in the 2010s. And although numerous advocacy organizations had spent decades writing papers on the general harmlessness of marijuana, academic essays did not cause marijuana legalization—rather, Cheech and Chong movies, Snoop Dogg's music, and other social and artistic influences helped humanize marijuana users so that people would no longer view that specific vice as a crime.

A movement to humanize opioid users began after the former opioid-using senator won the presidency. As the new government began working on the overdose crisis, the tone of the conversation had changed. Now that addicts and users had come out of the closet, they traveled to Washington, DC, in a caravan, culminating in a rally on the National Mall of hundreds of thousands of drug users and their supporters. The theme of the rally was "drug addicts are human beings," and signs were spotted saying, "Why do alcoholics get treatment and we get cages?" and "I became a drug addict in prison . . . think about that."

After a year of hearings and legislative dealmaking, the full legalization bill was brought to the floor. It became a full legalization bill, rather than just an opioid legalization bill, because thinking had changed on heroin and other opioids—long considered the most destructive and addicting drugs. Consequently, it had become untenable to treat cocaine, LSD, methamphetamine, or other popular recreational drugs any differently.

The bill passed narrowly and was signed by the president. It was the beginning of a new era.

* * * * *

Because of America's constitutional structure, when drugs were fully legalized at the federal level, states had the option of treating drugs however they wished. A variety of regimes emerged. Some states maintained prohibition for a few years, only to realize that their citizens were simply going to legalization states to purchase their drugs. A few still have prohibition today.

Other states decided to decriminalize drug use, as Portugal did. Drug users who possess small quantities of drugs for personal use are not punished criminally, but drug dealers and manufacturers still are. In decriminalization states, drugs are not available in stores, but some states have allowed drug users to acquire them from authorized medical services.

Finally, many states decided to simply legalize drugs, sales and all, but they chose different rules that dictate how drugs can be purchased and who can purchase them. After all, alcohol is not simply "legal." Only people of a certain age can purchase it, and only from licensed bars or retailers. Manufacture is also limited in various ways, from restrictions on home production to licensing systems. Other laws also restrict alcohol, such as prohibitions on drunk driving and liability for servers who overserve intoxicated customers.

States put varying age restrictions on purchasing different drugs, from up to age 25 to purchase heroin to as low as age 16. For other drugs, age restrictions fell somewhere in between. Most states passed stricter penalties for any type of drugged driving, and some created liability for those who used drugs with someone who they knew or had reason to know would soon be getting behind the wheel. Finally, some states restricted some hard drugs to prescription only, particularly heroin and methamphetamine.

Legalization produced some anticipated and some unanticipated results. When the president signed the bill, he gave a passionate speech about what to expect, and he was careful not to promise too much:

> Let me be clear, there will be more drug users after this law goes into effect, there will be more traffic accidents due to drug use, and there will be negative health effects. But all those things are true of alcohol legalization, and no one is seriously advocating banning alcohol because

of those effects, at least not anymore. We tried alcohol prohibition and it didn't work, and now we've learned the same about drug prohibition. Like alcohol, we will try to mitigate the negative consequences of drug use, but we won't punish everyone who likes to indulge occasionally. It's not possible for a society not to have a drug problem; rather, we must choose what kind of drug problem we have. We choose to have a drug problem where we treat our fellow citizens like human beings.

Fifteen years later, we can now assess how our "noble experiment" has fared.

The Nature and Form of Drug Use Changed Dramatically

Prohibition makes drugs stronger and therefore more dangerous, even absent adulteration. America's experiment with alcohol prohibition in the 1920s changed not only the way alcohol was consumed but also what alcohol was consumed. The day before alcohol prohibition went into effect in 1920, the most popular drinks were beer and wine. The day after alcohol prohibition was lifted, the most popular drinks were again beer and wine.

During Prohibition, however, the most popular drinks were various forms of high-potency spirits, usually either smuggled in from countries like Canada or produced in the form of so-called bathtub gin, which could often be tainted. According to our best estimates, spirits accounted for about 40 percent of alcohol sales before Prohibition but rose to 90 percent of sales almost immediately after it was enacted.[25] The cost of beer increased an estimated 700 percent over its pre-Prohibition price, whereas the cost of spirits increased 270 percent.[26]

This phenomenon is known as the "iron law of prohibition." When prohibited, drugs with higher potencies are preferred over those with lower potencies because of the need for more efficient smuggling. Smuggling a small barrel of gin into a speakeasy is much easier than smuggling a cartload of beer.

That is one reason why fentanyl began to adulterate the country's heroin supply before legalization.[27] The potency of fentanyl made it ideal for smuggling, even if it was less than ideal for drug users. As we have seen, although some users may demand fentanyl, many not only dislike the drug's effects but also understandably fear its dangers. Nevertheless, with black markets, they are often left without a choice.

Prohibition changes drug markets so drastically that one cannot easily infer what a legal drug market would look like by examining a black market. Under alcohol prohibition, some bars essentially served only Everclear. After legalization, bars served a variety of alcoholic drinks to meet the tastes of customers, most of whom wished to moderate their alcohol use to meet both their desires and their responsibilities. The same has proved true of most heroin, meth, and cocaine users.

Consequently, since legalization, we have seen a significant change in the potency of the drugs that are being consumed. Many users, even longtime addicts, prefer less potent drugs much of the time, saving the hard stuff for special occasions—the opioid, cocaine, or meth equivalent of doing tequila shots only if you're off work tomorrow.

Initially, the high-potency drugs that users were most familiar with were the hottest sellers, particularly heroin, meth, and
cocaine. And the drugs on the shelves were extremely high-grade,
given that they had been manufactured by pharmaceutical companies rather than diluted by black-market dealers or tainted with
drugs like fentanyl. Companies that produced the drugs for retail
outlets were understandably fearful that, in the initial weeks of
legalization, users would go to the stores, purchase high-grade
heroin or methamphetamine, and overdose from the unexpected
potency.

In addition, various states passed consumer protection laws
that allowed users and victims' families to sue pharmaceutical
companies for selling drugs that created an "unreasonable and
undisclosed" danger of overdose. The companies began selling
high-potency drugs in very small quantities with strong warning labels. One company—hoping to prevent extremely intoxicated users from consuming more drugs and overdosing—sold
high-potency heroin in a box that could be unlocked only by
completing a puzzle on a smartphone app. The puzzle would be
easy for those who were sober but quite difficult for those who
were high. Another company sold high-grade heroin packaged
with naloxone, an opioid antagonist that can reverse an overdose.
And perhaps most inventively, one company offered a Fitbit-type
bracelet that monitors a user's heart rate and respiration and sig-
nals emergency services if they drop too low.

But after the first few years, the demand for drug products radically changed. Heroin addicts like to get high, of course, but,
like cigarette smokers, they also need to take some sort of opioid

consistently to avoid withdrawal. Many don't always want to be high but, under prohibition, they had few options to curb their cravings other than high-potency heroin. Soon, however, they had multiple options: opium lollipops and other candies, inhalers, vaporizers, slow-release patches, sodas, teas, and too many more to list. The same was true with cocaine and methamphetamine. New products hit the shelves with the speed of new potato chip flavors. And as the sales of those products rose, the proportion of revenue from high-potency drugs dropped.

These changes had some precedent. The first wave of opium use in the United States was in the form of smoked opium. Introduced by Chinese immigrants, smoking opium grew in popularity throughout the late 19th century, particularly in the West, and the fabled opium den became its symbol. Municipalities began cracking down on opium dens and opium smoking in the 1870s. San Francisco passed an ordinance in 1875, as did Virginia City, Nevada, in 1876.[28] Municipal and state laws were often weakly or selectively enforced, so it wasn't until 1909, with the passage of the federal Smoking Opium Exclusion Act, that the legal response to smoking opium began to significantly affect the market. By 1917, a small tin of smoking opium, which usually sold for $20, averaged $70. By 1924, it was $200.[29]

But opium smokers had alternatives. Heroin was introduced by the pharmaceutical company Bayer in 1898, and morphine had long been available. Opium smokers began switching to heroin and morphine when smoking opium became too expensive or because they feared criminal consequences. One study recorded 78 addicts who had started as opium smokers, 68 of whom had become morphine users by 1917.[30] In Philadelphia, a marked shift to heroin by opium smokers was reported; a study of addicts in New York City's Tombs prison found that 80–90 percent of white addicts had switched to heroin after 1916.[31] Some of this shift was due to longtime opium addicts increasing their tolerance for the drug; however, much of it was due to the lack of available alternatives.

Intravenous heroin use also emerged around 1915–1925.[32] That shift was partially a response to the damage that prolonged snorting can do to the nasal septum and partially a response to the decreasing purity of the drug.[33] Intravenous delivery gave users a more immediate high and was more efficient than snorting the drug, particularly if the drug was not pure. Said one addict, "You didn't need no vein until they cut it."[34]

The perhaps surprising conclusion is that, before legalization, we didn't fully know what the demand for opioids would look like, because government policies had long distorted the market. When smoking opium began to become popular, municipal, state, and eventually federal laws pushed people toward morphine and heroin. Then the Harrison Narcotics Act of 1914 limited morphine and heroin to medical use only, and the Anti-Heroin Act of 1924 banned the drug entirely. The iron law of prohibition kicked in, and only high-potency drugs were available on the black market. If, before prohibition, users were addicted to lower-potency sources of opium such as laudanum—a tincture often containing about 10 percent opium—then, after prohibition, all that was available to them was heroin or morphine. This situation not only put them in greater danger of overdose but also made their addiction more severe.

After 15 years of legalization, the picture is becoming clearer. People are still addicted to heroin, methamphetamine, cocaine, and other drugs, of course, but addicts' numbers are dropping. Now, more people use or are addicted to low-potency drug products. But as long as the forces of prohibition are not pushing them toward higher-potency, more dangerous, and more addictive drugs, then that number seems to be stable.

Drug Use Increased, but Problematic Drug Use Decreased

As the president said, and as most experts predicted, rates of drug use rose after prohibition, but not as dramatically as people had expected.[35] In countries where drug use was merely decriminalized, as in Portugal, drug use didn't tend to rise. But legalization increased access to drugs through retail stores, product innovation, and commercialization. By removing many of the barriers to drug use—primarily fear of criminal penalties, fear of tainted drugs, inability to find drugs, and price—legalization increased the number of people willing to take drugs.

But that's not necessarily a bad thing. Unless we regard all drug taking as a wrong per se, then increasing the use of drugs actually brought a social benefit. In the beginning, some had difficulty understanding this fact, because they still regarded using meth, heroin, cocaine, and other hard drugs as categorically different from drinking alcohol. They had difficulty believing that such drugs could be taken casually and responsibly.

But it soon became clear that most people could take a little opium to enliven a night out or a little cocaine to keep the night going and then get to work on time the next morning, perhaps with the help of some amphetamines. If those drug users enjoy their experiences on drugs without causing problems for either their lives or society, it is difficult to argue that taking those drugs away produces a social benefit.

Most people understand this fact when it comes to alcohol. The primary cost of banning alcohol would be, and was, taking an enjoyable drug away from people who use it to augment their pleasure—from tailgating to wine-and-cheese parties, happy hours, and myriad other situations in which alcohol is used to increase amusement and pleasure. Dry weddings are less fun than open-bar weddings for a reason.

And people slowly came to understand that the same applied to the newly legalized drugs. Moreover, as described earlier, since the legal market created an explosion of less potent options for using drugs, drug use was integrated into various social situations. Psychedelics are used in art exhibits. There are "opium-cooking parties" and new-concept opium dens that resemble hookah bars.

All of this change represented a shift away from the more problematic use of heavy drugs, namely, the clandestine use of extremely potent drugs by addicts in unsavory locations, as was common under prohibition. The increasing social acceptability of drug use, combined with the varieties of available low-potency drugs, meant that addicts could come out of the shadows, so to speak, and not lose themselves in a hypodermic needle.

This transformation dramatically curbed many of the downsides of problematic drug abuse. As alcoholics have long known, the shame of being an alcoholic is one of the biggest barriers to seeking treatment. Attendees at Alcoholics Anonymous meetings are encouraged to introduce themselves as alcoholics and to have no shame in their condition. When hard drugs were illegal, the shame that accompanied addiction was compounded by the illicit and often hidden nature of the habit. That factor created a vicious cycle.

Addiction is just as much a product of social disconnection as it is of the seductive nature of hard drugs.[36] Prohibition heightened that social disconnection and pushed users to hide their habits. Problematic drug use can certainly cause social disconnection by itself, but abusing a prohibited drug makes that disconnection even worse. Users lost jobs, alienated friends and family, and discarded meaningful connections to hobbies and personal passions. Top that off with a criminal conviction that dramatically harmed employment prospects, educational opportunities, and much more, and it's no wonder that, for many addicts, the drug became their only source of pleasure, and they spent their days searching for ways to secure the next fix.

There are still addicts now, just as there are still alcoholics. And many of them find themselves in similarly dire situations. But by removing the barriers to acquiring safe drugs, taking away the threat of criminal prosecution, allowing them access to low-potency drugs that can help them curb their withdrawal symptoms, and lowering the social opprobrium that accompanied illicit drug use, we offered a more accessible and positive path to overcoming their addiction.

Overdose Deaths Dropped Significantly and Continue to Drop Steadily

We still have overdoses, quite a few actually, just as we still have significant medical problems from alcohol abuse. Although fentanyl-tainted heroin can and did cause many overdoses, plain, untainted heroin can still kill, often unpredictably. That is especially true when drugs are mixed.[37]

Immediately after legalization, not surprisingly, overdoses from tainted heroin declined significantly. Other types of overdoses seemed to increase, however. The new accessibility of drugs and the low price, at least compared with prelegalization, meant that many people indulged too heavily and too often. Initially, the problem was bad enough that drugstores began tracking purchases and refused to sell to people who bought large amounts of drugs in a single day or a span of days. The businesses did so because dram shop laws—laws that impose liability on businesses and servers who provide alcohol to those who are obviously intoxicated—were expanded to include drugs.

Overdoses continued to fall as numerous forces combined to help mitigate dangerous drug use. One, as mentioned, was the availability of low-potency drugs that were unavailable during prohibition. Others, also previously mentioned, were the various factors that helped bring addicts out of the shadows and offer them paths to recovery. Also, naloxone, the opioid antagonist that can reverse an overdose, became widely available and is now prominently sold in drugstores, just like hangover pills are sold in liquor stores.

Legalization was never championed as a way to stop all overdoses, so they're still a problem and will continue to be. What we eliminated were overdoses that were directly caused by prohibition. And by slowly changing the nature of drug use, we're beginning to see other types of overdoses decline.

Effective Social Systems of Drug Control Emerged and a Variety of Innovative Products Came to the Market to Help Addicts Quit

Prohibition is not the only way to influence how and whether people use drugs. Cigarettes have been legal for centuries; yet, despite their being highly addictive, levels of smoking have fallen precipitously since the mid-20th century. Some of that decrease was due to increased taxes and other forms of regulation; however, most was due to people seeking healthier behaviors and to an increase in the social condemnation of smoking.

Such social controls are more effective in a legal market, where users spend less time hiding their drug use and using drugs only with other drug users—that is, people who won't condemn their behavior or report them to law enforcement. The legalization law included funding for public health campaigns that inform users of the dangers of drugs, as well as warning labels similar to those on cigarette packs. But warning labels are not as effective as social forces—whether friends telling users that they've been taking too much or just the general opprobrium with which certain social circles treat some types of drug use.

Much like drinking soda became the target of social forces in the early 21st century, taking pure heroin, high-potency cocaine, or other strong intoxicants is viewed as uncouth in many social situations. Just as colleagues may be OK with someone ordering a glass of wine during an extended weekday lunch, calling for Jägermeister shots would be condemned.

Drunk driving is another example of how social forces helped mitigate a type of problematic drug use. Although criminal penalties for drunk driving were increased and the legal blood alcohol limit was lowered, social norms and shaming were just as important in decreasing incidents of drunk driving. Since legalization, we have seen increased social pressure to avoid driving and other dangerous activities when under the influence. Incidents of drugged driving increased immediately after legalization but have been falling ever since.

Finally, whereas drug dealers under prohibition had little incentive to help their customers quit, businesses began producing cessation aids after legalization. Like smoking cessation aids, a big market exists for those who want to quit drugs. Methadone has long been the most prominent drug for helping curb opiate cravings and, hopefully, gradually cure addicts. The wider availability of methadone—which can help many addicts but was often hard to come by during prohibition—mitigates harmful drug use.

And more products were to come. Legalization created a large and visible market of addicts who wished to be cured, and many health insurance plans began covering cessation aids. Businesses, seeing a profit opportunity, began researching new drugs and methods and soon produced nasal sprays, patches, gum, a long-lasting injectable form of naloxone, and many more. Helping addicts quit had become good business.

Policing and Criminal Justice Radically Changed

At the height of the drug war, hundreds of thousands of people were in prison for various drug offenses, and more than a million were under some type of supervision by the criminal justice system—such as parole or probation.[38] It is impossible to know how many lives were unnecessarily ruined over the course of the drug war, but the number would be staggering.

Letting drug offenders out of prison was, of course, one of the most immediate benefits of ending prohibition. After legalization, a federal law was passed that released all federal prisoners whose most serious offense was drug possession or low-level dealing. The vast majority of incarcerated drug offenders were in state rather than federal prisons, however, and states had to individually pass laws dealing with their incarcerated drug offenders.[39] Some released almost all of them and even erased conviction records. Suddenly hundreds of thousands of people could see a brighter future for their lives, something better than a jail cell and the difficult task of trying to live, work, and thrive with a felony conviction.

The benefits of deincarceration were obvious, and many people supported legalization because they could no longer stomach seeing their fellow humans put in cages for indulging a mere vice. Incarceration not only cost the government billions of dollars but also destroyed human productivity and potential. Yet other, less obvious benefits for our criminal justice system soon emerged.

How much the drug war changed the nature of policing itself is often forgotten. Traditionally, crimes have victims. When investigating an assault, murder, or rape, police can speak to witnesses, take evidence, and pursue the perpetrator through traditional means. After a robbery, victims typically invite the police into their houses and ask them to search for evidence to solve the crime.

When crimes have no victims, however, policing completely changes. With drug use, the supposed victim is also the perpetrator, and he or she doesn't want the supposed "evidence" of the "crime" to be discovered—that is, the drugs. Since no one is reporting the "crime" and no one is inviting the police into private places to discover evidence, the police need to "invite" themselves in somehow. Consequently, the drug war greatly eroded Americans' civil liberties.

Because of the drug war, police could fly helicopters over houses to search for drugs in backyards without a warrant. Because of the drug war, police could execute no-knock warrants in which heavily armed SWAT teams carried out violent raids on people's homes, often by breaking down the door with a battering ram and sometimes using explosives, such as flash grenades.[40] Because of the drug war, people could be detained at the border for significant periods, having their body cavities searched and other indignities forced upon them. Because of the drug war, police could claim to smell marijuana in a car and then seize the car under the theory of civil forfeiture.[41] Because of the drug war, police could shake down groups on the street–often young African American males–on the assumption that someone had drugs, and they would sometimes plant evidence if no one did.

Enforcing prohibition, particularly against something that is popular, inevitably makes the relationship between law enforcement and citizens antagonistic and fraught. Moreover, given the large sums of money that the illegal drug trade generated, corruption was inevitable. After all, who is going to know when a police officer slips a wad of bills into his pocket during a drug raid?

After prohibition ended, law enforcement officers around the country were unsure what to do. Law enforcement organizations and prison guard unions were some of the biggest opponents of legalization. For them, prohibition was a jobs program. Thousands of officers walked into work the day after legalization to find that their main job had been eliminated. They were superfluous.

But they weren't. America's murder clearance rate—that is, the rate at which homicides are solved—dipped to 61.6 percent in 2017, and in some cities, such as Baltimore, Chicago, and Detroit, the clearance rate was under 30 percent.[42] And police were no better at solving other crimes: aggravated assault, 53.3 percent; rape, 34.5 percent; burglary, 13.5 percent.[43] Meanwhile, during the drug war, 62 percent of SWAT team raids were for drug searches.[44] Police officers who had spent their careers tracking down drug users and pursuing traffickers could focus on interpersonal crimes, and predictably the clearance rates began rising.

Of course, when drugs were illegal, many of those homicides were directly or indirectly related to prohibition, particularly in cities like Baltimore, Chicago, and Detroit. It is nearly impossible to guess how many other crimes were directly or indirectly related to prohibition; however, clearly the CEOs of Budweiser and Coors do not fight street wars over territory. After legalization, the crime rate in the inner city began dropping steadily. In some cities, it dropped precipitously. And although gangs still exist, as they always will, legalization has removed their biggest source of revenue and the biggest source of intergang violence. The drug war was one of the worst things to ever happen to the inner city, and, unfortunately, the effects of decades of prohibition have not been alleviated after a mere 15 years of legalization.

* * * * *

But here, in the real world of 2020, drugs of course haven't been legalized. The wave of marijuana legalization that began sweeping the country in 2012 has been a welcome development, but we need to do more.

Instead, in 2016, the last year for which we have data, 44,700 people were sitting in American state prisons for simple drug possession, and another approximately 152,500 were in state prison for other drug offenses, such as selling, trafficking, or manufacturing.[45] An additional 81,900 were in federal prison for drug offenses.[46] In 2017, there were 1,632,921 arrests for drug law violations, of which 1,394,514 (85.4 percent) were for possession only.[47] In 2016, more arrests were made for marijuana possession than were made for all violent crimes.[48] In fact, marijuana possession arrests account for 5 percent of all arrests in the United States, which works out to about one marijuana arrest every minute.[49]

The preceding has been an attempt to imagine both the costs and benefits of fully legalizing drugs. Americans need to reassess how we treat our fellow citizens who have unpopular vices. We must ask ourselves whether the symbolic crusade of prohibition is worth the money it costs and the lives it destroys. Drugs can destroy lives, certainly, but the drug war itself can and has destroyed lives, communities, civil liberties, and even countries. Drug addicts are human beings, and they don't deserve less care and treatment than alcoholics.

Drugs won the drug war. As our hypothetical president said, "It's not possible for a society not to have a drug problem; rather, we must choose what kind of drug problem we have."

5

The Funding of Science

Terence Kealey

Until 1940, the United States inhabited a golden age of libertarian science, when under research laissez faire it became the richest, most technologically advanced, and most powerful country in the world. In 1940, however, it adopted the research *dirigisme* of the countries that were successively to lose World War II (France and Germany) and the Cold War (the Soviet Union).

Happily, however, since 1965, the federal government has been quietly pulling back its funding for research, and we are now about to embark on a second golden age of libertarian (or near-libertarian) science.

The First Golden Age

The first research golden age originated in the English Agricultural and Industrial Revolutions, which were the products of laissez faire in science. It culminated in the United States' rise to global economic supremacy, which was also achieved under laissez faire in science. That first research golden age ended for

Britain during the World War I and for the United States during World War II.

The roots of that first research golden age were nurtured by the Anglo-American love of freedom from the state, and its prophet was Adam Smith. In his 1776 book *Wealth of Nations*, Smith argued that governments need not fund scientific or technological research. Industry, he said, produced all the new technology it needed:

> If we go into the workplace of any manufacturer and . . . enquire concerning the machines, they will tell you that such or such a one was invented by a common workman.[1]

Moreover, Smith continued, pure science flowed out of the advances made in industry, not in the universities; and inasmuch as industry needed pure science, it produced all it needed.[2]

France and the German states, on the other hand, defaulted into absolutism, and their science was funded and controlled by the state. Absolutism found its science-funding and science-directing prophet in Francis Bacon, who in his 1605 *Advancement of Learning* had argued that industrial technology depended on pure science, which only governments would fund.

Bacon's so-called linear model thus proposed:

Whereas Smith's model proposed:

Who Was Right, Smith or Bacon?

During the 18th, 19th, and early 20th centuries, the globe engaged in a vast experiment, the results of which are clear: economic growth came by research laissez faire. The globe's two lead countries in succession were the United Kingdom (during the 19th century) and the United States (during the 20th century). So around 1890, U.S. gross domestic product (GDP) per capita overtook that of the UK, France, and the German states. However, France and the German states not only failed to overtake the UK (during the 19th century), they also failed *even to converge* on the UK's GDP per capita.[3]

The science policy lobby has, nonetheless, long propagated the myth that Germany overtook the UK economically during the 19th century, even though that myth has been repeatedly discredited. Table 5.1, for example, provides economic historian Paul Bairoch's gross national product per capita data.

Bairoch's data on the different national levels of industrialization are similar.

Table 5.1

Gross national product per capita (in 1960 U.S. dollars)

	1830	1913
United Kingdom	370	1,070
West Germany	240	775
France	275	670
United States	240	1,350

Source: David S. Landes, *The Wealth and Poverty of Nations* (New York: Norton, 1998), p. 232.

The economic history thus shows that research laissez faire—not *dirigisme*—correlates with increases in income, productivity, and wealth.

Federal Government Funding for Geopolitical Research during the Golden Age

In the decades following its founding in 1789, the federal government did subsidize some research, in that it created agencies whose missions might involve the funding of science (including the Library of Congress, 1800; the Office of the Coast Survey, 1807; the Office of the Surgeon General, 1818; the Army Medical Department, 1818; and the forerunner of the Naval Observatory, 1830). But those agencies' research was limited to their geopolitical missions: the federal government did not fund science for its own sake; it funded only geopolitical science, and the federal government's geopolitical ambitions were then limited.

The federal government's first foray into science for its own sake was, unexpectedly, foisted on it by an Englishman, James Smithson, who in 1835 donated $550,000 in his will

> to found at Washington under the name of the Smithsonian Institution, an Establishment for the increase and diffusion of knowledge among men.[4]

Because the money was gifted to the federal government, its acceptance was resisted by the defenders of states' rights: thus, Senator John C. Calhoun from South Carolina said that the money "must be returned to the heirs," while Senator William Campbell Preston, also from South Carolina, asserted that "every whippersnapper vagabond . . . might think it proper to have his name distinguished in the same way."[5]

Moreover, Andrew Johnson of Tennessee, who was then in the House of Representatives, was outraged when Congress voted not only to accept the donation but also to supplement it with the taxpayers' money, which he denounced as picking the "pockets of the people." Smithson's money was nonetheless accepted, and the pockets of the people were duly picked. (Today, the Smithsonian receives just over half its annual income of $1.5 billion from the federal government as an appropriation from the taxpayers.[6])

Agriculture

The largest research-associated mission the federal government adopted in peacetime before 1940 was agriculture. American agriculture had long been bedeviled by overproduction, and as economic historian Eric Jones wrote in his classic book *The European Miracle*:

> European farming methods were preternaturally productive in the New World. Time and again European travellers complained that American farmers wasted manure. Their dung heaps rose to tower over the red Palatine barns of the colonies; why were they not spread on the land?[7]

They were not spread on the land because farmers had access to too much virgin land, so they produced too much food. Consequently, spreading the manure would not have been a cost-effective activity. Moreover, the private sector—whether in the form of Eli Whitney's cotton gin (1793), Cyrus McCormick's mechanical reaper (1831), or Joseph Glidden's barbed wire (1874)—continued to transform productivity. And because of the overproduction, farmers were poor, so they looked to the federal government for relief—which Representative Justin Morrill (R-VT) sought to provide.

Morrill was a follower of Henry Clay's American Way, which was in its turn based on the *dirigisme* Alexander Hamilton was to elaborate in his "Report on Manufactures" of 1791, and he supposed that governments should overrule markets and manage economies. And in 1859, Morrill piloted a land-grant college bill through Congress, because he thought the farmers' poverty spoke of market failure. Yet then-president James Buchanan believed in markets (how would subsidizing its education solve agriculture's overproduction?), as well as in crowding out, so he vetoed the bill:

> This bill will injuriously interfere with existing colleges . . . [that] have grown up under the fostering care of the states and the munificence of individuals. . . . What the effect will be on these institutions of creating an indefinite number of rival colleges sustained by the endowment of the federal government is not difficult to determine.[8]

Only with the election of Abraham Lincoln, who, like Morrill, was a follower of Henry Clay, were the land-grant colleges established in 1862. Yet American agriculture is still bedeviled by the problem of overproduction.

War, the Episodic Federal Mission

It was also under Lincoln that, in 1863, the National Academy of Sciences (NAS) was incorporated as a military initiative to help build the ironclads and other technologies the North needed to help win its war. But once that war was settled, Congress found no more use for the NAS, which it did not dismantle but instead proceeded to ignore. And that was to be the story of the federal government's funding of military science—until 1940: federal support would be intense during wartime, followed by its neglect upon the resumption of peace.

There was, consequently, a brief revival of government research funding for military purposes during World War I, when institutions such as the Naval Consulting Board (chaired by Thomas Edison) were created, but—again—most such institutions were soon allowed to die after 1919. That holds true in the United States but not in the UK, because Britain abandoned laissez faire in science after WWI, and its government started to fund research. In contrast, the federal government in Washington did not.

U.S. Research in 1940

By 1940, therefore, the government was funding only 23 percent of American research and development (R&D), half of which went to agriculture (still facing overproduction) and half of which went to defense (which has only about a tenth of the economic value of civil research[9]). The federal government's R&D was, therefore, economically marginal.

The remaining 77 percent of U.S. R&D was supported by the private sector (industry, universities' own resources, and foundations). Yet by 1940, the United States had been the richest—and thus the most technologically advanced—country in the world for some 50 years, and it had produced the Wright brothers, Thomas Edison, and Nikola Tesla, among other extraordinary

technologists. The purest of scientists, too, had flourished without the government; Albert Einstein, for example, worked at
Princeton with private funds between 1933 and his death in 1955.

The market and civil society thus fully met the United States'
research needs before 1940.

The Truman Doctrine and the Federal Funding of Science for Its Own Sake

It was, as ever, for military reasons that in June 1941, the federal
government created a new science body, the Office of Scientific
Research and Development (OSRD), which four years later
employed some 6,000 scientists on programs ranging from the
Manhattan Project to antibiotics.

Yet by July 1945, with the threat of peace looming, the OSRD
feared the apparently inevitable demobilization. So that month,
its director, Vannevar Bush, published the book *Science: The Endless Frontier* to argue that OSRD's researchers should continue
to enjoy their salaries and jobs because—he claimed—the federal
government's funding of science would build economic growth in
peacetime the way it had built atom bombs in wartime.

It is now generally forgotten that few people believed Bush's
economic arguments (which is why, contrary to myth, *Science:
The Endless Frontier* dedicated most of its space to the military
applications of research). In those days, people understood that
the United States had grown under laissez faire in research, and
people generally dismissed arguments for government funding of
science as only special pleading by scientists and by corporations
looking for corporate welfare. That was why upon assuming office

Franklin Roosevelt cut back on government-funded research: by 1934, he'd cut the Agriculture Department's research budget (the federal government's largest research budget) from $21.5 million annually to $16.5 million (at the cost of 567 jobs in 1934 alone), and he more than halved the Bureau of Standards' research budget, from $3.9 million (1931) to $1.8 million (1934). But after 1945, the United States was about to go on a permanent war footing.

In his Farewell Address, George Washington had warned against "permanent alliances" and against "excessive partiality for one foreign nation, and excessive dislike for another" (often summarized as his warning against "foreign entanglements"). And until 1947—short wars excepted—that had remained U.S. policy (cf. the United States' refusal to join the League of Nations). Yet in 1947, the British, nearly bankrupt, suspended *Pax Britannica* and prepared to abandon Greece and Turkey to Soviet incursions. Whereupon President Harry Truman codified his doctrine (strengthened in 1948 and transformed into membership in the North Atlantic Treaty Organization in 1949), which might be summarized as *Pax Americana*: America, like Britain before it, was now permanently at war with international transgressors.

Modern war needs science, and modern war needs scientists. In 1942, 1943, and 1945, the U.S. Senate Subcommittee on War Mobilization held hearings on America's shortage of wartime scientists (the peacetime complement had been fully adequate for peace but not for war). And that subcommittee's chair, Harley M. Kilgore, subsequently led the congressional campaign for peacetime science. In 1948, therefore, the federal government's longstanding but modest mission in public health was expanded into the National Institutes of Health (NIH). And in a dramatic break with the past, the National Science Foundation (NSF) was created in 1950 to fund solely academic science.

Truman did not conceive of the NSF as a producer of science but of scientists, who—having been trained—would be deployed into defense. That is why in 1947 he vetoed the first NSF bill, because it met only the aspirations of researchers (its director, for example, was to be appointed by the scientists and trustees of the NSF itself, and its grants were to be distributed by peer review). But Truman wanted a geopolitical science, and in the words of his veto:

> This bill contains provisions which represent such a marked departure from sound principles for the administration of public affairs that I cannot give it my approval. It would in effect vest the determination of vital national policies, the expenditure of large public funds, and the administration of important government functions in a group of individuals who would essentially be private citizens. The proposed National Science Foundation would be divorced from control by the people to an extent that implies a distinct lack of faith in democratic processes.[10]

But by 1950, with the Cold War heating up, Truman accepted a compromise NSF: the president of the United States would appoint its CEO, but the NSF would distribute research funds to the universities by peer review, whence young researchers would emerge trained for military purpose.

Deforming the Universities

Before 1940, most research in the United States was performed where it was economically relevant, namely, within industry. The universities, then, were primarily liberal arts colleges—they were essentially institutions for teaching and scholarship and for speaking truth unto power—so they had to be inducted into applying for government grants. Thus did Fred Stone of the NIH, for example, tell how during the 1950s "it wasn't anything to travel 200,000 miles a year" to help the universities create and submit grant applications.[11] That thus imperiled the universities' autonomy and therefore their academic freedom.

In his famous 1961 farewell speech, President Dwight D. Eisenhower—who for five years had been president of Columbia University—linked the threats the "military-industrial complex" posed on society with the threats the "scientific-technological elite" posed to the universities:

> A steadily increasing share [of research] is conducted for, by, or at the direction of, the Federal government [so] the free university, historically the fountainhead of free ideas and scientific discovery, has experienced a revolution in the conduct of research. Partly because of the huge costs involved, a government contract becomes virtually a substitute for intellectual curiosity. . . .
>
> The prospect of domination of the nation's scholars by Federal employment, project allocations, and the power of money is ever present—and is gravely to be regarded.

Yet in holding scientific research and discovery in respect, as we should, we must also be alert to the equal and opposite danger that public policy could itself become captive of a scientific-technological elite.[12]

But Eisenhower was to be outflanked by two key papers.

Inventing a New Economics of Science

As late as 1942, it was possible for Austrian political economist Joseph Schumpeter to argue that markets were self-sufficient in research ("industrial mutation incessantly revolutionizes the economic structure *from within*"[13]), but ideas of industrial self-sufficiency did not satisfy the geopolitical ideologies of the 1940s. So new ideas had to be found. Enter RAND.

To promote his idea of an NSF, Vannevar Bush joined with the U.S. Air Force and the Douglas Aircraft Company in 1945 to help create Project RAND (**R**esearch **AN**d **D**evelopment; now the RAND Corporation), one mission of which was to lobby for federal funding of science for geopolitical reasons. Bush, the U.S. Air Force, and Douglas were of course highly self-interested, but nonetheless RAND got its money. To secure it indefinitely, RAND invested in an economics-of-R&D project to . . . well, let RAND's own historian continue the narrative:

> RAND's economics-of-R&D project also yielded two of the foundational papers in the field: Richard Nelson's "The Simple Economics of Basic Scientific Research" and Kenneth J. Arrow's "Economic Welfare and the Allocation of Resources for Invention." . . .

Nelson's and Arrow's papers provided appealing economic theories as to why the nation would systematically underinvest in basic research. Their theories had clear policy implications: the U.S. government should invest more in basic research owing to "market failures" in the private sector. These theories have been largely internalized within the now dominant neoclassical economic tradition.[14]

So a self-interested RAND sponsored the research that argued that science was a public good.[15]

Science Installed as a Public Good

In 1954, economist Paul Samuelson published a key paper in which he started to formalize the concept of a public good as being (a) nonexcludable (i.e., a public good couldn't be limited to one person) and (b) nonrivalrous (i.e., one person's use of a public good need not stop someone else from using it).[16] Such a 1954 description was ready-made for Nelson and Arrow in 1959 and 1962, respectively, to argue that science was a public good, because science is (a) published and (b) one person's use of a scientific idea (the laws of thermodynamics, say) does not preclude another person from using it.

Yet science is transparently not a public good.[17] When Edwin Mansfield and colleagues, for example, examined 48 products that had been copied within the major industries of New England during the 1970s, they reported the costs of copying were on average 65 percent of the costs of innovation.[18] The reason was the copiers had to rediscover for themselves the tacit knowledge embedded in the original innovation, a rediscovery so laborious that in some cases, Mansfield and his colleagues found that copying an innovation cost the copiers more than it had cost the original innovators. Moreover, Levin and colleagues' survey of 650 R&D managers provided similar results for the costs of industrial copying.[19]

Yet Mansfield, Levin, and their colleagues had reported only the marginal costs of the actual copying. And Rosenberg[20] and Cohen and Leventhal[21] have shown that companies seeking success in the market need first to sustain the fixed costs of a research staff whose activities are directed toward maintaining their own expertise (in pure science as well as in applied science). And since Griliches[22] and Mansfield[23] have shown that—contrary to myth—a positive correlation exists between the amount of pure science that companies publish and their profits (i.e., pure science is profitable for private industry), those costs will not be trivial.

As economist George Stigler has shown, moreover, companies also need to bear the costs of information;[24] and they also need to bear the costs of failed imitation attempts. We may therefore not know for certain what the average costs of copying in industry are, but they appear to be so high that research, in industrial practice, is excludable in the sense that it is not available to free riders.

Another Natural Experiment

Nonetheless, following the publication of the Nelson and Arrow papers, the federal government's support for R&D surged, and by 1964, the federal government was funding 67 percent of all U.S. research: companies wanting to do research would write grant applications, as if they were charitable not-for-profit foundations needing public support. And the economic consequences were . . . zero. The long-term rate of U.S. GDP per capita growth did not rise.

That was an inconsequence seen globally. Thus in 2007, on reviewing the literature on R&D, Leo Sveikauskas of the U.S. Bureau of Labor Statistics concluded:

> The overall rate of return to R&D is very large. . . . [B]ut, these high returns apply *only* to privately financed R&D [in industry].[25]

In 2003, with regard to using a different methodology and having studied the growth rates of the 21 leading world economies between 1971 and 1998, the Organization for Economic Cooperation and Development (OECD)—which is an intergovernmental economics research unit—had also found:

> Business-performed R&D . . . drives the positive association between total R&D intensity and output growth. . . . The negative results for public R&D are surprising and deserve some qualification. Taken at face value they suggest publicly funded R&D crowds out . . . private R&D.[26]

Even earlier, Walter Park of the American University in Washington, DC, and I had independently made the same discovery, namely, that the public funding of research crowds out its private funding.[27]

The vast expansion in NIH funding also seemed to be inconsequential, and on June 15, 1966, upon launching Medicare, President Lyndon Johnson complained that the "hundreds of millions of dollars that have been spent on laboratory research" had apparently yielded no benefit to patients. "Presidents, in my judgment, need to show more interest in what the specific results of medical research are."[28]

An Open Secret

Discreetly, governments have now recognized that their funding of research is economically irrelevant. Thus in 1981, the public sector across the OECD funded, on average, 44.2 percent of R&D, whereas it now funds only 28.3 percent of R&D,[29] and the total continues to fall. A recent survey across the major research countries of the OECD has "documented a major trend across the most advanced countries: a systematic retreat of public R&D compared to R&D financed by industry."[30] And in a classic example of crowding out, from 1981 to 2013, publicly funded R&D among the lead OECD countries fell from 0.82 percent to 0.67 percent of GDP, whereas industry-funded R&D rose from 0.96 percent to 1.44 percent of GDP. That is, a fall of 0.15 percent of GDP in publicly funded R&D has provoked a rise in industry-funded R&D of 0.48 percent.

I call this an "open secret," because the facts are publicly available, but hardly anyone talks about them: the suggestion that governments need not fund research is simply not welcome, so the downsizing of the governments' support for it has been done with minimal public debate.

U.S. Government—Again—Funding Mission Research Only—Hurrah!

Just as in 1940, the federal government is again funding only 23 percent of U.S. R&D, only for specific missions. Thus, half of the federal government's annual outlay of $122 billion for R&D is on defense ($64 billion), with $30 billion going to health, $11 billion to space, and $11 billion to energy. And those missions of defense, health, and space and of reducing our energy dependence on fossil fuels from the Middle East clearly enjoy popular support.

The federal government's only apparent nonmission research is the annual $5.5 billion for the NSF, but that too is mission based. Its purported mission is to fund the basic science that, in the so-called linear model, is the claimed origin of the applied science that industry needs. But the linear model is now utterly discredited among economists of science and policymakers, which is another open secret that is rarely discussed publicly.[31] In fact, the real mission of the NSF's $5.5 billion is to buy off a powerful lobby that would otherwise clog the op-ed pages of the newspapers on both sides of the aisle with the claim that the federal government's neglect of university science would destroy the economy. And at $5.5 billion annually, it's a trivial cost.

However, a legitimate justification exists for the government funding of science, even though it is 100 percent and 360 degrees opposed to the conventional justification: namely, to challenge—not support—industry. We know, for example, that cigarettes cause lung cancer, not because of the assiduous research of the tobacco companies but because of Adolf Hitler. The Führer was a teetotaling, tree-hugging, eugenicist vegan (he bought into the whole progressive package circa 1933), and among his obsessions was a conviction that cigarette smoking had to be harmful. Upon assuming power, therefore, Hitler instructed his epidemiologists to find the evidence, which they did.[32] (Physician Richard Doll in Britain later claimed credit for the discovery, which had not spilled over widely from the Nazi medical literature, but Doll had been one of the few Britons to have discreetly read the original research reports.)

But even if the government funding of science is healthy because it challenges industry, it nonetheless carries its own risk, namely, crowding out philanthropic research. During the 19th century and the first half of the 20th century, philanthropists in the United States and the UK funded research with marked generosity, yet that funding fell away postwar, after governments stepped in. As Martha Peck, executive director of the Burroughs Wellcome Fund said in 1993, "We've seen foundations turn away from research . . . the perception has been that science is getting it from other sources."[33]

The falling away of government support for R&D has since seen, however, a happy revival of philanthropic research money. And just as the Wellcome Trust (founded in 1936; current endowment £23.2 billion) was once the largest charity of any type on the globe, that palm now goes to the Bill and Melinda Gates Foundation (founded in 2000; current endowment $44.3 billion).

Conclusion

The growth and survival of the myth that science is a public good were fostered by (a) the scientists themselves, who preferred to work on their own agendas at the public's expense rather than to industry's direction at the shareholders' expense; (b) industrialists, who are always on the lookout for handouts from the federal government; (c) the politicians, who see research as an inexpensive way of portraying themselves as latter-day Medicis supporting latter-day Galileos (witness Bill Clinton's claiming in 2000, on behalf of the federal government, the credit for the first draft of the sequencing of the human genome, even though most of its cost had been borne by the Wellcome Trust, a British charity, and Craig Venter's Celera, a for-profit company); and (d) the general public, who like the idea of science being a democratically accountable popular activity.

But the myth was always doubted by presidents (including Andrew Johnson, James Buchanan, FDR, Harry Truman, Ike, and LBJ), who privileged evidence over theory. Also discreetly skeptical have been the discrete denizens of treasuries across the OECD.

In 1994, I predicted that the welfare state's ever-increasing pressure on public funds would cause governments, globally, to cut their budgets for R&D, which would be wholly good, because the subsequent rise of private money would more than compensate for the public sector's retraction.[34] For my pains I received little but abuse,[35] yet the prediction has come to be more than good.[36] We are embarked on a second research golden age.

Consider space exploration, which started in Massachusetts with Robert Goddard (1882–1945). Goddard, a professor at Clark University, developed the first modern rockets (liquid fuel, 1925; gyro stabilizer, 1932; altitude reaching 9,000 feet, 1937).

Those developments were funded privately by the Guggenheims and Hodgkins as not-for-profit ventures. But in view of the geopolitics, the state—in the shape of the Nazis, the Soviets, and the National Aeronautics and Space Administration (NASA)—would appropriate Goddard's work and supplant the funding of the foundations. Today, however, thanks to entrepreneurs like Elon Musk, Jeff Bezos, and Richard Branson, space exploration is about to enter its third funding regime, namely, that of the private for-profit sector. Under those circumstances, should the taxpayer not challenge the continued funding of NASA?

Or consider molecular biology. Its most exciting current development is CRISPR-Cas9 (clustered regularly interspaced short palindromic repeats–CRISPR-associated protein 9), which is a genome editing tool that can edit DNA with almost magical precision. But its discovery owed little or nothing to the centrally planned model of Francis Bacon and everything to the entrepreneurialism Adam Smith proselytized. In the words of Eric Lander of the Massachusetts Institute of Technology:

> Breakthroughs often emerge from completely unpredictable origins. The early heroes of CRISPR were not on a quest to edit the human genome—or even to study human disease. Their motivations were a mix of personal curiosity (to understand bizarre repeat sequences in salt-tolerant microbes), military exigency (to defend against biological warfare), and industrial application (to improve yogurt production).[37]

Thus did CRISPR—which may prove revolutionary in the evolution of all the organisms we value (including ourselves)—emerge as something of an afterthought when yogurt manufacturers picked up on loose ends left over by biological warriors who had themselves picked up on loose ends left over by saltwater microbiologists. This process is best left to competition between the marketplace, civil society, and geopolitical defense research; it cannot be planned.

Or consider electronics, which emerged from the marketplace, not from government-directed labs. Michael Faraday discovered electromagnetic induction in 1831 at the privately funded Royal Institution; in 1883, working in his private laboratory at Menlo Park, New Jersey, Thomas Edison discovered the thermionic effect that underlay the development of diodes and triodes; William Shockley invented the semiconducting transistor circa 1950 while working at the private Bell Labs. Today, with Amazon spending $22.6 billion on research in 2017 and Alphabet $16.6 billion (and Microsoft $14.7 billion, 2018; Facebook $10.2 billion, 2018; Intel $13.1 billion, 2017; Apple $11.6 billion, 2017; Oracle $6.3 billion, 2017; Cisco $6.1 billion, 2017; Qualcomm $5.5 billion, 2017; IBM $5.4 billion, 2017), that industry's future in the care of the private sector remains assured.[38]

Adam Smith had few illusions about industry. He may have described the division of labor as the source of wealth, yet he nonetheless knew it failed us as humans:

> In the progress of the division of labour, the employment
> of the far greater part of those who live by labour, that is,

the great body of the people, comes to be confined to a few very simple operations, frequently to one or two.

In consequence, Smith wrote:

> The man whose whole life is spent performing a few simple operations . . . generally becomes as stupid and ignorant as it is possible for a human creature to become. . . . His dexterity at his own particular trade seems . . . to be acquired at the expense of his intellectual, social, and martial virtues. But in every improved and civilized society this is the state into which the labouring poor, that is, the great body of the people, must necessarily fall, unless government takes some pains to prevent it.[39]

Those pains had to include the government's provision of education, Smith concluded, because the stupid and ignorant human creatures that industry generated could not be entrusted with the schooling of their offspring.

Equally, Smith would have endorsed the government's funding of science to monitor potential threats from industry, such as smoking, but he would have been unsurprised that the past two centuries have confirmed his argument of 1776: research for economic growth and curiosity should be entrusted solely to the market and to the voluntary institutions of civil society.

6

Regulatory Science

Patrick J. Michaels

For decades, many areas of science have been systematically distorted in order to advance regulatory policies that can deprive people of their property, and even their health. In the regulatory science arena—which includes areas such as climate change and regulation of ionizing radiation and other carcinogens or of fine particulate emissions—research is generally funded by the federal government.

Many distortions arise from the incentive structure for scientific advancement, noted in detail below. Others, often involving property issues, are based on a misuse of scientific authority, which itself derives from scientists who have benefited from the incentive structure. Again, these issues will be examined in detail.

Nonetheless, such distortions do not necessarily apply to all areas of regulatory science, nor are federal efforts always pernicious. A shining example of scientific success in an issue with substantial political overtones was the identification of the causative agent for AIDS and the development of treatments that greatly prolong the life of those with that condition. Here, we are interested in the opposite situation, which is dismally frequent.

The near-monopoly nature of science funding in certain fields induces distortions. Later in this chapter, I will provide a more market-based solution that should serve to diversify the scientific enterprise in the regulatory arena. But first we will examine four scientific distortions that should respond to our prescription: (a) the regulatory paradigm for ionizing radiation and carcinogens; (b) the "regulation by committee" of the mining of highly significant deposits of uranium in Virginia; (c) the distortion of the law to prevent exploitation of the world's largest copper, gold, and molybdenum deposits; and (d) the increasing divergence between observed and modeled tropical temperatures. By exploring how each of these areas is distorted by the federal government's de facto monopoly on funding research, and the incentives that funding creates, I hope to provide a clearer, more concrete picture of the kinds of problems a market-based and more open system of scientific funding will solve.

Ionizing Radiation and Carcinogens: Using the Wrong Dose–Response Model

An example of regulatory science gone bad involves ionizing radiation and carcinogens. Ionizing radiation comes from the portions of the electromagnetic spectrum with sufficient energy to remove an electron from an atom, which makes the atom a positively charged ion that is more reactive. X-rays, gamma rays, and the ultraviolet portion of sunlight are common examples.

Carcinogens, possible causes of cancer, include ionizing radiation as well as a tremendous number of natural and anthropogenerated compounds in our environment.

In a Cato Institute book titled *Scientocracy*, University of Massachusetts toxicologist Ed Calabrese writes:

> Current regulations are based upon a deliberate misrepresentation of the scientific basis for the dose response for ionizing radiation-induced mutations by the former leaders of the radiation genetics community. These actions culminated in a successful attempt to manipulate the scientific community and the general public of the U.S. and world community by the prestigious U.S. National Academy of Sciences (NAS) Biological Effects of Atomic Radiation Committee (BEAR I)–Genetics Panel in 1956 when it recommended that the dose response for radiation-induced mutation be changed from a threshold to a linear dose response.

> . . . This model, called the "linearity–no dose threshold" (LNT) searches for the lowest exposure to a carcinogen or ionizing radiation that is associated either with substantial mutations or cancer itself. That should be the starting point for any dose–response model, but it is not. Instead, a line is drawn backward from the detection threshold data point to the origin on the graph. The implication is obvious. By forcing the response through the origin, any exposure—including the most minuscule—is claimed to be dangerous.[1]

Calabrese has extensively documented that strong evidence existed against the LNT when it was adopted for radiation.[2] He continued:

> During the process of their assessment, the BEAR I[3] Genetics Panel would falsify and fabricate the research record concerning the estimate of radiation-induced genomic risk, as I have documented in detail.[4] It made a decision not to share the profound degree of uncertainty amongst the Panel members but rather, to misrepresent it by removing and changing data concerning estimates of genetic mutations in the U.S. population at a certain level of radiation exposure.

One must remember the times. The BEAR I panel met during the heyday of atmospheric testing of nuclear weapons. One constituent of the widely dispersed fallout from those tests was strontium-90. With a half-life of 28.8 years, strontium-90 is metabolized the same as calcium (being in the same column on the periodic table). Consequently, it is incorporated into animal bones and cow's milk, which is consumed by growing children. By calling even the first ingested atom dangerous, the BEAR Committee heightened public fear and pressure for an atmospheric test ban. One can only imagine that the BEAR Committee thought it was performing virtuous public service by using the LNT model.

As Calabrese has repeatedly shown, the dose–response model is wrong. In fact, low doses of some forms of ionizing radiation, like sunlight, can confer health benefits, such as the final synthesis of vitamin D. It is also now known that our cells self-repair DNA, and that repair more than protects against the harmful effects of low-dose radiation.

Calabrese has meticulously documented that BEAR I was heavily influenced by Nobel Prize winner Hermann Muller's work and his dominant personality.[5] Membership on panels like BEAR I is only awarded to people of considerable academic accomplishment, that is, those who have been very successful in the federal funding game, producing significant publications and therefore attaining academic promotion. The professional literature defines the dominant paradigm, which was (and remains) the LNT model. The price of an invitation to BEAR I was professional prestige and acceptance of the LNT model.

Use and Misuse of Authority by the National Academy of Sciences and Federal Committees

It is common for the National Academy of Sciences (NAS), via its subsidiary the National Research Council (NRC), to commission committees of prestigious academics to examine complicated issues like environmental risk. These committees are highly influential and can promote policies that may result in deprivation of people's property rights, as we show here regarding large, privately owned deposits of uranium and copper.

In 1863, President Lincoln requested and signed legislation creating the NAS to "investigate, examine, experiment, and report upon any subject of science." Of course, at the time, he was really interested in new technologies and ideas to successfully prosecute the Civil War. Another believer in expansive government, and again a wartime president, Woodrow Wilson created the NRC (initially called the National Research Foundation) as the research arm of the NAS.

Because they are usually prominent scientists, NRC committee members for a given task are vetted and well-known by the NAS. In controversial areas, a majority view will be "balanced" by one or a few dissenters. By selecting the participants, the NAS gets the results it wants: the incentive structure of science creates biased bodies of literature, and the creators of that literature form biased review bodies. Federal agencies also provide a veneer of authority by forming committees analogous to those of the NRC but tasked with recommending policy options in particular provinces of the regulatory sphere.

Uranium Mining in Virginia: Authority and Misleading Science

On March 28, 1979, two remarkable things happened. Marline Uranium discovered what turned out to be the largest known uranium deposit in the United States, in Pittsylvania County, Virginia, hard along the North Carolina border. Virtually the entire deposit sits on and underneath a single private property, known as Coles Hill, for its owner, Walter Coles Sr. On the very same day, reactor number 2 at Three Mile Island, Pennsylvania, experienced a cooling malfunction that resulted in a partial meltdown. The release of radiation was very limited, but public reaction was stoked by a concurrent (and totally fictional) movie about a nuclear meltdown, *The China Syndrome*. The hoopla eventually resulted in a 1982 ban on uranium mining that can only be lifted by new Virginia legislation.

Exploitation of a new uranium deposit wasn't economically feasible until uranium's price began to rise early in the 21st century. Instead of selling mining rights and reaping an instant profit, Walter Coles tapped his son, Walter Jr., a Wall Street fund manager, to raise enough money to start up a new company, Virginia Uranium, which traded on the Toronto Stock Exchange. Coles raised considerable capital, but the success of the company depended on the lifting of the moratorium.

Coles wanted to play it straight. He proposed that the NAS commission a report on the state of science and technology regarding mining his deposit. He believed it would be fair and impartial, and Coles footed the entire bill for the report. The National Research Council empaneled a committee to do the report, *Uranium Mining in Virginia: Scientific, Technical, Environmental, Human Health and Safety, and Regulatory Aspects of Uranium Mining and Processing in Virginia (UMV)*.

The NRC selected 14 prominent individuals to sit on the committee. Four were viewed as being likely to support exploitation, as they either had consulted in defense of the industry concerning environmental matters or had been involved in mining themselves. An ecosystem hydrologist and a uranium geochemist on the committee were harder to predict, although the hydrologist was a board member of a local environmental activist organization near his home institute, Frostburg State University, in the rugged Maryland panhandle. The vitae of the other eight clearly indicated that they were predisposed against exploitation, including that many were strict believers in the LNT model.

On December 19, 2011, the NRC released the report, knowing full well that one paragraph would be extensively cited:[6]

> If the Commonwealth of Virginia rescinds the existing moratorium on uranium mining, there are steep hurdles to be surmounted before mining and/or processing could be established within a regulatory environment that is appropriately protective of the health and safety of workers, the public, and the environment. There is only limited experience with modern underground and open-pit uranium mining and processing practices in the wider United States, and no such experience in Virginia.[7]

The core arguments creating the "steep hurdles" were geophysical: largely climatic and to a lesser extent tectonic. The climate argument can be summarized as "there have been some big floods in Virginia" and plenty of hurricane strikes. The main climate reference was a non-peer-reviewed *University of Virginia News Letter* article that I coauthored in 1982 in my role as the then–state climatologist.[8]

The body of the *UMV* text repeatedly refers to "extreme" climate-related events (26 instances), and the notion of "extremes" captured the public discourse as a reason to keep the moratorium in place. In town hall meetings, newspaper editorials, and news stories, the specter of contamination of the water supply of Virginia Beach (175 air miles from Coles Hill) by a flood-induced impoundment failure of modestly radioactive mine tailings was repeatedly raised.

In *UMV,* the NRC made little attempt to compare its geophysical analysis of Virginia with conditions in other areas of the country or with the parts of the world where uranium mining or processing has taken or is successfully taking place. Further, no attempt was made to differentiate the localized Coles Hill climate and seismic risk from those of a general survey of the state. In reality, the climate extremes expected at Coles Hill are much less than those experienced elsewhere where uranium is mined. *UMV* contained so many geophysical exaggerations that I published a peer-reviewed article on the topic.

The section on hurricanes is typical of the distortion that mars *UMV:*

> In the period from 1933 to 1996, 27 hurricanes or tropical storms made landfall in Virginia . . . bringing with them the threats of flooding, high winds, and tornadoes.[9]

The relevant citation for that statement is an obscure publication from the National Weather Service Forecast Office in Wakefield, Virginia, titled "Historical Hurricane Tracks, 1933–1998, Virginia *and the Carolinas*" (emphasis added). Examination of the historical tropical cyclone tracks from the National Hurricane Center reveals that only eight tropical storms (and no hurricanes) made landfall in Virginia itself from 1933 through 1998; 19 were in North and South Carolina.[10] *UMV* is clearly misleading in its documentation of Virginia's general tropical cyclone history, an inaccuracy that leads to the assessment of a greater risk than is actually present in the state's current climate. But who is going to check the august NRC for accuracy?

UMV represents a remarkable distortion that can only be characterized as abuse of scientific authority. It had consequences, too. Virginia Uranium (now Virginia Energy Resources) traded in the $5 range before *UMV* was published. Following its publication, the price dropped to about $0.04 per share. The estimated $7 billion valuation of the Coles Hill deposit became worthless because it could not be mined.[11] In effect, the misleading arguments in *UMV* resulted in a massive taking from the Coles family.

The Virginia Uranium fiasco is an *indirect* result of federal funding. All members of an NRC panel are distinguished in some fashion, meaning they have published enough research to be promoted. When the NAS wants an answer (actually, a specific answer), a potential panelist's research and public record determine where they are likely to lie on a particular issue. NRC committees are hardly selected randomly.

But other, related bodies can directly use scientific authority against private property: panels selected by various federal agencies. We need to look to Alaska for a prime example.

Alaska's Pebble Mine

In southern Alaska, about 150 miles west of Anchorage, lies what is currently thought to be the largest known copper, gold, and molybdenum deposit on earth. It is on private land zoned by the state of Alaska for mining. The deposit is drained by a small creek that empties into pristine Lake Iliamna, by volume the seventh-largest lake in the United States. Lake Iliamna ultimately drains into Bristol Bay, home to the world's largest wild sockeye salmon fishery. The deposit is known as the Pebble Mine.

In Pebble, the U.S. Environmental Protection Agency (EPA) colluded with environmental organizations to create what could best be termed a science fiction to prevent the exploitation of private property. It is a textbook case of an empowered agency creating "science" with the sole purpose of executing a policy.

The permitting process for a mine like Pebble is governed by the 1970 National Environmental Policy Act (NEPA). An application for a mining permit is made to the U.S. Army Corps of Engineers and has to include a detailed environmental impact statement. In anticipation, by 2012, Pebble's owner, Northern Dynasty Minerals of Vancouver, had already spent about $150 million in baseline ecological studies of the site, including the local hydrology and geology.

Instead of having the Pebble project proceed with its own environmental impact statement, the EPA substituted its own assessment of the impact of the Pebble project on the Bristol Bay watershed—in place of the formal and comprehensive NEPA environmental impact statement decision process.

The EPA's statement appeared in the form of a draft report. In May 2012, the EPA issued "An Assessment of the Potential Mining Impacts on Salmon Ecosystems of Bristol Bay, Alaska." On April 20, shares of Northern Dynasty Minerals (NAK on the New York Stock Exchange) traded at $5.80; the stock was considered a fairly conservative investment and certainly a staple in many Canadian retirement accounts. After discovering the massive deposit, NAK acquired major financial backing from one of the world's largest mining concerns, Anglo-American, which invested over $500 million in startup expenses for NAK.

By May 25, NAK sold for $2.48. The *draft* EPA report had stripped nearly 60 percent of the stock's value in a month.

According to the EPA, it became involved in the permitting of the project because of petitions against the mine from Native Alaskan tribes in 2010. Verbal statements from EPA employees and official agency documents reveal the existence of an internal EPA "options paper" that makes clear the agency opposed the mine on ideological grounds and had *already decided* to veto the proposal in the spring of 2010. The draft Bristol Bay report, a scientific figleaf, was not released until two years later.

The EPA designed a fictional Pebble mine in its ultimate (2014) "Bristol Bay watershed assessment," which it then used to preempt the real Pebble under the Clean Water Act. This fictional mine was a worst-case mine design.[12] The EPA charged a senior biological scientist named Philip North to design an open-pit "mine" that would have no chance of being approved when reviewed by a professional mining engineer.

The mine plan fabrication is an egregious example of federal agency deception and distortion of "science" reported in a "scientific assessment." The application of this process to deny a person or corporation of property rights is hardly unique, as illustrated by the Virginia Uranium story. In this case, however, it was the direct action of a federal agency concocting a "scientific" rationale rather than a team of established scientists handpicked to sit on an NRC panel. This example is more about the broad scope of federal influence than the specific power of money in the careers of successful scientists.

Global Warming: How Incentives Distort

In academia, achievement of promotion and permanent positions requires large numbers of peer-reviewed publications, which, in climate research, can only be produced with massive financial support. Consequently, scientists seeking advancement must largely support whatever paradigm currently reigns in their field. Federal funders are cautious and are guided to that caution by those they rely on for advice. Large science programs challenging existing paradigms are rare.

Individual proposals that are counterparadigms are also rarely approved, as the peer review will likely be highly critical. Peer reviewers tend to support research that doesn't stray too far from the dominant paradigm, as they likely have done the same in their careers. Therefore, scientists looking to challenge the status quo have difficulty finding the money they need to support their work. Consequently, to succeed, they revert to the existing paradigm. There is a further problem: given the costs involved in climate research, and given that research pushing established boundaries runs a higher risk of producing no publishable results, funders naturally feel more comfortable approving proposals that hew closer to already-established findings or paradigms. The cost of this caution is a reduction in scientific diversity, which is often a prerequisite for scientific breakthroughs.

In the world of climate change, the reigning paradigm is that large computer simulations—known as atmospheric general circulation models or total earth system models—are capable of producing reliable and realistic forecasts of climatic regimes that can be used with confidence to support various policies.

One would think that these models should be systematically tested, but the models suffer from having all been "tuned" to mimic the evolution of surface temperature since 1900.[13]

This tuning makes independent testing of surface temperature predictions very difficult. As an alternative, economist Ross McKitrick and climate scientist John Christy isolated the strongest model signal above the surface, which is an enhanced warming that increases with height in the tropical atmosphere. Because it is far from the surface, it wasn't tuned in. As a family, they found that the models systematically predict between two and three times as much warming as has been observed over the past 60 years.[14]

Political power and large financing accrue when a perceived need exists for large-scale regulations because of some existential threat. Global warming is often portrayed as such. And federal agencies, which tend to regress to existing paradigms, will preferentially fund models that produce large rates of warming with large consequences from that warming. They will also studiously avoid funding research that hypothesizes lessening effects or increasing adaptation, as dilution of a threat imperils future funding. It is noteworthy that the critical test described by McKitrick and Christy was not federally funded.

Gavin Schmidt—director of the National Aeronautics and Space Administration's Goddard Institute for Space Studies, who is also in charge of its climate model—recently documented the incredible number of parameters that are "tuned" in climate models.[15] Clearly, one can produce pretty much any amount of future warming (or cooling) with such broad latitude.[16] Pierre Hourdin, head of the French climate modeling team, notes that models are tuned to give what he calls an "anticipated acceptable result."[17]

Given the newly revealed plasticity of the models, there is an incentive to tune them to output significant warming. Without those forecasts, large funding for the paradigm—which believes in the utility of the highly tuned models—would dry up. As a result, the model-driven paradigm is one of substantial and consequential warming.

The problem with overtuning a model is that it can induce instabilities. The models are all tuned to simulate the warming of the early 20th century, almost a half degree Celsius from the 1910–1945 period, as largely a function of human changes in the atmosphere. But, in fact, atmospheric carbon dioxide was only slightly elevated from its nominal 1850 background in 1910, so the only way that a model could simulate this much warming would be with a sensitivity to temperature that is too high. This tuning is what likely generates the disparity between simulated and observed temperatures away from the tropical surface.[18]

It turns out that only one model, the Russian INM-CM4, tracks the observed history. That is also the model with the least 21st-century warming. In other words, with one exception, there has been a massive systematic failure in the universe of climate models. The fact that they continue as the basis for policy is testimony to the power of incentives and the inability of a community to apply obvious corrective measures because of those incentives.

A Modest Libertarian Proposal

It is good to speculate on an ideal libertarian world. However, it's fair to stipulate that the federal government is going to continue to fund regulatory science and also to stipulate that scientists will continue to respond to the incentives that will result in advancement and permanent employment.

Let's also stipulate that the incentives to remain funded are strong, and they are creating biased canons of knowledge. Stanford's Daniele Fanelli provided strong evidence for this fact when he uncovered a significant and large increase in the number of papers reporting support for a stated (and usually funded) hypothesis.[19] Further, he noted, along with coauthor John Ioannidis, that the addition of an American author to an international team doubles the likelihood of a positive result.[20] A positive finding is one in which the data support a previously stated hypothesis. In fact, hypotheses rather than facts are largely the recipients of public largesse.

That's strong evidence that scientists in fact do try to please their funders.[21] So here is a modest recommendation to fix regulatory science.

Establish a Cap-and-Trade System for Science Funding

A more diverse and richer science will emerge from a more diverse and richer source of funders. Imagine that a finite amount of federal money is available for research on global warming. Currently, in a highly competitive environment, scientists will strive for the most lurid and headline-grabbing results, and they are preferentially published in the flagship journals like *Science* or *Nature*.[22] But certainly other parties are interested in funding global warming science—maybe one of the major energy producers. If they were to contribute, say, 10 percent of the total global warming research outlay, the federal contribution could be dropped by the same amount. One can envision similar buy-in by the enormously wealthy World Wildlife Fund (with an annual budget of approximately $325 million[23]), or major foundations like the Carnegie Endowment and the MacArthur Foundation.

Contributors then get proportional representation on the various supervisory boards as well as a choice of which ones they want to sit on. This benefit gives them important input into the programmatic direction of funded science areas. Making this membership public will encourage investigators with differing points of view to apply, and it can be assumed that their incentive is still continued funding. So like most scientists, they will continue to do research and cite research that supports their continued success.

Diversifying the Canon

Funded results are usually published—otherwise funding has a way of drying up. Funding a broader base of bias will in fact diversify science, whereas not diversifying will narrow the scope of the canon.

Consider global warming and deaths related to urban heat waves. Everyone interested in the field remembers the great French heat wave in August 2003, with nearly 15,000 excess deaths. There was plenty of blame to go around. August is the prime vacation month in France, and so many physicians weren't working. Further, many of the elderly lived in homes without air conditioning, which had been vacated by vacationing children. The more frequent such heat waves become, the more deaths there would be—or so it would seem.

But opposing evidence also exists. Large numbers of deaths result in greater pressure for adaptation (including more air conditioning) and for increasing public health awareness and health care availability. Three years later, in July 2006, a longer and even hotter heat wave hit France, but about 4,400 *fewer* deaths occurred than would have been expected for that long stretch of high temperatures.

We surely see many more papers—which means much more funded research—on increasing (or prospectively increasing) deaths rather than on decreasing mortality rates. The fact is, from the 1960s through the 1990s—despite warmer temperatures (which would have occurred even without global warming, thanks to the urban heat island effect)—population-adjusted heat-related mortality *declined* in all studied U.S. urban areas, except in one (Seattle) where heat waves are rare.[24] But no substantial related literature is studying whether we are reducing deaths below the prospective elevated background because of warming. But if you fund it, they will come. In fact, the paper showing reduced mortality was so groundbreaking that it won the Association of American Geographers "Paper of the Year" award in the "climate" section in 2005.

Or consider Ed Calabrese's revolutionary research on dose response, which provides strong evidence that the current regulatory model—where the first photon of ionizing radiation or the first molecule of an ultimate poison is just as deadly as the bajillionth—is wrong. The only reason he has been so successful is that the military has an abiding interest in organismal responses in the low-dose ranges that service members are often exposed to.

So the U.S. Air Force has been funding Calabrese's work for years, not the National Institutes of Health, which largely funds work within the existing paradigms.

The regulatory science literature is richer and more diverse thanks to Calabrese's more than 600 publications countering the LNT model. Scientific progress and scientific diversity go hand in glove.

Diversifying the Academy

Applying cap-and-trade to regulatory science funding should diversify the associated permanent faculty, as more diverse funding will diversify publications and therefore broaden the span of knowledge within universities and their departments. This approach can be good, both by fertilizing academic discussion within a faculty and by fostering student interaction with mentors more diversified in their research.

To return to the discussion of climate, disproportionate funding has been disbursed to modeling efforts. And judging from the volume of literature, very little has gone to rigorous testing of climate models (although within that sparse literature, evidence exists for systematic problems). Generally, those advocating for more testing will be programmatically supported preferentially by funding sources within the cap that are not taxpayer based, something that cannot happen in today's funding model. Generally speaking, those advocating testing (or complaining about the lack of it) are marginalized within the community. This modest proposal will demarginalize quantitative skepticism, something that does not happens now because of the current incentive structure.

Summary and Conclusions

Regulatory science is being distorted by incentives for professional advancement interacting with a monopoly provider of paradigm-supporting funding. The result has been distortion of the canon of knowledge and the consequent distortion of rational policy outcomes. In addition, and across many areas of regulatory science, a monolithic paradigm structure is inhibiting the research diversity that is necessary to advance science. The prime examples in this chapter deal with global warming and regulation of ionizing radiation and carcinogens.

A related problem is that professional advancement confers authority, which is often used by prestigious organizations like the National Academy of Sciences and its associated National Research Council to pursue policy objectives that can be harmful to property rights and even human health. Prestige-based panels populated by various agencies, like the EPA, have the same unfettered power. Here are three examples: the EPA's preemptive veto of the Pebble Mine under the Obama administration,[25] the BEAR I Committee's adoption of the LNT model for radiation (subsequently broadly applied to toxic chemicals and other carcinogens), and the NRC's misleading geophysical arguments devaluing the largest uranium deposit in the United States.

In response, I propose to substitute a cap-and-trade system for regulatory science research funding, in which public funds, which are currently spent largely in the service of existing paradigms, are partially displaced by more diverse interests. This approach should have the salutary effect of diversifying existing research, rewarding a more diverse faculty with promotion and advancement, creating a more diverse academy, and enhancing scientific progress.

Criminal Justice

Clark Neily

The purpose of criminal law is to identify conduct that threatens the fabric of civil society and to make clear that such conduct will not be tolerated. The kind of conduct that makes civil society impossible falls into several categories that are familiar to most libertarians: (a) using unjustified force against others, (b) taking other people's property by force or fraud, and (c) interfering with other people's ability to engage in conduct that does not violate anyone else's rights. In essence, a sound criminal code seeks to express and implement John Stuart Mill's harm principle, which provides, "The only purpose for which power can be rightfully exercised over any member of a civilized community, against his will, is to prevent harm to others."[1]

A well-functioning criminal justice system seeks to discourage people from violating the relatively few prohibitions that are truly necessary to protect the fabric of civil society. But instead of focusing on the relatively few, genuinely anti-social criminals, our system outlaws a vast array of nonwrongful conduct and thus saddles itself with the responsibility of dealing with an enormous number of "transgressors," only a fraction of whom are actual criminals.

Furthermore, by outlawing activity that is not truly wrongful, the government itself actually creates crime, both by designating people who continue engaging in the proscribed conduct as criminals and oftentimes, as with drug prohibition, by ensuring the existence of one of the most powerful generators of criminal activity known to man: black markets. As a result of these misguided and illiberal policies, the government ends up creating a great amount of crime that would likely not otherwise occur and designating as "criminals" a huge number of decent, peaceful, and otherwise law-abiding people. Faced with the ensuing deluge of transgressors, the government responds by ditching many of our system's most important protective mechanisms and replacing them with more efficient—but often wildly unjust—workarounds.

To appreciate just how thoroughly hacked and unjust our system has become, imagine yourself in the following situation.

You are a young black man driving back to Denver from a friend's farmhouse just outside Boulder, Colorado. Besides a small vegetable garden, your friend also grows several hundred marijuana plants for a nearby medical cannabis dispensary, which is perfectly legal under state law. For a belated birthday gift, your friend offers you a dozen marijuana plants, which you accept and place in the trunk of your car. On the way home, you pass an aggressively nondescript gray sedan with tinted windows and multiple antennae. The sedan pulls out and follows you down the highway for several miles. Looking back in the rearview mirror, you see blue lights flashing from behind the sedan's grill. You are being pulled over, but you have no idea why. Here's what can happen next—and every bit of it is considered perfectly legal by the U.S. Supreme Court.

The police officer approaches the driver's side window and asks if you know why he pulled you over. You don't, but you're smart enough not to guess. The officer says he decided to pull you over for "driving while black," so he followed you until he saw you commit a traffic violation—namely, driving one mile per hour over the speed limit. The officer asks for consent to search your car; you decline. He calls for a canine unit, which arrives just as the officer is handing you a warning for exceeding the speed limit. The officer walks the drug-sniffing dog around your car and it "alerts" near your trunk. The officer takes you out of your car, handcuffs your arms behind your back, and places you in the back seat of his unmarked police car. He pops your trunk, sees the marijuana plants, and advises you that you are now under arrest.

"But marijuana's legal in Colorado," you protest. "Furthermore, you just admitted you decided to stop me for 'driving while black,' which is unconstitutional, so any evidence you found as a result of the stop is fruit of the poisonous tree and therefore inadmissible." (It turns out you've watched a lot of *Law & Order*.)

The officer responds, "Well, I'm part of a federal task force, so I'm authorized to enforce federal laws, and marijuana possession is still a federal crime. As for pulling you over for 'driving while black,' the Supreme Court has held that purely pretextual traffic stops do not violate the Fourth Amendment, which means it's irrelevant why I actually pulled you over. The fact that I could have pulled you over for driving one mile an hour over the speed limit means the stop is valid under the Fourth Amendment and the evidence is admissible. Nice try, though."

At this point, you play your last card. "Ah, but this marijuana was neither bought nor sold—it was given to me as a gift—and it was grown right here in Colorado and never crossed a state line. So the federal government lacks the authority to criminalize my possession of these plants under the Commerce Clause—or any other constitutionally enumerated power."

"Very impressive," the officer says. "But you see, the Supreme Court's got my back there too. A 1995 case called *Gonzales v. Raich* held that Congress may criminalize the purely intrastate, noncommercial distribution of marijuana using its power to regulate commerce among the states. Now I'll grant you that's not the most intuitive reading of that particular passage, but let me ask *you* a question: Are you starting to notice a pattern here at all? Because I'll let you in on a little secret, partner—this is how the system works and this is how it's going to be from now until you decide what charges you want to plead guilty to. Trust me, things will go a lot smoother for you if you just sit back and accept the inevitable. All right, my friend—let's go ahead and get you processed."

Of course, this is a stylized and somewhat absurd hypothetical. But it captures the essence of the system from a defendant's standpoint. The constitutional deck *is* stacked against you, the playing field *is* persistently tilted in favor of the government, and, for most defendants, the outcome *is* all but inevitable. At the risk of stating the obvious, ours is not remotely a libertarian criminal justice system. But is there any such thing, or are those two concepts—libertarian and criminal justice—mutually exclusive?

As explained below, most people—including most libertarians—believe some kind of criminal justice system is necessary to protect peaceful members of society from persistent rights violators. But the goals of a truly just and well-functioning system would be much more modest than those of our present system, and such a system would restore several features that we have largely eliminated, including: (a) robust protection for substantive and procedural rights, (b) strong accountability for those charged with enforcing the laws, and (c) high levels of citizen participation in the administration of criminal justice. After describing several of our current system's most serious pathologies, I will offer some ideas for how we could change the system to more faithfully reflect our historical commitment to justice, liberty, and limited government.

The first problem to consider is the proliferation of illegitimate legal prohibitions, or what we might call "unconstitutional over-criminalization." The scope and substance of criminal law are of course not set in stone. No Platonic ideal criminal code outlaws precisely the right sorts of conduct while leaving people free to do everything not specifically proscribed. Thus, creating a criminal code—that is, a set of laws dictating what people may and may not do and providing punishments for those who transgress—is an inherently political endeavor. But because we live in a constitutional republic rather than a pure democracy, the government is limited in what it may proscribe.

Some of those limits—such as laws censoring speech—are familiar and fairly well-theorized by the courts, whereas other constitutional limits on government power are either ignored outright by the courts or so undertheorized that they are effectively rendered meaningless. In addition to the judiciary's failure to develop a philosophically serious theory of criminal sanction, strong incentives drive legislators to create far more prohibitions than are desirable or defensible, resulting in a recipe for overcriminalization.

Clearly, from a purely philosophical standpoint, one must have a good reason to interfere with another person's freedom of action, and to initiate force against another person without sufficient justification is immoral. What is less clear—at least as far as the Supreme Court and many leading constitutional theorists are concerned—is whether this basic moral obligation applies equally to government. In other words, must government have a good reason to lock people up in cages, or may it do so more or less on a whim? Unfortunately, the Supreme Court has answered this vital question with what amounts to an institutional shrug. Accordingly, the courts have come to treat the arrest and incarceration of citizens as a fairly trivial imposition on their liberty that government may—except in a few settings—impose for no particular reason at all.

As already noted, powerful dynamics cause government officials to criminalize far more conduct than is socially optimal or morally defensible.[2] That's because when voters feel anxious or outraged about something—whether it's the opioid epidemic or a bubble-driven financial crisis—legislators have two basic choices.

Either they can do the hard work of studying the problem to fig-ure out what actually caused it and determine what, if anything, government can realistically do to make things better. Or they can simply pass a law making it illegal to do whatever it is that people think may have caused the problem and start locking peo-ple up as a means of assuring constituents that the problem is being addressed—whether or not it really is.

Take marijuana, for example. For most of our history, the culti-vation or consumption of cannabis was not illegal; in fact, cannabis was historically used in various medicines, such as cough syrup. But, eventually, marijuana use became associated with certain countercultures, and the white establishment came to fear, then demonize, it. But now the pendulum is swinging back, and after a half century or so of severely punishing people for possessing and distributing marijuana, most states have either partly or wholly decriminalized it. The federal government has not followed suit, however, and the penalties under federal law for cultivating or distributing marijuana are severe.[3]

But as more than 60 percent of Americans now realize, those laws exist for no good reason; in fact, the decision to criminal-ize marijuana—but not far deadlier substances such as alcohol and tobacco—is essentially arbitrary. Yet judges not only have upheld the constitutionality of criminalizing marijuana—even when prescribed by doctors to desperately ill people for whom no other treatment has worked—they also continue to participate in the enforcement of those laws by imposing morally indefensible prison sentences on people who violate them. That, in a nutshell, is the face of unconstitutional overcriminalization.

America's criminal justice system was designed to deal with the relatively small number of genuinely anti-social people who exist in a generally healthy and well-functioning society at any given time. But because our policymakers have chosen to criminalize vast amounts of nonwrongful conduct that many perfectly decent, otherwise law-abiding citizens wish to engage in—and will continue to engage in despite the prohibition—our criminal justice system finds itself completely overwhelmed with a task it was never designed for, namely, identifying, arresting, prosecuting, and punishing a vast number of mere transgressors, only a fraction of whom are actual criminals.

It would be impossible to document in a single chapter the myriad ways in which our system cuts corners and abandons painstakingly prescribed constitutional procedures for adjudicating criminal charges. But the essence of the issue is reflected in a single, astonishing statistic: some 95 percent of criminal convictions today are obtained by guilty pleas instead of by jury trials. As Orwell, Dostoevsky, and countless others have observed, many regimes throughout history have excelled in extracting confessions of guilt from their citizens for crimes real or imagined. Unfortunately, America has become a leading member of that ignominious club. We call this process "plea bargaining," but that is really a misnomer—what we really have is a system of coerced confessions that has almost completely supplanted the criminal jury trial and transformed America's criminal justice system into little more than a conviction machine.

Article III of the U.S. Constitution provides that the trial of all crimes shall be by jury. So central was the jury trial to the

Founders' vision of just government that it is the only right mentioned in both the original Constitution and the Bill of Rights. Not coincidentally, the Bill of Rights devotes more words to the subject of juries than any other, because the one thing that virtually every leading thinker of the American Founding appears to have agreed on was the critical role of juries in limiting the power of government.

Alexander Hamilton noted that the Federalists and the Anti-Federalists, "if they agree in nothing else, concur at least in the value they set upon the trial by jury; or if there is any difference between them it consists in this: the former regard it as a valuable safeguard to liberty; the latter represent it as the very palladium of free government."[4] Likewise, Thomas Jefferson considered "trial by jury as the only anchor ever yet imagined by man, by which a government can be held to the principles of its constitution."[5]

Notwithstanding the ineluctably clear command of the Constitution, the jury trial is now practically extinct in America. As noted, more than 95 percent (and more than 97 percent in the federal system!) of criminal convictions today are obtained through plea bargains, using a process that would certainly have alarmed and astonished the Founders.

The story of how a practice that was unknown at the Founding and viewed with great suspicion and even disdain by 19th-century American and English jurists came to supplant the constitutionally prescribed method for adjudicating criminal charges is a fascinating one.[6] But for present purposes, it is enough to briefly describe the two dynamics that transformed American criminal justice from a primarily adversarial system into a primarily transactional one. The first dynamic is coercive plea bargaining; the second is a radical devaluation of the jury trial compared with its role at the time of the Founding. These will be discussed in turn.

One of the most powerful levers prosecutors have is pretrial detention. Simply put, those who are locked up awaiting trial are cut off from family, friends, and other sources of support. They will have a much more difficult time securing and working with counsel to prepare their defense. And given the dirty, dangerous, and generally miserable conditions of so many of the nation's jails, defendants will likely entertain just about any offer that promises either an immediate release or a transfer to a more sanitary and professionally run prison, which is where people who have been convicted of crimes typically serve their sentences.

Another powerful lever is prosecutors' ability to stack charges against a defendant—including charges that carry a mandatory minimum prison sentence—and then offer to drop some of those charges or recommend leniency to the judge at sentencing. Other countries, such as England, impose strict limits on the differential between the length of sentence prosecutors may threaten defendants with if they go to trial and lose versus the discounted sentence prosecutors may offer if defendants confess. However, American prosecutors have unfettered discretion to make draconian threats while offering a comparatively trivial punishment if the defendant will simply agree to plead guilty.[7]

To appreciate just how much pressure prosecutors can bring to bear, consider the case of young computer genius and internet pioneer Aaron Swartz. Swartz was arrested for breaking into a computer closet at the Massachusetts Institute of Technology and connecting a laptop carrying a program he had designed to download articles from the JSTOR academic database. Despite the fact that Swartz caused no permanent damage to any of the systems, and despite JSTOR's disavowal of any "interest in this becoming an ongoing legal matter" once its data were secured, federal prosecutors hit Swartz with a 13-count federal indictment that threatened him with 35 years in prison and a $1 million fine. They offered him six months if he agreed to plead guilty.

Tragically, the pressure was so great and his mental state so fragile that Swartz killed himself during plea negotiations. Outrageous and inhumane as they may seem to the casual observer, clearly nothing was particularly unusual about the tactics used in Swartz's case: U.S. Attorney Carmen Ortiz defended the conduct of her prosecutors as "reasonable" and fully consistent with Department of Justice policy.

The third and fourth major levers of coercive plea bargaining are the complexity of the system and the persistent inadequacy of public defender services. On the one hand, criminal procedure has become so complex that ordinary laypersons cannot simply represent themselves effectively in a criminal trial as was the customary practice at the time of the Founding. That means all criminal defendants, and certainly defendants in felony cases, are well advised to retain counsel. But lawyers—especially good ones—are notoriously expensive, and the vast majority of criminal defendants simply cannot afford one. Accordingly, some 80 percent of criminal defendants are represented by government-furnished counsel—either a public defender or a court-appointed private practitioner who will typically receive a fixed fee, often one that is set at some archaic and shockingly low amount, for his or her services.

On the other hand, although some public defender offices are quite good, many are not, and virtually all are desperately over-worked.[8] The problems with public defenders are well-known and well-documented, and they include a persistent lack of funding that translates into crushing caseloads and inadequate support services, such as investigators and expert witnesses.

Another problem with public defenders is the fact that they are repeat players who carry dozens or even hundreds of cases simul-taneously, often against the same small set of prosecutors. Because taking all of those cases to trial would be impossible, a public defender knows that most of the cases will have to plead out. This approach results in a potential conflict of interest, because public defenders have a strong incentive to maintain sufficiently good relations with the prosecutors to ensure favorable plea offers for all of their clients, even if such an approach may result in less than fully zealous advocacy for particular defendants who might benefit from a more aggressive defense.[9]

As suggested earlier, another dynamic is at work here besides coercion: a radical devaluation of the criminal jury trial as an institution. To understand what happened, one must appreciate that there are two distinct ways to conceive the role of a criminal jury. The first is to think of it as a purely fact-finding body whose sole purpose is to increase the likelihood of a factually accurate verdict: Did this defendant sell a prohibited substance to that undercover officer—yes or no? The second is to think of the jury as playing at least one other, perhaps more important, role in our system of criminal justice: to check the abuse of government power by refusing to allow unjust convictions. The former conception is a relatively recent invention and is essentially mythical; the latter reflects the true role of juries in our system and the consistent understanding of their function both at the American Founding and through more than 1,000 years of our common-law history.

Perhaps not surprisingly, the government transformed both the understanding and the role of juries in our system. That fascinating history is presented in compelling detail in the book titled *Jury Nullification: The Evolution of a Doctrine*.[10] That transformation boils down to a successful campaign by prosecutors and judges to undermine the time-honored institution of conscientious acquittal (often referred to pejoratively and less accurately as "jury nullification") and to deprive jurors of information that might incline them to embrace it in a particular case. Such information might include the punishment the defendant will receive if convicted or the substance of any plea offers made to the defendant, like the six months prosecutors offered Aaron Swartz after threatening him with 35 years in prison.

As a result, whereas Founding-era juries generally knew what punishment the defendant would receive if convicted and understood their time-honored right—even duty—to acquit factually guilty defendants to prevent injustices, modern juries are carefully vetted by prosecutors and supervised by judges to ensure that they remain ignorant of both points. Consequently, "the jury today is, in the words of [Yale law professor] Akhil Amar, a 'shadow of its former self.'"[11]

Thus, the profoundly pathological combination of unconstitutional overcriminalization, coercive plea bargaining, inadequate representation, and neutered juries has radically transformed our criminal justice system. Instead of focusing on genuine criminals and proving their guilt beyond a reasonable doubt in an open and adversarial system, prosecutors spend most of their time racking up convictions by extracting confessions from the guilty and the innocent alike.[12]

So what would a well-functioning and truly just criminal justice system look like and how would it differ from ours?

First and foremost, it would recognize the criminal sanction for what it is: a public policy tool of last resort that should be deployed only when the failure to do so would threaten the very fabric of civil society and prompt private citizens to take matters into their own hands in the form of vigilante justice. Second, it would restore citizen participation to its rightful place at the heart of the criminal justice system, both by ensuring that all or most convictions are obtained through jury trials rather than guilty pleas and by enabling civil juries to hold police and prosecutors liable for abusing their power. Third, it would seek to level the playing field between citizens and law enforcement to ensure that the adjudication of criminal charges is a genuinely fair and adversarial process. And finally, it would impose appropriate constraints on specially empowered actors within the system, particularly police officers and prosecutors, to ensure that they are properly incentivized to avoid abusing their authority and properly accountable to their victims when they do. Here's how this might look in practice.

The first line of defense against overcriminalization would be a judiciary that properly interprets the Constitution as requiring the government to have a very good reason for putting people in cages. As discussed, that would be a radical departure from current jurisprudence, which requires the government to provide neither a good nor even an honest explanation for enforcing most criminal laws. A properly robust standard of judicial review would strike down a substantial number of existing criminal laws, including many, if not all, drug prohibitions. Ending the so-called war on drugs would reduce crime and enable police and prosecutors to devote their attention to actual, rights-violating crimes such as homicide, rape, robbery, and theft. The second major reform would be to vastly reduce the prevalence of plea bargaining by eliminating (or at least substantially constraining) several of the most coercive levers in the prosecutorial toolbox. As previously discussed, those levers include pretrial detention, inadequate legal representation, and the so-called trial penalty, that is, the often massive differential between what punishment prosecutors can threaten defendants with and what they can offer to induce a plea.

Such reform would result in pretrial detention becoming the exception, not the rule. Inadequate legal representation would be addressed by requiring roughly equal funding for defense counsel as for prosecutors and also by allowing defendants to hire counsel of their own choosing using government-funded vouchers instead of simply assigning defendants a government-employed public defender. The trial penalty would be addressed by imposing a hard cap of, say, 10 to 20 percent on the discount between the sentence threatened in an indictment and the sentence offered in plea bargaining.

Another key reform in this area would be a prohibition on bribing witnesses. Bribing witnesses is, of course, already illegal, and indeed a federal law makes it a felony to offer "anything of value to any person for or because of testimony" to be given by that person at any trial or hearing.[13] Incredibly, however, that statute has been interpreted by the courts as inapplicable to a single group of lawyers (prosecutors) in a single type of judicial proceeding (a criminal prosecution).[14] As a result, prosecutors may—and routinely do—pay for witness testimony using not just material inducements but also the one thing more valuable than money: freedom in the form of reduced or dismissed charges. The government's use of "snitches" has had a predictable and well-documented corrupting influence on criminal prosecutions and has led to a considerable number of false convictions. Compelling reasons exist for making it illegal to bribe witnesses, and those reasons apply equally to prosecutors.

The third major reform we should implement is to restore citizen participation in the administration of criminal justice. That reform would in turn require two distinct changes to current policy. The first change involves restoring the criminal jury to its Founding-era role as not merely a finder of fact but also a preventer of injustice. The second policy change would be to eliminate various immunity doctrines that enable government agents—including particularly police and prosecutors—to avoid civil liability for abusing their authority.

To reiterate, a crucial distinction between Founding-era juries and modern juries is that the former typically understood what punishment defendants would receive if convicted, whereas the latter generally do not. Indeed, prosecutors now go to extraordinary lengths to prevent jurors from learning what will happen to defendants if they are convicted, including not just the length of the prison sentence, but also collateral consequences, such as loss of various civil rights or deportation for noncitizens.

Another important distinction is that Founding-era jurors would likely have been both familiar with and supportive of "jury nullification," more accurately referred to as "jury independence" or "conscientious acquittal." All of those terms refer to a jury's decision not to convict a defendant whose factual guilt has been proved beyond a reasonable doubt when the jury believes it would be unjust or otherwise inappropriate to do so. This situation might include defendants who have been charged with conduct that jurors believe should not be illegal in the first place, such as simple marijuana possession; defendants who have been charged with a crime that should be punished, but not as harshly as the government proposes; and defendants who appear to have been unfairly singled out or otherwise targeted by the government for inappropriate reasons, such as retaliation for political dissent.[15]

But while conscientious acquittal has a long and storied history in the Anglo-American legal tradition that predates even the Magna Carta, it is subject to various misconceptions and caricatures, including the idea that it empowers jurors to "nullify" democratically enacted laws. In fact, jurors have no such power, and a moment's reflection shows how nonsensical the concept is. Unlike judges, jurors are not called upon to assess the constitutionality of laws and there is no mechanism by which they can strike down, or "nullify," any piece of legislation. Instead, the only power a jury has is to acquit a particular defendant of particular charges under the circumstances of a particular case. If a mother is charged with marijuana possession and child endangerment for administering cannabinoids to her epileptic son at the direction of his pediatrician and a jury acquits her, has that jury "nullified" laws against child endangerment or marijuana possession? Plainly not, and it is preposterous to suggest otherwise. Indeed, some or all of those same jurors might well vote to convict a different mother who fed her healthy child a marijuana-laced brownie "just for the fun of it." Simply put, conscientious acquittal (aka "jury nullification," a misnomer) is not about undermining duly enacted laws; rather, it is about checking the government's abuse of power when the government seeks to enforce those laws in a manifestly unjust way.

Unfortunately, the current status of conscientious acquittal in American courts remains unclear. On the one hand, the Supreme Court has held that criminal defendants are not entitled to have jurors instructed that they are permitted to acquit the defendant for any reason, including their belief that it would be unjust to convict a defendant whom they believe to be factually guilty.[16] On the other hand, it remains an open question in most jurisdictions whether the trial judge has the discretion to advise jurors about their power to engage in conscientious acquittal if the defendant requests such an instruction.

A related question is whether individuals who are not involved in the case may provide jurors with general information about conscientious acquittal as well as specific information about the particular case on which they are serving. Federal and state laws prohibit jury tampering, but those laws are not models of precision, and their wording leaves significant doubt about which communications are covered and which are not. As a result, people have been prosecuted for activity as prosaic as simply handing out jury nullification literature outside courthouses. And most prosecutors believe it is illegal to share case-specific information, such as probable sentence length or the substance of any plea offers made to the defendant by the prosecution before trial.

But even assuming such information is covered by existing jury-tampering statutes, the question remains whether communicating it to an empaneled juror (or anyone else for that matter) might be protected by the First Amendment. The short answer is yes, because dictating to people what they may say to empaneled jurors (cautioning them to arrive early at the courthouse to secure parking, for example, which is fine, versus advising them that the defendant in their case is facing a 25-year mandatory minimum sentence for having a gun in his car during a drug deal, which is not fine) is a classic content-based restriction on expression and as such must meet the highest level of judicial review: strict scrutiny.[17] To satisfy strict scrutiny, the government must demonstrate that it has a compelling interest in restricting the speech in question, and that the means chosen to restrict the speech are narrowly tailored to that interest.

That poses a fascinating question: Does the government have a compelling interest in ensuring that no one communicates to jurors regarding such public—and publicly available—information as what punishment the defendant will receive (or what the likely range of punishments will be) if they convict and the fact that American courts have repeatedly acknowledged the legitimacy of conscientious acquittal even if they have not actually embraced it as something they wish to see jurors actually contemplate in specific cases?

To ask that question is to answer it: the government has no interest in keeping jurors ignorant of most publicly available information about the cases they are participating in, and certainly not when the only reason for doing so is to prop up an essentially mythical vision of the criminal jury as a purely fact-finding body. And although the legal doctrine in this area is quite thin—not to mention undertheorized and even glib—the Cato Institute has launched a strategic amicus campaign designed to vindicate people's right to educate jurors about their historic role in checking the abuse of government power—including the pervasive unconstitutional overcriminalization and coercive plea bargaining that have largely stripped our criminal justice system of both its efficacy and its legitimacy—and to equip them with information relevant to that duty.

A key question is how prosecutorial behavior might change with the advent of properly informed juries. The short answer is that we can't say for sure because it is a practice that has not been tried in living memory. But we can surmise that prosecutors would have to exercise far greater caution, both in their charging decisions and in their conduct of plea negotiations, lest they incur the ire of a jury that has come to believe the prosecutor has exercised her authority in bad faith in a transparent effort to coerce the defendant into pleading guilty. Some prosecutors are fond of saying, "If you can't stand the time, don't do the crime," to which the defendants who enjoy the protections of a properly informed jury might respond, "If you can't toe the line, don't threaten the time."

The second jury-related policy change is to restore the ability of citizens to impose civil liability on public officials who abuse their power by violating people's rights. In fact, a federal law on the books (42 U.S.C. § 1983, colloquially referred to as "Section 1983") seeks to do precisely that by creating a cause of action for people who suffer the "deprivation of any rights" at the hands of any state or local official. Unfortunately, the Supreme Court has largely gutted Section 1983 by inventing a variety of immunity doctrines that make it difficult—and in some cases impossible—to hold government actors liable for their misconduct.

The three cornerstones of this near-zero-accountability policy for law enforcement are qualified immunity, absolute prosecutorial immunity, and the elimination of employer liability for government agencies such as police departments and district attorneys' offices.

The first of those policies, qualified immunity, radically narrows the scope of Section 1983 liability by effectively inserting the words "clearly established" before "any right." That means that to bring a lawsuit against a public official, would-be plaintiffs must show not only that the conduct in question violated their rights (as the literal language of the statute provides), but also that a pre-existing case in the relevant jurisdiction had sufficiently similar facts that no police officer or other public official could have had any doubt that the particular act in question—whether it be ramming a car off the highway, throwing an unarmed woman to the ground for walking away from a voluntary interview with police, or conducting a strip search of a child without parental consent—is impermissible. And if there is no case directly on point, then the citizen cannot sue, and, perhaps equally important, a jury will have no opportunity to convey to the relevant official the community's sentiment about the propriety or culpability of the act in question.

The next accountability-destroying doctrine is called absolute prosecutorial immunity. Like qualified immunity, it was invented out of whole cloth by the Supreme Court and was effectively appended to the text of Section 1983, which makes no special provision or exemption for prosecutors (or any other government official for that matter). Absolute prosecutorial immunity is precisely what it sounds like: a complete bar on suing prosecutors for anything they do within the scope of their job as a prosecutor. Incredibly, that includes deliberate acts of malfeasance, such as knowingly and even vindictively prosecuting an innocent person and even suborning perjury to help secure an unjust conviction.

The Supreme Court's twin rationales for absolute prosecutorial immunity are both risible and empirically unfounded: first, the Court asserts, in the face of voluminous evidence to the contrary, that other mechanisms besides civil liability suffice to hold prosecutors accountable for their misconduct. And second, the Court fears, again without evidence, that prosecutors would be unduly distracted if they could be sued by people whose rights they are claimed to have violated in the course of a criminal proceeding— even to the point that some people might choose not to become prosecutors if, like every other professional, they could be sued for injuries they cause through their negligent or willful misconduct.

Finally, the Supreme Court has decided that the standard common-law doctrine of employer liability, or *respondeat superior*, should not apply to police departments and other public employers. Thus, if a Domino's Pizza driver smashes into your car in an act of road rage while delivering a pizza, you can sue Domino's for any injuries its driver causes you while acting in the course and scope of his employment—in this case, delivering a pizza. By contrast, if a police officer runs you off the road for no good reason, you cannot sue the officer's employer, the police department he works for. Again, the text of Section 1983 contains no basis for this so-called *Monell* doctrine[18]—it is simply another special privilege invented out of whole cloth by the Supreme Court to help shield government officials and agencies from accountability.

A libertarian criminal justice system would eliminate all of these immunity doctrines because they are unjust and counterproductive. Instead of immunizing and indemnifying police for their misconduct, as we do now, a libertarian system would emphasize personal responsibility and require police to purchase professional liability insurance, just like doctors, lawyers, and engineers must. Besides providing better redress to victims, this approach would harness the power of the market to reward rights-respecting police who manage to do their jobs without violating people's rights with lower premium costs while forcing rights-violating officers to internalize the costs of their misconduct in the form of higher premium costs—just like unsafe drivers and malpractice-prone doctors are penalized for their behavior. Indeed, because insurance companies are so adept at identifying risk, there is every reason to believe the worst offenders would eventually render themselves uninsurable and thus unemployable, which is precisely what we want. These positive dynamics would, of course, be reinforced by eliminating the *Monell* doctrine and imposing employer liability on police departments and district attorney offices. Among other things, this would give supervisors a strong incentive to weed out marginal applicants for those positions, maintain high standards of training and conduct for those who are hired, and exhibit a much lower tolerance for "bad apples."

There is a less obvious benefit to substantially increasing police and prosecutors' exposure to civil liability that bears further consideration. In our current system, police spend a remarkable amount of time ravaging low-hanging fruit. Thus, there were more arrests in 2015, 2016, and 2017 for marijuana possession than for all violent index crimes (murder and nonnegligent manslaughter, rape, robbery, and aggravated assault) *combined.*[19] This is plainly a misallocation of law enforcement resources that is presumably occasioned in part by officers' relative indifference to the quality of a given arrest as long as they have a sufficient quantity of arrests. Given that officers receive roughly the same credit for a marijuana bust as for taking down an armed robber or closing a cold rape case, we should expect police to focus on the easiest arrests, not the most socially beneficial ones that are harder and more time-consuming to solve.

But what if every interaction with a citizen carried the very real risk of personal liability for the police officer? And what if every prosecution carried a similar risk of liability for the prosecutor? It seems plausible to suppose that police and prosecutors would shift their focus to genuinely bad people—true criminals whose behavior actually hurts other people or otherwise threatens the very fabric of civil society—both because the value of getting those people off the street is worth the financial risk *and* because genuinely bad people have a much lower chance of winning a damages award against a police officer or prosecutor who may have engaged in some borderline conduct to make the arrest or secure the conviction. By contrast, people who were not hurting anyone and were simply minding their own business or engaged in peaceful commerce with others when law enforcement chose to involve itself—they would make much more sympathetic civil-rights plaintiffs, and the kind of people police and prosecutors might choose to steer clear of unless absolutely necessary. Can we be sure the incentives would align that way? No, we can't be sure. But given the system we have now, it would be worth experimenting to see if they might. Most people—including most libertarians—agree that operating a criminal justice system is a legitimate and indeed vital function of government. To be legitimate, however, a criminal justice system must punish only those people who truly deserve punishment, and it must do so in a way that is proportionate to the magnitude of their wrongdoing. Importantly, it must do those things in a substantively fair way, one that also has the appearance of fairness. Across all of those axes, America's criminal justice system is failing miserably. Fortunately, we know how to do better—all it takes is the will to do so.

8

Intelligence and Surveillance

Patrick G. Eddington

Intelligence: From the Bible to the Modern Age

Now Joshua sent men from Jericho to Ai, which is near
Beth-aven, east of Bethel, and said to them, "Go up and
spy out the land." So the men went up and spied out Ai.

—Joshua 7:2, New American Standard Bible

Since the creation of the first human kingdoms thousands of
years ago, rulers have used their most trusted servants to gather
information on potential enemies—foreign and domestic. By
Caesar's day, Rome had well-developed military and political
intelligence capabilities.[1] During the American Civil War, both
sides employed frontline scouts (on foot and on horseback) as well
as clandestine operatives located deep in enemy territory.[2] Union
forces took the first step in the realm of aerial reconnaissance by
using balloons for close observation of Confederate formations.

Between the end of the Civil War and the outbreak of the Spanish-American War, Army intelligence largely withered aside from mapmaking and maintaining cavalry scouts. The Navy fared slightly better, establishing what would become the Office of Naval Intelligence in 1882 and slowly building a cadre of U.S. Navy officers periodically posted abroad to monitor foreign naval, military, and political developments.[3] America's emergence on the global stage in the late 1890s presaged the expansion of America's intelligence apparatus.

The Creation of the Modern American National Security State

It was not until the early 20th century that the United States developed the human, technological, and legal tools to give it some measure of advance warning about possible foreign dangers. But as Americans would learn the hard way, those capabilities were a double-edged sword: they could be used abroad or at home.

From the end of the Civil War until 1908, the U.S. Secret Service was the lone civilian investigative and intelligence component of the federal government. During the Spanish-American War, Secret Service agents not only spied on Spanish government officials in North America but also busted up an alleged Spanish spy ring operating on American soil.[4] But the Secret Service also turned its gaze on Americans, especially in the wake of President William McKinley's assassination in September 1901.

McKinley was killed by Leon Czolgosz, a mentally unstable self-proclaimed anarchist. After McKinley's death, the Secret Service was at the forefront of a national crackdown on known or suspected anarchists, with the names, addresses, and associates of those accused of anarchist beliefs maintained in ledgers at the Treasury Department, the parent entity of the Secret Service.[5]

President Theodore Roosevelt made overly aggressive use of the Secret Service for a range of investigations, including against political opponents in his own party, usually under the guise of anti-corruption investigations. The agents were typically detailed to other federal departments or agencies who requested them. The backlash came in the spring of 1908, when Congress banned the Secret Service from paying the salaries of Secret Service agents detailed to other agencies; the move effectively limited the Secret Service to protecting the president and chasing counterfeiters.[6]

Roosevelt was undeterred. He ordered Attorney General Charles Bonaparte to create a cadre of federal investigators within the Justice Department using generally appropriated funds. Launched on July 26, 1908, the new unit was known as the Bureau of Investigation (BoI). By November 1908, the BoI was spying on American journalists; by the spring of 1909, it was spying on American socialists.[7]

Once America entered World War I, the BoI, the Secret Service, the Army's Military Intelligence Division, and the Office of Naval Intelligence engaged in domestic spying against a huge range of individuals and groups. As historian Roy Talbert Jr. noted:

> The enemies were varied: Socialists, pacifists, supporters of pacifists, Germans, German-Americans, Americans suspected of being pro-German, Americans suspected

of being neutral, the [Industrial Workers of the World], black activists, and labor agitators active in too many sensitive industries.[8]

Armed with new, draconian laws such as the Espionage Act,[9] the Trading with the Enemy Act,[10] and the Food Control Act,[11] federal agents investigated Americans with little or no probable cause, disregarding the Fourth Amendment. Newspapers were either censored by the edition, or in the case of the socialist *Milwaukee Leader*, banned from the mails entirely.[12] Hundreds were convicted under the Espionage Act, often on the basis of spurious gossip or outright falsehoods gathered by civilian and military intelligence and law enforcement officials.

After the war, Congress repealed some of the laws used for political persecution—the Sedition Act and the Food Control Act—but the Espionage Act and the Trading with the Enemy Act were left in place. In doing so, Congress effectively codified tools the BoI, the Secret Service, and military intelligence agents could use against alleged domestic enemies in peacetime or in war.

Congress: Witch Hunt Enabler and Partner

Indeed, during the interwar period, the BoI—renamed the Federal Bureau of Investigation (FBI) in 1935—as well as its military counterparts, conducted domestic surveillance against various individual Americans and groups—African Americans, organized labor, and, as war came to Europe and the Pacific from the mid-1930s on, German Americans and Japanese Americans.[13] Also during this period, the "Congressional witch hunt" style of investigation came into vogue, starting with the Fish Committee in 1930.

Named after Representative Hamilton Fish III (R-NY), the committee investigated the professional, and even to some degree the personal, lives of those it alleged had Soviet or other communist connections. In its final report in early 1931, the Fish Committee branded the American Civil Liberties Union (ACLU) as being "closely affiliated with the communist movement in the United States" and stated that "fully 90 per cent of its efforts are on behalf of communists . . . ."[14] The advocacy organization represented a range of Americans. And although the ACLU certainly had defended a large number of alleged or actual communists in federal courts, the committee produced no evidence that it was controlled or funded by the Soviets.

The Fish Committee's charges against the ACLU were wildly misleading at best, and outright lies at worst. But the greatest damage to the rights of Americans was caused by the precedent of the Fish Committee itself. A congressional committee had been authorized and used to attack Americans, individually or based on group affiliation, for their political beliefs.

Hitler's rise to power in Germany in the early 1930s subsequently triggered the creation of yet another "investigative" committee—the McCormack-Dickstein Committee, which operated between 1934 and 1935.[15] That committee was followed in 1938 by the Special Committee on Un-American Activities, better known as the Dies Committee for its chairman, Representative Martin Dies (D-TX).[16]

Both the McCormack-Dickstein and Dies Committees employed investigators to look into the activities of individual Americans and groups—and the McCormack-Dickstein Committee went so far as to place informants inside alleged or actual pro-Nazi groups, essentially usurping traditional federal law enforcement functions. Commenting on the legacy of the Dies Committee, author August Raymond Ogden rather understatedly observed, "It stands in the history of the House of Representatives as an example of what an investigating committee should not be."[17]

Instead of learning the correct lessons from the Dies Committee experience, Congress doubled down on the committee's tactics by permanently reauthorizing the House Un-American Activities Committee (HUAC) in 1945, which would for the next 30 years cooperate closely with the FBI in investigating Americans with alleged "subversive" or communist ties. As the official House of Representative website's brief history of HUAC notes, "At the height of the Cold War rivalry between the United States and the Soviet Union, HUAC's influence soared and contributed to a climate of domestic fear stoked by its sensational and often unsubstantiated investigations."[18]

Federal Courts: Eviscerators of the Bill of Rights

As the size of the federal law enforcement and intelligence apparatus grew, federal courts issued a series of decisions that chipped away at the core protections embodied in the Bill of Rights.

The 1914 decision *Weeks v. United States* made it illegal for investigators to seize from a person's home and use in court, without a warrant, things like telegrams or cables. But the case did not address whether federal authorities could simply go to Western Union and demand—without a warrant—copies of the telegrams or cables of an American.[19] In fact, federal agents did precisely that in the run-up to WWI, after which companies like Western Union *volunteered* to supply such information to the BoI and the Secret Service.[20]

During WWI, the Supreme Court ruled the Espionage Act constitutional, a decision that resulted in the prosecution and persecution of political figures such as former Socialist Party presidential candidate Eugene V. Debs.[21] A decade later, in *Olmstead v. United States*, the Court ruled that federal wiretaps conducted off the property of a person under surveillance that intercepted the subject's personal telephone calls did not violate the Fourth Amendment.[22] And during World War II, in *Korematsu v. United States*, the Court upheld the conviction of the Japanese American plaintiff for his refusal to evacuate his home on the West Coast under Executive Order 9066. Detailed intelligence reports confirming that the overwhelming majority of Japanese Americans posed no security threat were not provided to the Court.[23]

During the Cold War, federal courts generally continued to affirm the right of federal law enforcement and intelligence agencies to collect information on Americans. That began to change in the late 1960s.

In December 1967, the Supreme Court reversed its finding in *Olmstead*, declaring in *Katz v. United States* that (in the words of Justice Potter Stewart) the Fourth Amendment "protects people, not places" and that it applies to oral statements as well as tangible objects.[24] Four years later, the first of a series of domestic surveillance revelations would ultimately lead to the creation of the Senate Select Committee to Study Governmental Operations with

Respect to Intelligence Activities, better known as the Church Committee, after its chairman Senator Frank Church (D-ID).[25]

The multihearing, multivolume investigation conducted by Church and his colleagues laid bare the radical domestic surveillance and political repression orchestrated by the FBI, the National Security Agency (NSA), and the Central Intelligence Agency (CIA) from 1945 onward.[26] Although the FBI's campaign to discredit Dr. Martin Luther King Jr. became one of the best-known episodes of abuse, it was only one of many carried out against Americans from virtually every walk of life.

As a result of the Church Committee's findings, Congress created dedicated intelligence oversight committees in each chamber and also passed the Foreign Intelligence Surveillance Act (FISA) in 1978—a law designed to prevent mass warrantless surveillance of Americans.

The FISA statute created the Foreign Intelligence Surveillance Court (FISC) to review executive branch applications ostensibly for foreign intelligence–related surveillance—the first time Congress had created a court designed to operate in complete secrecy and without the normal adversarial process used in Article III federal courts.[27] For decades, the FISC operated without the public really understanding what kinds of surveillance it was approving and what that meant for the sanctity of Americans' communications.

Al Qaeda's unprovoked attack on the United States on September 11, 2001, ushered in a new, radical era of federal surveillance. Just six weeks after the attacks and with minimal debate, Congress passed the USA PATRIOT Act, a bill that vastly increased the scope and kinds of information federal authorities could collect, often without needing a court-approved warrant.[28] During the same period, the NSA began a secret, warrantless surveillance program named Stellar Wind that bypassed the FISC entirely for over two years.[29]

The *New York Times* exposure of the Stellar Wind program in December 2005 touched off a years-long debate over newly out-of-control executive surveillance powers carried out in the name of "national security."[30] The ensuing debate produced the so-called Protect America Act (which essentially simply made the previously illegal Stellar Wind program legal),[31] but critics managed to insert an expiration provision into the law that triggered another legislative showdown in 2008.

The result was the FISA Amendments Act,[32] a bill that supporters claimed would preclude the kind of mass surveillance that had targeted Americans under the Stellar Wind program. The law, originally passed in 2008, was renewed in 2012. For a time it appeared that the debate over federal surveillance powers was winding down.

However, all of that changed in June 2013, when NSA contractor-turned-whistleblower Edward Snowden revealed to the world that the FISC had been approving mass surveillance of the telephone calls of Americans.[33]

In the months and years after Snowden's initial revelations, Americans engaged in the largest, most sustained public debate about federal spying powers since the Church Committee nearly 40 years earlier. Indeed, Snowden's revelations—and others that followed—demonstrated that the very structure designed to prevent mass surveillance against Americans had led to that very mass surveillance—exactly what Bill of Rights defenders had always feared.

The question remains: What, if anything, can be done to rein in federal surveillance and related political repression while still avoiding 9/11-like disasters?

Toward a Liberty-Centric Approach to Security

The Founders constructed the Fourth Amendment with great care and deliberation. The idea that people or their property should be searched and seized only when the government has real probable cause to believe they have committed a crime was foundational to the American Revolutionary experience. Warrantless seizures and searches were the proximate cause of the Revolution.

The Founders never intended their experience under the British crown to be repeated by the new government they created. That they failed has nothing to do with the text of the Fourth Amendment. It has everything to do with subsequent chief executives, courts, and Congresses failing to uphold that text. Despite the damage done to the Fourth Amendment, and thus to our rights, the damage can be undone, and fairly simply.

A key step is to repeal both the PATRIOT Act and the FISA Amendments Act. In the case of the former, we know that the law has not stopped a single terrorist attack on this country.[34] In the case of the latter, no executive branch official has ever been able to demonstrate that the massive, continuing collection of the overseas phone calls, text messages, and related digital data of innocent Americans has made us one bit safer. That Congress has continued to renew both acts shows how little learning takes place on Capitol Hill . . . which brings me to the core problem: Congress and the American voter.

As the old saying goes, "The people get the government they deserve." The failure of American voters to make the protection *of their own liberty* a top issue with politicians is *the* cause of the loss of our Fourth Amendment rights.

American voters *could* choose House members who would impeach executive branch officials or federal judges who order or allow warrantless mass surveillance of citizens. American voters *could* choose senators who would only appoint judges who take a strict approach to the Bill of Rights in general and to the Fourth Amendment in particular. American voters *could* elect a chief executive who unconditionally pledges to uphold the letter of the Bill of Rights and to expose and stop any unconstitutional surveillance activities he or she discovers upon assuming office.

Assuming all of those conditions could be met—and, in fact, they could—what would intelligence collection in a truly liberty-centric government look like?

First, the FBI would be prohibited from initiating suspicionless "assessments" of individuals—de facto investigations that require no criminal predicate to initiate.[35] In a foreign intelligence context, the FBI should investigate Americans only when it has met the Constitution's probable cause standard that a crime has been or is being committed.

Second, Congress should pass legislation barring government at any level from requiring electronic device manufacturers to create flaws in their software or hardware—so-called encryption backdoors—to facilitate government surveillance. In the digital age, our smartphones, tablets, and computers contain essential data on our lives: our personal and business contacts, our most cherished photographic and video memories, our private and business communications. The international standard for protecting those communications uses encryption—a process involving the conversion of our data into a protected code to prevent unauthorized access.

The ability to conduct secure communications via encryption protocols—especially for online purchases—is a cornerstone of the 21st-century economy. Protecting those communications is already a complicated and difficult task. Even with the best intentions, software designers make mistakes, including mistakes in encryption protocols. Government-mandated flaws in encryption would increase, not reduce, cybercrime—and in the process make us all more vulnerable to cyberattacks. If we are to have confidence in our digital communications and in the protection of our rights, Congress must outlaw so-called encryption backdoors forever.

Third, to ensure compliance with this new liberty-centric approach, the Government Accountability Office (GAO)—Congress's agency watchdog—should be tasked to monitor FBI, CIA, and NSA compliance with the Fourth Amendment. GAO personnel would be stationed at each of these agencies, with unfettered access to the intelligence collection sources, methods, and databases used by each, to ensure that no data on innocent Americans were being collected, stored, or otherwise used in violation of the Constitution.

The GAO would also be tasked with conducting ongoing audits of Intelligence Community programs and activities to ensure that they actually work at getting information on foreign actors potentially threatening the United States. We know from past GAO audits that the Pentagon has squandered tens of billions of dollars on various programs—wasting taxpayer money and making the country less, not more, safe. The same rigor should be applied to all Intelligence Community programs as well.

In this life, nothing is perfect. We have no guarantee that those in government charged with protecting our rights will, in fact, do so. That reality is all the more reason that the recommendations outlined above are so important. Implemented together, they would create a more robust and redundant constitutional safeguards network that would make it harder for authoritarian-minded government officials—elected, appointed, or in the civil service—to violate our rights with impunity.

Making the right choices on who is allowed to exercise federal law enforcement and surveillance power is arguably the most important civic responsibility of every American. Creating a truly liberty-centric future begins with each of us demanding that elected and appointed officials honor our constitutional rights—or face the consequences. Those wishing to live as a free, self-governing people have no other choice.

9

Unshackling Our Freedom to Trade

Daniel J. Ikenson

The consensus among economists is that by expanding the size of the market to enable more refined specialization and economies of scale, free trade creates more wealth than any system that restricts cross-border exchange. Nearly all agree that the intellectual case for specialization and free trade articulated by Adam Smith in *The Wealth of Nations* in 1776 and the law of comparative advantage expounded by David Ricardo in *On the Principles of Political Economy and Taxation* in 1817 have endured the test of time to remain beacons of economic thought.

Possibly even more compelling than the economic argument for free trade is the moral case, which finds its roots in John Locke's articulation of natural rights. The moral case posits that people are free to pursue their own industry and are entitled to the fruits of their labor, which include the right to exchange their output with whomever they choose and on whatever terms they agree to.

To exchange is a natural right and, when executed voluntarily on agreed terms, is inherently fair.

In contrast, when government intervenes to change terms and influence outcomes on behalf of one party or one set of interests at the expense of others, it subverts the rule of law and encourages the diversion of productive resources from economic to political ends. Instead of investing in new factories, service centers, machines, workers, and research and development across the country, businesses are incented to invest in Washington because they perceive politics to pay bigger dividends.

Free markets are essential to our prosperity. Free trade is the extension of free markets across political borders. Making markets freer and expanding them to integrate more buyers, sellers, investors, and workers both deepens and broadens that prosperity. True free traders abhor domestic trade barriers and want them removed regardless of whether other governments remove their own barriers, because the benefits of trade are the imports we obtain, not the exports we give up. The benefits are measured by the value of imports that can be purchased for a given unit of exports—the more, the better. Trade barriers reduce those benefits, which include greater variety, lower prices, more competition, better quality, and the innovation spawned by those and other factors.

To oppose free trade is to favor not only suboptimal economic outcomes but also intrusive, immoral actions by governments. Unfortunately, although the case for free trade is a moral and economic one, trade *policy* is a creature of the political realm. For centuries, politics—where demagoguery, subterfuge, and coercion are the currency—has obscured the case for free trade.

That said, we have made progress. Increasingly, the politics have been constrained. By historical standards and relative to present norms in most other countries, the U.S. government's trade restrictions are a modest intrusion. Many of the most obvious restrictions on our freedom to trade have been significantly curtailed. From its peak in 1932, the average U.S. tariff fell from about 60 percent to about 4 percent in 2017, and most quotas have been abolished.[1] At the end of 2017, Americans were freer to engage in international trade than at any time in U.S. history.

But before we prematurely declare "mission accomplished," we still have a long way to go. Amid our abundance, most of us fail to notice the extent to which government continues to abridge our freedom to trade. It is in that oversight that we fail to imagine life in a world truly free of trade restrictions.

Why Do We Trade?

To grasp the significance of a future free from government restrictions on our liberty to trade, it is important to understand and appreciate why we trade in the first place. Imagine life without trade. Imagine a life of solitude. To attend to your own subsistence, you wake each morning before sunrise to make your clothes, build and repair your meager shelter, hunt and harvest your food, concoct rudimentary salves for what ails you, and toil in other difficult and tedious tasks. Forget luxuries. Forget leisure. All of your time would be consumed trying to produce basic necessities merely to subsist. Life would be nasty, brutish, and short.

Fortunately, most members of modern societies choose not to live that way. In fact, one of the defining features of modern society is that most of its members recognize—actively or tacitly—the benefits of institutions, such as cooperation. Most of us don't attempt to make everything we wish to consume. Instead, we specialize in a few, or a couple, or just one value-added endeavor—one profession. What makes specialization possible is our commitment to the concept of exchange, which is the ultimate expression of cooperation.

The purpose of exchange is to enable each of us to focus our productive efforts on what we do best. Rather than allocate small portions of our time to the impossible task of producing everything we need and want, we specialize in what we do best, produce more of it than we need, and exchange that surplus for other things we need or want but haven't produced.

The law of comparative advantage explains why this arrangement enables us to produce, and thus consume, more output than would be the case in the absence of specialization and trade. If Aaron can produce $100 worth of venison in eight hours but only $50 worth of clothing in eight hours, he has a comparative advantage producing venison. By specializing in venison production, Aaron forgoes $1 worth of clothing to obtain $2 worth of meat. But to forgo production of clothing, Aaron needs some assurances that he can obtain clothing by exchanging surplus venison.

Because Paul, who lives nearby, is more efficient at producing clothing than venison—he can make $40 of clothing but only $30 of venison in an eight-hour day—he specializes in clothing production and forgoes producing venison at all, knowing he can obtain it through exchange with Aaron. Paul has a comparative advantage producing clothing.

How do we know Aaron and Paul are better off by specializing and exchanging? By specializing, their combined output is $140 per day ($100 of venison and $40 of clothing). Had they chosen to live in solitude and not exchange, they could still produce $140 per day, but Aaron would have only venison and Paul would have only clothing. Any attempt by either man to produce a combination of these products would yield less total output. If each devoted four hours each to venison and clothing production, for example, their combined daily output would be $110. Aaron would produce $50 of venison and $25 of clothing; Paul would produce $15 of venison and $20 of clothing.

Moving from a two-person economy illustration, in the modern economy, we specialize in an occupation and exchange the monetized form of the output we produce most efficiently for the goods and services we produce less efficiently. It's the same concept on a grand scale.

Enlarging markets entails the reduction or elimination of barriers that inhibit the free flow of goods, services, capital, and labor. The larger the market, the greater is the scope for specialization, exchange, and economic growth. Just as consumers have a greater variety and a better quality of items to purchase with their monetized output, producers have access to a greater variety and a better quality of inputs for producing most efficiently.

During the past few decades, a truly global division of labor emerged, presenting opportunities for specialization, collaboration, and exchange on scales once unimaginable. The confluence of falling trade and investment barriers, revolutions in communications and transportation, the opening of China to the West, the collapse of communism, and the disintegration of Cold War political barriers has spawned a highly integrated global economy comprising most of the world's nearly 8 billion people with vast potential to produce greater wealth and higher living standards than ever before.

The factory floor is no longer contained within four walls and one roof. Instead, it spans the globe through a continuum of production and supply chains, allowing businesses to optimize investment and output decisions by matching production, assembly, and other functions to the locations best suited for those activities. Because of foreign direct investment in the United States and the United States' direct investment abroad, quite often "we" are "they" and "they" are "we." And because of the proliferation of disaggregated, transnational value chains, "we" and "they" often collaborate on the same endeavor.

In the 21st century, competition is more likely to occur between entities that defy national identification because they are truly international in their operations, creating products and services from value-added activities in multiple countries. In this regard, expanded world trade, which has resulted from elimination or reduction of both natural and artificial barriers, has reinforced good governance—or at least better governance. Because investment in design, production, assembly, distribution, and other supply chain activities flows to countries where government policies are less intrusive, less burdensome, and more predictable, governments have tended toward more liberal import and export regimes.

Usually without even thinking about it, Americans enjoy the fruits of international trade daily. Nearly every thread of clothing we own is made abroad. We take to the roads in vehicles assembled from parts manufactured in myriad countries. We book hotel rooms, order takeout, and purchase music and gifts for family and friends using smartphones assembled abroad from components made in third countries and running on technology developed in the United States.

We have more to spend, save, and invest because retailers pass on some of their cost savings in the form of lower prices, which are made possible by retailers' access to thousands of foreign producers, who design and sell products that would never have been commercially viable without the cost efficiencies afforded by transnational production and supply chains. Because of trade, we enjoy imported fresh produce that was once unavailable out of season. Many of us deposit paychecks that are larger than they would otherwise be on account of our companies' growing sales to customers abroad, or we enjoy salaries and benefits provided by employers that happen to be foreign-owned companies.

A recent study from the Peterson Institute for International Economics estimated that the payoff to the United States from trade expansion—attributed to policy liberalization and improved transportation and communications technology—between 1950 and 2016 was about $2.1 trillion and that U.S. gross domestic product (GDP) per capita increased by $7,014 (both measured in 2016 dollars).[2]

Many of us take these benefits for granted—or at least we fail to attribute them to lower trade barriers. Although we tend to take notice of the "destruction" from trade, we are too often impervious to trade's "creation." We observe the clothing factory that shutters because it couldn't compete with lower-priced imports. The lost factory jobs, the nearby businesses that fail, and the blighted landscape are all obvious. What is less discernible is the increased spending power of the divorced mother who must feed and clothe her children. Now, she not only can buy cheaper clothing, but also has more resources to save or spend on food, health care, and computers, which improves her family's standard of living and underpins growth elsewhere in the economy. The adjustment costs of trade are immediate and observable, whereas the benefits of trade are obscured because they are dispersed and accrue over time.

Consider Apple, which relies on low-wage labor in China to assemble its devices. Apple may be depriving some U.S. workers of the opportunity to perform those low-end functions in the supply chain, but the production cost savings enables Apple to price iPods, iPhones, and iPads within the budgets of a large swath of consumers. If the government had compelled Apple to produce and assemble all components in the United States (something that both Presidents Obama and Trump have espoused), the necessarily higher prices would have prevented those devices from becoming ubiquitous, retarding or suppressing entirely the emergence of spinoff industries, such as those producing accessories and apps, which have created enormous value and employment opportunities throughout the U.S. and global economies.

Essentially, trade-barrier reductions begat transnational production and supply chains, which enabled the commoditization of powerful smartphone technologies, which created mass markets for new products and services, as well as new ways for billions of people around the world to communicate, shop, learn, and organize. Uber, Airbnb, Venmo, and so many other resource-saving innovations and conveniences might never have come to fruition had government restrictions on our freedom to trade been what they once were.

Indeed, we have made significant progress in restoring our natural right to trade, and the benefits of that progress are undeniable, if not obvious. But we still have a long way to go. Today, large swaths of the U.S. economy remain off limits to foreign competition. In other words, the government continues to restrict our freedom on a fairly significant scale.

How Does Government Restrict Our Freedom to Trade?

More than 150 years ago, the French classical liberal economist Frédéric Bastiat observed:

> Between Paris and Brussels obstacles of many kinds exist. First of all, there is distance, which entails loss of time, and we must either submit to this ourselves, or pay another to submit to it. Then come rivers, marshes, accidents, bad roads, which are so many difficulties to be surmounted. We succeed in building bridges, in forming roads, and making them smoother by pavements, iron rails, etc. But all this is costly, and the commodity must be made to bear the cost. Then there are robbers who infest the roads, and a body of police must be kept up, etc.

> Now, among these obstacles there is one which we have ourselves set up, and at no little cost, too, between Brussels and Paris. There are men who lie in ambuscade along the frontier, armed to the teeth, and whose business it is to throw difficulties in the way of transporting merchandise from the one country to the other. They are called Customhouse officers, and they act in precisely the same way as ruts and bad roads.[3]

In Bastiat's time, rapid technological progress in transportation led to a dramatic decline in freight costs, sparking the first great wave of globalization. Connecting cities by road and rail was intended to reduce the cost of travel and commerce. Just as reducing tariffs creates larger markets and greater scope for specialization, so does connecting those markets with physical infrastructure. Bastiat's equating natural, geographic trade barriers (distance, marshes, rivers, ruts, and bad roads) to administrative or manmade trade barriers (customhouse officers guarding the frontier) was spot on. And it is just as apt today.

In 2017, U.S. Customs and Border Protection collected $33.1 billion in import duties—the "revenue" generated by assessing tariffs (which are taxes) on imported goods. Although the U.S. president and other politicians often invoke the need for trade reciprocity or calls for leveling the proverbial "playing field" as justification for imposing tariffs on goods imported from abroad, the fact is those tariffs are actually taxes imposed on American businesses and consumers. It is U.S. importers who pay the tariffs or duties or taxes to the U.S. government. Those taxes raise the cost of production for U.S. companies that rely on imported inputs and the cost of living for U.S. households, whose real income is reduced by the resulting higher prices on retail store shelves.

In 2017, about half of the value of U.S. imports consisted of raw materials, intermediate inputs, and capital equipment—the purchases of U.S. producers to manufacture their own output. Higher costs squeeze manufacturing profits, reducing the incentive and the ability to expand production, create more value, and employ more labor. This reality particularly handicaps smaller businesses seeking to challenge entrenched incumbents because the latter are more capable of absorbing the higher transaction costs. Just as tariffs on intermediate goods hurt small firms more than large firms, tariffs on final goods hurt lower-income households more acutely than they hurt middle- and upper-income households.

Spread across the $2.3 trillion value of all U.S. imports in 2017, the average applied tariff rate came to 1.4 percent.[4] Nearly 70 percent of all goods imports came in duty free; therefore, the average tariff rate on the 30 percent of products subject to tariffs was 4.1 percent.[5] Of course, that average conceals certain important points. Lower-income households spend a higher proportion of their resources on goods and the majority of goods consumed in the United States are imported. Among the most heavily "tariffed" products are clothing, footwear, foodstuffs, and building materials, such as lumber, cement, steel, paint, flooring, furniture, appliances, and nails. U.S. trade policy subjects life's basic necessities—food, clothing, and shelter—to some of the most regressive taxes in the United States. And things may get worse before they get better. In 2018, President Trump started a trade war. As a result, Americans are less free to trade today than we were in 2017. Although it's difficult to measure this "loss" of freedom, the president has imposed punitive tariffs ranging from 10 percent to 25 percent on about $320 billion of imports, which could result in U.S. Customs and Border Protection's collections more than doubling to $70 billion. Is this bad, coercive, interventionist policy? Yes. Is it a huge burden? On some industries and households, yes, and any good libertarian or free trader would oppose Trump's tariffs, as well as the tariffs that were already in place before Trump's presidency.

As in Bastiat's time, today we continue to observe that geography and distance present impediments to trade that we seek to overcome with ingenuity and determination, while we seemingly tolerate the manufactured trade barriers that mitigate or negate the benefits of that ingenuity and determination. But unlike Bastiat's time, the most insidious trade barriers in the 21st century are those that exist not at the frontier but behind the border, in the form of domestic laws and regulations.

Throughout the U.S. services economy, the government continues to limit our choices to domestic sources. In industry after industry, foreign suppliers are precluded from fully competing for our dollars, which is another way of saying that we are denied the liberty to exchange on our own terms. We have "Buy American" rules, which restrict the pool of companies and products eligible for government procurement spending to domestic firms and U.S.-made products. And that mitigates the disciplining effects of competition on price and ensures that more taxpayer dollars get squandered.[6] We have laws forbidding foreign air carriers from competing on U.S. domestic routes, which raises the cost of business travel and leisure and reduces the quality of service.[7] We have laws restricting waterborne transportation of cargo to ships that are U.S.-built, -owned, -flagged, and -staffed, which raises the cost of transportation and, ultimately, the retail prices of nearly everything bought and sold in America.[8] We have public health, safety, and national security regulations that are often invoked as fig leaves to conceal protectionist motives.[9] We have a vast network of preclusions and restrictions on foreign professional, health care, and education services, to list some.[10] And beyond medicine and education, occupational licensing requirements, generally, present major obstacles to our freedom to trade with both domestic and foreign suppliers across many different services industries.[11]

Ironically, protectionism is baked into our so-called free-trade agreements. It takes the form of rules-of-origin requirements, local content mandates, intellectual property and investor protections, enforceable labor and environmental standards, and special carve-outs that shield entire products and industries from international competition.

Tackling government's restrictions on trade in services has proved considerably more difficult than reducing tariffs on goods. Among the reasons for this disparity is that services trade barriers are less obvious and less quantifiable. But considering that services constitute a much more significant share of the U.S. economy than goods, the benefits from services trade liberalization should be much more substantial than the benefits realized from goods trade liberalization.

Where Free Trade Is Needed Most

The significant reduction of trade barriers during the second half of the 20th century encouraged a surge in cross-border investment and transnational supply chains that lowered production costs and retail prices and made the United States and the rest of the world richer. But that liberalization affected mostly trade in goods. As such, our great "success" opening up the U.S. economy to trade should be viewed more as incremental progress than as "mission accomplished." So far, trade liberalization has really restored only a small portion of our freedom to trade because the United States is a services economy, and protectionism remains in place throughout our most important services sectors. But that may soon change.

More than 70 percent of full-time-equivalent (FTE) U.S. workers are employed in the services sectors, including retail, transportation, health care, education, professional services, financial services, information, and hospitality.[12] In 2017, services accounted for more than $12 trillion (62 percent) of GDP and more than $9 trillion (70 percent) of household consumption expenditures.[13] For every dollar consumers spent on goods, they spent $2.20 on services. But only a tiny portion of that $2.20 was spent on services that were imported.

In 2017, consumers spent $9.2 trillion on services, only $550 billion of which were imported.[14] That amounts to about 6 percent or $0.13 of that $2.20. By contrast, U.S. consumers spent $4.1 trillion on goods in 2017, with imports of goods totaling $2.3 trillion that year.[15] Imports accounted for 57 percent or $0.57 of every dollar spent on goods. That wide disparity in import penetration—6 percent for services versus 57 percent for goods—suggests that the United States maintains fairly significant barriers to trade in services. Figure 9.1 appears to corroborate that theory.

One of the obvious takeaways from the figure is that, over the course of two decades, the prices of some goods and services decreased, whereas others increased—nothing too extraordinary there. On closer examination, however, it becomes clear that the

Figure 9.1

Price changes of selected U.S. consumer goods, services, and wages,
January 1997–December 2017

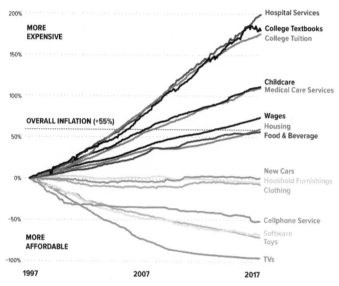

Source: Mark J. Perry, "Chart of the Day (Century?): Price Changes 1997 to 2017," *AEIdeas* (blog), February 2, 2018, http://www.aei.org/publication/chart-of-the-day-century-price-changes -1997-to-2017/.

price declines occurred predominantly for goods, which are commonly imported and thus subject to foreign competition. But when domestic suppliers are not disciplined by foreign competition in the market, which is very much the case throughout the services industries, they need not care as much about pricing competitively. Their customers are relatively captive, demand is more price inelastic, and so prices rise.

Health care and education services—which together account for more than one-quarter of U.S. GDP—have experienced some of the largest price increases over the past two decades. At $10,348 per year, U.S. per capita spending on health care exceeds that of any other country by far, yet the quality of service as measured by morbidity, mortality, life expectancy, and other health metrics is middle of the pack.[16]

Meanwhile, U.S. spending per full-time-equivalent student on elementary and secondary education is almost $12,400 (29 percent higher than the Organization for Economic Cooperation and Development [OECD] average of $9,600) and spending at the postsecondary level per FTE student was $29,700 (or 81 percent higher than the OECD average of $16,400).[17] Yet again, the quality of education services as measured by international test scores is middle of the pack.

Among the reasons for the high costs and middling quality in these two major industries are the limits imposed on competition through licensing and accreditation requirements, which restrict both domestic and foreign competition. These industries are not only ripe for reform, the benefits of competition are also sorely needed. Health care accounts for more than 18 percent of the U.S. economy and education (including postsecondary) accounts for more than 7 percent, yet only a tiny fraction of these markets is open to foreign health care and education service providers. Americans can import foreign services through four channels:

- By traveling abroad and consuming those services (as tourists, patients, or students, for example);

- By consuming services in the United States from an affiliate or subsidiary of a foreign-owned company (a restaurant, hotel, construction firm, or bank, for example);

- By receiving services from a foreign person who is performing those services in the United States (a consultant or accountant, for example);

- By cross-border supply of a service from the territory of a foreign country into the United States, typically delivered via telecommunications or postal infrastructure.

In the first three channels, both the provision and consumption of the service take place in the same country. In the fourth, the provider and consumer of the service are in different countries.

"Medical tourism"—which entails traveling abroad to receive medical care in the form of surgical or other procedures—is generally not subject to U.S. laws and regulations. Given the high cost of health care in the United States, it is not surprising that a growing number of Americans are partaking of this channel. The savings are so great—and the quality high enough—that some U.S. insurance companies are encouraging the practice and covering the travel and treatment costs. Some medical tourists go abroad for treatments that are not available or approved in the United States. According to Patients Beyond Borders, an estimated 1.4 million Americans went abroad for medical procedures in 2016.[18]

But even if more health insurance plans cover medical procedures performed abroad, the logistical impracticalities of sick people traveling to foreign countries for medical care attenuate growth prospects in this part of the industry.

Likewise, Americans consume foreign education services primarily through the same channel—by going abroad. According to the Association of International Educators, 332,727 U.S. students enrolled in foreign universities in 2016–2017, which represents about 1.6 percent of all U.S. students enrolled at institutions of higher education in the United States.[19] But in most cases, this mode of consumption is not chosen as a lower-cost alternative. Rather, it is a unique experience for which students and their parents pay premiums.

Meaningful competition in health care and education services of the magnitude that can discipline prices and free up vast amounts of resources will require growth in the delivery of services through the second, the third, and, especially, the fourth channel. The fourth—where the provider is abroad and the consumer is in the United States—probably has the greatest promise, because the cost of delivering services over the internet is lower and decreases with technological advances.

A major obstacle to liberalization of these service sectors is the domestic providers, who are protected by licensing requirements, accreditation systems, and a web of state and national laws. But the government has no legitimate reason to impede U.S. consumers from procuring medical and education services from foreign providers. Given the skyrocketing costs and looming crises in these industries, it is imperative that the reforms necessary to open these markets be implemented as soon as possible.

How Will Free Trade Shape the Future?

Competition improves quality, innovation, and opportunities for more rapid adoption of life-enhancing and life-saving technologies. Yet, for the vast majority of things Americans consume, the supply options are limited to domestic sources only. Imagine that. With all we have learned about the benefits of trade, and as enlightened as we like to think we are, the United States— which is home to 1 out of every 20 people on Earth—has not yet opened up its services markets to competition from 95 percent of the world's potential providers. Instead, we accept rules that require water and air transportation services in the United States to be provided only by U.S. companies using U.S. crews. Financial services, legal services, and other professional services, on which Americans spend hundreds of billions of dollars every year, are all largely restricted to U.S. companies. That is just astonishing.

The potential for the internet to deliver affordable, high-quality telemedicine and online education programs to broaden the supply of medical treatment and education services is great and realistic. As Simon Lester wrote in a 2015 Cato policy analysis on health care and trade:

> Reform is coming to the field of medical services. Telemedicine can never completely replace in-person care, of course, but it will be a common and widely used method in the near future. Governments are beginning to recognize this, and domestic regulatory systems will have to be changed to accommodate it.[20]

Imagine having a life-saving operation at your local hospital or medical office performed by automated medical instruments controlled by the world's renowned expert in Singapore.

In an earlier Cato policy analysis on online education, Lester concluded:

> The growth of online higher education is going to be extremely disruptive to the existing industry structure. There will be many complaints from those with a vested interest in the current system. But just as the music, book, and movie industries have had to do, traditional higher education institutions need to adapt to the online world.[21]

Consider how much easier and more affordable it will be for your daughter to acquire the skills necessary to perform state-of-the-art surgeries, when she can learn from and interact with experts around the world through online classes and seminars.

Health care and education services—which account for one-quarter of U.S. GDP but rank among the least efficient sectors in the economy—will soon be open to significant foreign competition. As discriminatory regulations protecting domestic incumbent providers are removed to enable foreign competition, and the costs of delivering high-quality health and education services over the internet continue to fall, we should expect to see significant productivity gains and dramatically declining prices in these sectors. That is essentially what happened with manufacturing during the second half of the past century. Artificial barriers to goods trade (tariffs, quotas, import licenses) were eliminated or significantly reduced, which enabled global producers to disaggregate production and supply chain operations and to achieve greater economies of scale, all of which had the effect of driving down costs and thus prices. Meanwhile, advances in transportation—including quite significantly the advent of the shipping container and more efficient container ships—produced revolutions in transportation and logistics, which also contributed meaningfully to the decline in the prices of delivered goods.

The services sectors, by and large, have yet to experience a productivity revolution. Given the much greater importance of services to the U.S. economy, even modest productivity gains could generate significantly greater value added in the economy than could be accomplished from a much larger increase in productivity in manufacturing.

In other words, with increased focus on liberalizing services trade by reducing discriminatory regulations and tapping into new technologies and the powerful reach of the internet to deliver those services, the potential for favorably changing the trajectory of economic growth—while reducing the burdens imposed on the public by massive entitlements (of which health care costs are a major element)—is within reach. As usual, the key ingredient to realizing these fruits is first to realize the freedom to trade.

10

Immigration

Alex Nowrasteh

Most of this book imagines a more libertarian future, but I've decided to imagine a more libertarian past. My hope is that this approach will help readers understand how a substantially more liberalized immigration policy might have worked in practice and hint at how such a policy would affect the world today. This chapter is a brief alternative history of the United States if it had never closed its borders. To the maximum extent possible, my fictional answers to these questions in the alternate United States are adapted from actual episodes in U.S. history and social science. In those cases, I provide citations.

Alternative history is a rich subgenre of fiction that begins with a so-called point of departure, which is a significant historical moment that differs from what actually happened but that is preceded by factual history. Good alternative history is not utopian, thus the alternative history presented here is not utopian nor is it a vision of a perfect society molded by free immigration.

There are certain aspects of this world—such as other policies chosen by the U.S. government to "compensate" for a lack of control over immigration and other social changes—that I do not like and would never endorse but that are more likely under such an immigration system than under the one that actually regulated immigrant entry to the United States. The history of the United States is complicated, especially as it relates to immigration, so I provide a brief explanation of the facts in the shaded boxes.

Ultimately, alternative history cannot stand alone as an argument for a different policy in today's world. This chapter is not an empirical paper that builds a rigorous model that can be tested. Instead, this format offers an alternative conclusion constructed by informed history and related social science. It is a rough model of human behavior—and a lot of fun. It may not convince you to support liberalized immigration or to believe that the United States and the world would have been better off with a substantially more open immigration policy over the past 130 years; however, I hope it will at least make you think of just how influential immigration has been on virtually every aspect of our nation's past and how its importance will continue far into the future.

Expanding Immigration and Domestic Reforms: 1889–1913

When Congress passed the Chinese Exclusion Act in 1882, the public supported it. Residents in the western states, labor unions, and many other Americans were worried about the growing numbers of Chinese immigrants. So Congress restricted immigration for an entire group of people for no other reason than that they were from a particular country and were not liked by American voters. A previous law in 1875 barred the immigration of criminals and some other specifically defined individuals. But never before was a restriction based on an arbitrary government determination that the population of an entire nation could never become American citizens.

The Chinese Exclusion Act was ultimately challenged; the Supreme Court famously overturned it in the case of *Chae Chan Ping v. United States* in 1889. The Court found that the U.S. Constitution contained no broad grant of power that permitted Congress to restrict immigration—unless it was necessarily and properly related to another enumerated power, such as restricting the movement of foreign spies and criminals, or in accordance with the Law of Nations.[1] As the Court wrote:

> The Constitution enumerates the powers that sovereign states have enjoyed since time immemorial but did not include the power to ban the immigration of aliens. . . . The power to restrict immigration must be nested in other enumerated powers such as the power to make war. . . . The highest duty of the sovereign is to preserve the Constitution, which cannot be a justification for blanket immigration laws that have no reasonable relationship to that constitutional charge.

Over the following several years, a series of federal laws restricting immigration were struck down except for those barring criminals.

Fact: The Supreme Court upheld the Chinese Exclusion Act in the *Chae Chan Ping* case and additionally ruled that the power of Congress is not limited when setting immigration policy. The Court argued that such a degree of power comes from national sovereignty rather than its being an enumerated power.

Chinese immigration to the West Coast picked up immediately after the courts toppled each federal law. The western states—led by California and its now infamous anti-immigrant rage—proposed numerous constitutional amendments to restrict immigration from Asia or to create a broader general grant of total congressional power over immigration. Southern states did not go along with the amendments, northern states with large immigrant populations opposed them, and industrialists were adamantly opposed to any restriction on the flow of consumers or workers to these shores—no matter their complexion, religion, or language. The only colors they cared about were green and gold, and the only language they understood was that of profit as preached from the church of commerce.[2]

Fact: These three groups were all pro-immigration until the early 1900s, when the southern states turned restrictionist because they realized that the new immigrants were unlikely to settle there.

Southern states were still dominated by planter elites who wanted labor. They teamed up, ironically, with an elderly Frederick Douglass, who made an impassioned natural rights appeal to defend the rights of the Chinese by reprising his famous 1869 speech in numerous venues North and South:

> There are such things in the world as human rights. They rest upon no conventional foundation, but are external, universal, and indestructible. Among these, is the right of locomotion; the right of migration; the right which belongs to no particular race, but belongs alike to all and to all alike. It is the right you assert by staying here, and your fathers asserted by coming here. It is this great right that I assert for the Chinese and Japanese, and for all other varieties of men equally with yourselves, now and forever. I know of no rights of race superior to the rights of humanity, and when there is a supposed conflict between human and national rights, it is safe to go to the side of humanity.[3]

The odd coalition of the defenders of free immigration had their work cut out for them. The Immigration Restriction League (IRL), founded in 1894, rallied around the battle cry of the nation being sabotaged by "Jews, Jesuits, and steamships," in the now infamous words of Prescott Hall, one of the IRL's founders. But no matter their efforts, Congress and the states could never agree on a constitutional amendment that would satisfy them all.

As with most controversial issues of the time, a growing economy in the late 1890s deflected much of the anti-immigrant animosity. And the rapid economic integration of Chinese and other East Asian immigrants, combined with a steady return migration, took the steam out of the IRL's national movement.

Fact: Congress narrowly failed to pass a law or override presidential vetoes to mandate literacy tests for immigrants until 1917. In the meantime, Congress passed and the president signed many restrictions on Japanese immigrants, other Asian immigrants, and African immigrants and enforcement measures to deal with illegal immigration, which was an unintended consequence of immigration restrictions.

The failure of their first attempt at a national constitutional amendment refocused the IRL's efforts on persuading state legislatures to restrict the entry of the Chinese and other Asians in the same way that they had restricted the entry of blacks before the Fourteenth Amendment. Western states enthusiastically adopted these so-called Chinese Codes, which set up an immediate confrontation with the federal government in San Francisco. Several Chinese families were essentially confined to the port until their relatives in California and the ships' captains successfully sued in federal court.

The court found that since the individuals had been legally admitted, the states had to recognize their rights to locomotion inside the United States. After several arduous court battles, the federal courts vacated the Chinese Codes in an 1897 court case that reaffirmed the right of locomotion inside the United States. The IRL lost this latest battle for restriction, but it did not give up.

Fact: The fictional Chinese Codes are based on state black exclusion laws that were invalidated by the Fourteenth Amendment and on the California Alien Land Act of 1913, which barred many Asian immigrants from owning agricultural land or holding long-term leases.

In the meantime, the economic boom of the 1890s and the explosion of the *USS Maine* in Havana focused U.S. public attention on other matters. Stoked by "yellow journalism," the United States fought a short and successful war against Spain, gaining most of her remaining empire in the process. During that brief conflict, the U.S. Congress passed a law that banned the immigration of Spanish nationals to the United States for the duration of the war, a precedent for later immigration restrictionism.

Fact: The United States fought the Spanish-American War exactly as I describe it here, except I added a debate over barring the immigration of Spanish nationals for the duration of the conflict. Immigration restrictionists were inventive at this time and probably would have leapt at any opportunity to close the border.

The major political fights over immigration in the last half of the 1890s and first decade of the 20th century concerned noncitizen voting rights on the state and local level. The new Progressive movement—founded by Americans who thought a more involved government could improve American society and economy—pushed for restrictions on the immigrant franchise on the basis of racial and ethnic theories popular at the time, which posited that the waves of immigrants from southern and eastern Europe and China were unsuited to republican government. Thus, they argued that state governments should have the power to restrict immigrant voting rights to protect the Constitution.

Fact: The justifications here differ little from those actually used. States did move to restrict the franchise of noncitizens during that time, and eugenics-inspired arguments for restriction were a major ideological factor until World War II.

The Progressives succeeded in repealing laws in many states that allowed noncitizens to vote.[4] However, opponents to their movement in the nonprogressive wings of the Democratic and Republican parties also rose in defense of noncitizen voting to protect the political power of existing machines and political arrangements. Native-born Americans of the so-called Old Stock ran these machines and were able to use immigrant votes to perpetuate their hold on political power.

Progressives were more successful in passing state-level sterilization laws that targeted immigrant and black criminals, as well as bans on alcohol that eventually morphed into a nationwide Prohibition movement, itself a thinly veiled attack on Catholic immigrants who clashed with the Protestant majority. Although those movements were eventually repudiated, a major Progressive achievement that endured was the reform of public schools to help assimilate immigrant and non-Protestant children.

At this time, the IRL teamed up with Progressives to start the so-called Americanization movement. They raised money and lobbied states to support civic education for immigrants and to fill the public schools with lessons in patriotism and American values, a big about-face as they had previously claimed that the new immigrants were unassimilable.[5] The popular sentiment at the time was summed up by the phrase, "If we can't keep them out, we had better make patriots out of them."

Although little evidence shows that the Americanization movement had any effect on assimilation, it provided a useful outlet for immigration restrictionists who were frustrated by the inability of Congress and the states to pass a constitutional amendment to ban immigration.[6] Large increases in immigration from Japan, China, the disintegrating Ottoman Empire, and the poorer parts of eastern and southern Europe prompted many states to adopt those progressive school reforms to satisfy nativist voters.

Fact: Anti-immigration Americans were discouraged by the inability of Congress to close the border, so they redirected their efforts toward assimilating those already here through the Americanization movement. However, little evidence shows that it helped boost assimilation, and some shows that it actually slowed it.[7]

The Progressive movement collapsed before World War I, as its push for amendments to the Constitution to create an income tax and to allow for the direct election of senators failed. The former failed as increased budget surpluses, having been created by robust economic growth fueled by wise policies and a surge of immigrant workers, made such a radical change unnecessary. The push for the direct election of senators floundered because many voters believed that such changes would undermine the state selection of senators that was a traditional bulwark against perceived Catholic and immigrant populism.

Fact: The Progressive movement did not collapse, and it succeeded in pushing through constitutional amendments to create an income tax as well as the direct election of senators.

America as a Refuge and Growing Power: 1914–1929

World War I, which began in August 1914, changed the face of the world and greatly expanded America's involvement in global affairs. Immigration from Europe, except from Italy, collapsed after the fighting began. European nations were eager to keep young men at home to fight; Europe's poor had new but temporary opportunities in war industries in their home countries; and the newly treacherous Atlantic crossing, patrolled by warring navies, all served to diminish the flow from the Old World.

American economic demand for immigrants continued to build as industry and agriculture expanded to fill the gaps left by European economies that retooled for war. Chinese and Latin American immigration surged to fill the growing demand for workers in industries across the country. Regions that were used to European immigrants were suddenly populated by large numbers of Chinese and Mexican workers for the first time, many of the latter also fleeing the revolution in their home country.

Before this time, Chinese immigration was largely circular, as immigrants worked here mostly for short periods and then returned home with their earnings. As Chinese immigrants began moving east from California, many began to settle permanently in growing northern and midwestern cities, thus forming the first Chinatowns east of the Mississippi. In addition, black Americans began to migrate from the rural South to northern cities, eventually totaling three million by 1970.[8]

Besides Italy, the major exception to the decline in immigration from the Old World was the exodus of Christian and Armenian immigrants from the genocidal policies of the Ottoman Empire. The economic boom and his policy of keeping America out of war allowed President William Howard Taft to end his second term with unrivaled popularity, leading to the landslide election of Republican Charles Evans Hughes in 1916. But even Hughes could not keep the United States out of the war forever.

Fact: There were no new Chinese immigrants, Mexicans did come in large numbers, fewer immigrants made it out of the disintegrating Ottoman Empire, and even more southern blacks migrated to the North.

America's entry into World War I prompted the federal government to turn a country of 150 million Americans accustomed to peace into a society on a war footing. Congress banned immigration from the Central Powers immediately after declaring war on them in 1917 as a response to German attacks on American shipping and the exposure of the Zimmerman Telegram, which proposed that the Mexican government invade the United States. The disastrous effects of this ban were not known until later, when it became clear that Congress's choking off the immigration of Armenians and other Christians from the Ottoman Empire allowed the Turks to slaughter almost a million of them.

Fact: The Zimmerman Telegram influenced the American government's decision to declare war on Germany. The Turkish government murdered an estimated 1.5 million Armenians. There were also only about 100 million Americans around the time the United States entered World War I.[9]

Building on precedent from the Civil War, Congress raised numerous army divisions populated by immigrants from specific countries. Those divisions—manned by immigrants of Polish, Chinese, Irish, Mexican, Italian, and Japanese descent—fought valiantly and earned citizenship more rapidly as a result of their service.

Their bravery convinced many Americans that the new immigrants had assimilated and had become Americans just like their own ancestors had. The other divisions of the American Expeditionary Force mixed Old Stock Americans with immigrants and their descendants on a scale never previously experienced, prompting their commander John J. Pershing to praise them in correspondence with local ethnic newspapers throughout the United States to boost morale on the home front.

Fact: The United States did not really raise ethnic army divisions populated by immigrants from specific countries for World War I. Furthermore, black American soldiers who served in World War I did not gain more respect after returning home and were even targeted more severely by lynch mobs than before the conflict.

Allied victory in Europe and the Versailles Treaty were marked by two big changes in immigration. The first change was the large number of immigrants from northern and western Europe who began to arrive in the United States from their devastated and impoverished homelands, the first such surge since the 1880s. This sudden wave prompted Congress to maintain wartime restrictions on immigrants from the Central Powers. Armenian American groups and the Hebrew Immigrant Aid Society filed lawsuits that resulted in federal courts striking down those laws as unconstitutional in 1920, which led to a large increase in German, Austrian, and Hungarian immigration as well as the revival of Arab, Armenian, and Kurdish immigration from the now-dissolved Ottoman Empire.

Bitter commentators at the time argued that American wartime restrictions allowed the Ottomans (and later the Turks) to kill almost a million Armenians and other Christians when many of them could have escaped to safety in the United States. "They had the ability to save themselves, and our government stopped them," lamented American newspapers as news of the genocide spread. Ethnic cleansing in western Turkey and the infamous population exchange between that country and Greece in 1923 diverted many of the displaced on both sides to the United States, whose economy had recovered after a brief and sharp postwar recession. The American public welcomed them with open arms as an attempt to overcome the shame of locking out so many Christians who were then slaughtered.

> Fact: In our world, Congress imposed severe restrictions on immigration in 1921 and even harsher ones in 1924, limiting immigration from Europe as well as maintaining a virtual moratorium on immigrants from Asia and Africa.

The Russian Revolution added another wrinkle to America's complex relationship with immigrants. Brutal communist revolutionaries seized control of Russia in 1917 and set about building their Marxist utopia, which convinced millions to flee and seek refuge in western Europe and the United States. Congress passed an immigration restriction barring communists, anarchists, and other supporters of violent revolution as a threat to the sovereignty of the United States—a claim bolstered by the stated intentions of Soviet leaders like Vladimir Lenin who wanted to spread worldwide revolution.

Although many communists believed that revolution would not come to America for some time because it was too ethnically, religiously, linguistically, and racially diverse to begin building a labor movement that could morph into a revolution—as shown by the repeated failures of Samuel Gompers to unify American labor unions—the courts upheld immigration restrictions based on threatening ideologies.[10]

Fact: Ideological restrictions to naturalization existed at this time, but restrictions on entry because of ideology did not become law until the 1950s. Samuel Gompers was also the most successful labor organizer in American history.

Fear of communism and other foreign threats represented by the renewed surge of immigrants from a devastated Europe and Middle East renewed Republican efforts in Congress and the states to pass a constitutional amendment to restrict immigration. Although Congress passed several such amendments, states with large immigrant populations voted down every state-level amendment. Republicans responded with the Naturalization Act of 1924, which permitted immigrants to naturalize if they were of good moral character and had resided in the United States continuously for 21 years but barred them from holding public office until they naturalized—the harshest such law ever passed in American history.[11]

The Democratic Party responded by beginning to repeal state laws that restricted the franchise to citizens, restoring voting powers to noncitizens in many states, which shored up Democratic support in cities and convinced Republicans that their only chance for future electoral success was to halt their renewed push for a constitutional amendment.

It was politically impossible to maintain anti-immigration positions in a country where immigrants or their children made up more than half of the population. The Republicans compensated for their political weakness among immigrants by near-unanimous support for an amendment that granted universal suffrage to women age 21 and older in an effort to appeal to native-born American women.

Fact: Republicans were the anti-immigration party, whereas the Democrats supported liberal immigration.

The economic boom of the early 1920s produced an unusually fierce election between Republican candidate Calvin Coolidge of Massachusetts and Democrat Al Smith of New York, the first Catholic candidate for office and a champion of immigrant rights. Coolidge won the contest thanks in large part to the growing economy and his promise to respect America's traditional open-door immigration policy—so long as it "kept America American," which was a reference to continuing the popular ban on communists and other radicals. Coolidge's vice president Charles Curtis was elected in a landslide in 1928 after Coolidge decided that he wanted to retire. That smooth transition was then marred by the stock market crash of 1929.

Fact: Coolidge was an immigration restrictionist, and he chose the progressive Republican Herbert Hoover as his vice president. The election of 1924 was not close.

Depression, Recovery, and World War: 1929–1945

We now know that bad domestic monetary policy and a rickety postwar international monetary order were the proximate causes of the Long Depression, but at the time everybody focused on the stock market crash.[12] The Dow Jones declined from a high of 581 in September 1929 to 425 in December of that year.[13] The consistent increase in housing prices—largely due to the immigrant flows during the Roaring Twenties that peaked at 3.5 million in 1928—shored up household finances and provided a large base of consumers for a partial recovery by 1932. But it was not quite enough to overcome all of the damage from a bad monetary policy that shrank the nominal gross domestic product (GDP).[14]

Fact: The housing market collapsed and the Dow Jones peaked at 381. The housing market also had much lower prices and recovered later.

Republicans did reform several federal laws during the early years of the Long Depression. First, the absence of an income tax combined with the prohibition of alcohol, previously a major source of revenue for the government, tightly squeezed the federal budget. Republicans avoided adopting the former by ending the latter through an amendment to the Constitution in 1931, which they did jointly with Democrats who were able to champion the repeal in order to shore up political support among their Catholic and immigrant voting base.[15]

Second, Republicans passed the Smoot-Hawley tariff in 1930 to raise revenue and protect American industry.[16] But the tariff did neither and helped close international markets to the products of American industry via retaliatory tariffs. To its credit, the Curtis administration avoided the persistent clamoring of a shrinking number of older progressive Republicans like Herbert Hoover to institute national make-work schemes or to create industry cartels. But avoidance of bad policies like those weren't enough to save the Curtis administration in the 1932 election. The subsequent rise in the price of consumer goods from the tariff and the persistently high unemployment, at about 12 percent in 1932, doomed Curtis's reelection.

Fact: Prohibition wasn't repealed until 1933, and Congress repeatedly raised income taxes to attempt to close the widening deficit.

Democrat Franklin Delano Roosevelt won the presidency in 1932 on a platform of stable money, free trade, and the passage of a constitutional amendment to create a national income tax to close the budget deficit. By the slimmest of margins, the Republicans held onto the Senate, scaring up the anti-Catholic vote in midwestern states by focusing on the prominent political deal between Roosevelt and his conservative Catholic vice president Al Smith, the first member of the Church of Rome elected to high office in the United States.

Fact: Roosevelt was more extreme; Smith was not on Roosevelt's ticket because he was too conservative and the two did not like each other; the 1932 election was not close; and Republicans controlled neither house of Congress. The first Catholic elected president was John F. Kennedy in 1960 and the first Catholic vice president was Joe Biden, who was elected in 2008.

The beginning of the Roosevelt administration was rocky as an epidemic of bank failures momentarily shook people's faith in the financial system. Disagreements between Roosevelt and Smith also prevented a unified Democratic Party from facing both the divided Congress and an electorate that expected new federal policies to help deal with the Long Depression.

As a result, only two portions of Roosevelt's so-called New Deal became law, with the help of moderate Republicans in the Senate. The first was a scaled-back farm subsidy program to aid struggling farmers. This program was popular because Old Stock Americans were the main beneficiaries, as immigrants and their children tended to live in cities. The second was the resurrection and passage of a national income tax amendment, which fell just a few states shy of passage at the beginning of Roosevelt's term. The income tax amendment that finally became law in April 1935 capped top rates at 10 percent but otherwise gave the federal government wide latitude in tinkering with an income tax code that soon became famous globally for its complexity and low rates. Never before had so much revenue been collected through such an anfractuous scheme.

Fact: The Democratic Congress rubber-stamped much of Roosevelt's New Deal and was not handicapped by the lack of an income tax or by any constitutional restrictions on its top rate. The 16th Amendment to the U.S. Constitution created the income tax in 1913. New Deal programs were geared toward aiding whites and Old Stock Americans, not blacks.

The rest of Roosevelt's New Deal failed in Congress. Although many passionate arguments were raised against the New Deal—from comparisons with Stalin's Soviet Union and Mussolini's Italy to cries that it violated the Constitution—the most politically effective argument was raised by Representative James Wadsworth (R-NY) in his famous 1933 "Welfare for the World" speech. Wadsworth claimed that immigrants would stream here from around the world to take advantage of government handouts and jobs, crowding out native-born Americans who were the intended beneficiaries, and that the government had no way to effectively fix this problem without closing the border.[17]

The New Deal died on an altar of free immigration, but the economy began to recover quickly in early 1935 anyway. Roosevelt won reelection in 1936, and the Democrats also took control of the Senate in that year. But the economic recovery dulled any latent desire for more radical reforms, especially after the Supreme Court limited the scope of the farm subsidies passed during Roosevelt's first term.

Fact: Arguments against the New Deal that were based on immigrant abuses did not occur, because the border was effectively closed to all but the richest immigrants. The Supreme Court eventually approved the New Deal, and a second depression in 1937 extended the economic misery for years.

Economic recovery dominated Roosevelt's first term, but foreign policy took center stage in his second. Japan's aggression against China mobilized Chinese Americans to raise money, arms, and volunteers to fight on behalf of the Chinese Nationalist government. Remittances from Chinese Americans fueled much economic growth and industrialization before the Japanese invasion, and many prominent members of the Chinese Nationalist government who had spent several years in the United States took some governance lessons back to their home country.[18]

By the 1930s, China's growing industrial base supplied modern war materials to its large but previously underequipped armies. Historians disagree about the particulars, but the close economic, cultural, and migratory ties between our two countries played a major role in China's resisting the Japanese invasion in the 1930s as well as the postwar communist onslaught.

Fact: China was unable to offer effective resistance to Japan and had little modern industry.

Although Asia played an important role in galvanizing the American public against Japanese aggression, most observers in the United States focused their attention on Europe and the rise of Adolf Hitler's National Socialist German Workers (Nazi) Party. Anti-Semitic and racial purity laws in Germany convinced over 80 percent of German and Austrian Jews to flee to the United States before the start of the war.

Nationalist movements in Poland, Hungary, Romania, the Soviet Union, and other eastern European countries convinced many Jews to flee their homeland—accelerating a Jewish outflow that had been quite large since the 1880s. This second Great Exodus saw about 275,000 Jews per year leave Europe for the United States, often with harrowing tales of being robbed of all their possession at the dock or train station and even the occasional public lynching. The number of Italian immigrants remained strong in the 1930s as Mussolini's despotic grip tightened, transforming a largely economic-inspired emigration to also include some individuals and groups critical of the fascist regime.

Fact: Very few German Jews or other victims of European nationalist movements in the 1930s were able to flee to the United States because of immigration restrictions that did not create exceptions for refugees.

Anne Frank, whose best-selling novelized diary of coming to America after being abused by Nazi officials, came as part of this wave in 1938 aboard the *MS St. Louis* during one of its dozens of trips delivering refugees to New York.[19] Tens of thousands of academics, scientists, and engineers fled *en masse* in the late 1930s. From Albert Einstein and Joseph Rotblat to Klaus Fuchs and their families, as well as countless others, America was a haven that offered them opportunity and safety.[20] No other country stuck to its tradition of offering refuge to the persecuted of the world during the dark 1930s, a fact that Americans to this day are still proud of and that erased some of the shame felt by many after the ill consequences of locking out Ottoman Christians during the First World War.

Fact: Anne Frank's family were denied visas to come to the United States. She and members of her family died in Nazi concentration camps, and her diary has been read by millions around the world. The *MS St. Louis* was infamous, as its attempt to land Jewish refugees in the United States was thwarted by the U.S. government, and most of the refugees were sent back to Europe, where many died in World War II.

On a rather smaller note ignored by most historians, the expansion of Jewish immigration in response to anti-Semitic regimes in Europe hobbled Roosevelt's last major push for the New Deal. Southern Democrats were especially apoplectic in their argument that "Roosevelt's soft-socialist New Deal will just attract more Jews, communists, and the bums of the world."

The economy had recovered fully from the Long Depression, which likely took some political steam out of Roosevelt's second New Deal push anyway. But southern Democrats and moderate Republicans would fund only Social Security, increased national defense spending, large construction projects aimed at rural areas where native-born Protestants of the Old Stock lived and worked, and agricultural subsidies for those farmers.

Although there was very little political interest in funding government make-work schemes or subsidies to help the New Americans, the private-option Social Security scheme was popular. Rumors had it that Roosevelt tried to kill the optional private component, which ended up being the most popular and sustainable portion of Social Security. But Congress passed the legislation with both the government and private systems included in 1937. Left-wing historians often view this action as the high-water mark of American government intervention. The Supreme Court struck down Social Security in 1939, and many Democrats still complain about that judicial stab in the back almost a century later.

Fact: Roosevelt did kill the private Social Security option, and the Supreme Court ruled the act constitutional.

The influx of Jewish and Chinese immigrants came at a terrible time for the Roosevelt administration from a political perspective. Eleanor Roosevelt spent much of her time welcoming the new refugees and speaking on their behalf, but a core group of Americans was unmoved by the plight of Jewish and Chinese refugees. They were threatened by the number of foreigners, especially non-Christians, who seemed to dominate the flow of new immigrants.

Charles Lindbergh became the face of the American movement to halt the flow of "non-Christian and non-Western" immigrants who threatened to "swamp our dear White Christian institutions with their Oriental paganism."[21] Many have speculated on the origin of Lindbergh's nativism, but he stirred up a mass populist movement against the policy of welcoming refugees and, especially, Eleanor Roosevelt's open embrace of them.

When Roosevelt's son James Roosevelt married Evelyn Chang, the daughter of a wealthy San Francisco real estate developer who immigrated from China in 1901, Lindbergh's conspiracy theorists went wild. Combined with this factor, southern Democrats and urban Catholic Democrats began to disagree on fundamental issues of segregation, the New Deal, and the building tensions in Europe and Asia. Disagreements over those issues ripped the Democratic Party apart on the eve of the 1940 election.

Fact: President Roosevelt did block a large increase in Jewish immigration for political reasons even though his wife championed their cause; James Roosevelt did not marry a Chinese American woman; and the Democratic Party was unified in the election of 1940. Charles Lindbergh was a vicious nativist, although his actual quotes differ from those above.

During the chaotic American political situation, Germany invaded Poland in September 1939. That sparked fears among the American public of a new wave of refugees from Poland, which would add to the almost three million Poles who had arrived since 1930. Those fears were unfounded, of course, as the Germans closed most exit routes from Poland, while the Soviets closed the rest after they invaded. A large number of Finns, immigrants from the Baltic states, and Jews from other eastern European nations entered the country and broke monthly immigration records from October 1939 through June 1940 in anticipation of the coming war.

Roosevelt looked helpless and proposed that Congress and the states rapidly approve a constitutional amendment to allow the president to temporarily ban immigration. Charges of Caesarism split the Al Smith Democrats and the urban Catholic vote away from the Democratic Party, guaranteeing a rout by the Republicans in the 1940 election.

Fact: Smith was anti-Roosevelt for other reasons, and no surge of immigrants occurred.

The new Republican president Wendell Willkie won on a "Keep America Open for Business and Out of the War" platform that only made some small nods to the anti-Democratic and anti-Semitic conspiracy theories that swirled around Roosevelt's implosion. But neither was important in his election victory, as the Democrats defeated themselves. After Willkie took power, Congress considered several immigration restrictions that were tailored to promoting national security and keeping the United States out of the war in Europe. Specifically, they made it illegal for Nazis and others likely to be spies, saboteurs, or ideological rabble-rousers to enter the United States.

The proposed restrictions made some Americans feel safer. However, Willkie's request for a large naval construction program and the raising of an army and air force to defend America from Axis aggression did much more to comfort the public.

When Japan sank the American fleet at Pearl Harbor on December 7, 1941, Willkie asked for and received a declaration of war with only a handful of dissenting voters from the pacifist congressmen and -women representing Montana and the Dakotas. Nazi Germany declared war on the United States four days later. Willkie had his work cut out for him as his administration went about mobilizing 250 million Americans for global war.

Fact: Willkie lost the 1941 election to Roosevelt, and the U.S. population at the beginning of World War II was only about 132 million.

The major battles of World War II are well known. Some ethnic- and immigrant-stocked infantry divisions were raised, as happened in the Civil War and World War I, but the infamous "Americanization Memo" limited their number to just a few symbolic units given support roles.

Better known were the American fighter squadrons manned by refugees and immigrants from countries occupied by the Axis powers. Fighter squadrons manned by Chinese American, Polish American, and Jewish American pilots fought with distinction in both theaters of war. Just as the Japanese American combat battalions fighting in Europe were the most decorated American units of the war, due to their desire to prove their loyalty while many of their family members were interned, Polish, Chinese, and Jewish fighter squadrons generally shot down more enemy planes than did other squadrons.

Fact: The U.S. military did have racially segregated units and some Japanese American combat units but no other intentionally ethnic units. The Japanese American 442nd Infantry Regiment was the most decorated in U.S. military history, and many fought while their families were interned. Other countries, like the United Kingdom, did have fighter squadrons flown exclusively by Polish pilots.

Despite those well-known exceptions, the American military was not divided by ethnicity or country of origin except for discrimination against blacks, a shameful policy abandoned in 1944. The authors and supporters of the "Americanization Memo" argued that mixing Americans in the armed services would help build a national identity during the war and create a more cohesive fighting force. That infamous memo would have far-reaching implications after the war, but many credited it at the time with building a more solid national identity that would knit together all the diverse ethnicities and countries of origin under the American flag.

Social scientists were unable to measure any shift in immigrant assimilation trends since the early 20th century, but the surges of Chinese and Jewish refugees before the war made Americans more uncomfortable than did the largely Christian and white immigrants who had arrived before.

Fact: The U.S. military did not desegregate until 1948.

Mexicans, Latin Americans, and Caribbean immigrants arrived in large numbers during the war to fill the void left by the tens of millions sucked into the armed services and the slowdown of immigration from Europe and Asia. Their work in war industries, mining, and agriculture helped make the United States the so-called factory of democracy that exported arms to our allies in fantastic quantities.

American troops serving abroad also helped jump-start immigration from areas of the world that had previously sent very few immigrants to the United States, such as North Africa, the Indonesian archipelago, India, and Iran. World War II started the phenomenon of American servicemen marrying local women who, in turn, brought members of their native communities with them to the United States.

Fact: Many temporary Mexican migrants did enter during and after World War II on the Bracero program, a temporary work visa for agricultural workers that continued until 1964.

Postwar Boom: 1946–1973

The joy of the Allied victory in World War II was soon followed by the dark specter of nuclear war. The American atomic bombings of Hiroshima and Kokura in August 1945 accomplished America's three goals of shortening the war, saving Allied lives, and terrifying the Soviet Union. An unexpected outcome was the fear of destruction in a global thermonuclear war, made suddenly more real because of the Cold War between the Soviet Union and the United States and the lesser powers in the soon-to-be-formed North Atlantic Treaty Organization.

The lingering economic destruction of World War II and fears of renewed war restarted European emigration in earnest. From 1947 to 1950, almost 20 million Poles, Germans, Italians, and other Europeans moved to the United States. The exodus was so large that the Soviet Union used its military to close the East–West transit routes to prevent the depletion of its newly conquered territories, from which anybody with enough money for a boat ticket or who was fortunate enough to have relatives in the United States fled. Western European countries were especially eager to smooth Eastern Europeans' transit to the United States in a misguided attempt to ease the burden of postwar recovery. The Soviets also constructed walls at common crossing points like Berlin.

Fact: The United States dropped atomic bombs on Hiroshima and Nagasaki. Kokura was an alternative target. At the beginning of the Cold War, a slight uptick occurred in European immigration, but it was a small fraction of that recounted above. The East Germans built the Berlin Wall in 1961.

The situation was less extreme in Western Europe, where the reintroduction of capitalist economic institutions reinvigorated growth. However, immigration from France, the Netherlands, the British Isles, and Norway all picked up before falling substantially in the early 1950s.

Young American men on occupation duty in Germany and Japan married local women in small but significant numbers that changed the character of post–World War II immigration. The stereotype of a Japanese American or German American housewife married to a World War II veteran came to dominate popular culture much more so than the more numerous Polish, Italian, Mexican, or Chinese immigrants at the time. That stereotype peaked in the TV show *Leave it to Beaver* (which ran from 1957 to 1963), when the best friends of parents Ward and June Cleaver were a former American serviceman and his Japanese wife.

Fact: *Leave It to Beaver* had no such character couple.

Every schoolkid knows that Jews were the major target of Nazi persecution in World War II. The Nazis murdered about 3.5 million Jews during the war and millions of others whom the regime determined were not worthy of life. That number would have been even higher if the emigration of Polish, Romanian, German, and other Eastern European Jews had stopped at some point before World War II.

The uninterrupted flow of millions of people from those countries to the United States—including a disproportionate number of Jews—ended up saving them from a worse fate that few could have predicted. Many of those immigrants contributed to funds to help the survivors of the Nazi Holocaust found the state of Israel or move to the United States. Interestingly, some U.S.-born Jews emigrated to help establish Israel in the 1940s, although immigrants from Israel to the United States supplanted American emigrants to Israel by 1951.

Fact: The Nazis murdered an estimated six million Jews and millions of others.

The United States reached a record population of 300 million in 1950, fueled by a largely Catholic American baby boom and the streams of immigrants and their children from Europe, Asia, and Latin America.[22] To avoid the policy mistakes that exacerbated the Long Depression, Republican and Democratic administrations supported the General Agreement on Tariffs and Trade (GATT). American ethnic lobbies pushed to include many countries in the Americas, southern Europe, and the Middle East that had been excluded from the first drafts of the planned GATT. The 44 original members of GATT agreed to halving tariff rates over the next decade and eliminating over 1,500 different tariffs.[23]

Fact: The population of the United States in 1950 was about 151 million, and the initial round of GATT included only 23 countries.

Chinese economic growth increased greatly after World War II. Chiang Kai-shek's corrupt Nationalist government was domesticated by rich Chinese American entrepreneurs, who were sick of seeing foreign powers take advantage of their ancestral homeland and who worried that Chiang's government would otherwise quickly fall to communism. Their remittances, foreign direct investment, and the selective return migration of Chinese American businesspeople helped stabilize Chinese government finances by 1947, reverse inflation, and prompt a virtual dollarization of large segments of China's economy.

U.S. government military aid combined with a division of American volunteers, nearly all second-generation Chinese Americans, helped the Nationalist army surround Mao Zedong's forces in the battle of Changchun. Mao escaped encirclement and fled to the Soviet Union, but his departure transformed the communist insurgency into a low-level terrorist organization mostly contained by Chiang Kai-shek's budding dictatorship.

The continued slow reforms of the Nationalist government transformed China from a poor rural country into the economic powerhouse it is today, with almost two billion citizens. That degree of development would have been unthinkable without the technical, financial, and military skills of Chinese Americans, who had the desire and wherewithal to aid the land of their ancestors and to tie the two countries closely together in the eventual alliance of powers that helped contain communist aggression in Asia.

Fact: Hyperinflation and a civil war eventually resulted in a poor China being conquered by Mao. China's population today is also only about 1.4 billion, a number far lower than the 2 billion I posit, because of the one-child policy and devastating famines caused by communist agricultural collectivization.

Several factors helped create a sense of cultural and national unity never before seen in American history: the proud legacy of winning World War II, postwar economic growth, the unifying power of the communist threat, the constant stream of refugees fleeing that threat, the huge pickup in interethnic marriages and resulting baby boom, and the continuation of the draft. Those factors combined to shrink the vigor of the American nativist movement with two small exceptions.

The first was the breaking of a handful of Soviet spy rings in the American defense industry that heightened fears of communism. Several of the spies were anti-Nazis who had communist sympathies, but some were refugees who had supposedly fled the spread of Soviet communism and turned out to be deep moles using that as a cover for infiltration.

The second was Catholicism's becoming the majority religion in the United States. Generations of immigrants from Catholic-majority countries—given extra force by the surges of Eastern European and Mexican immigration after World War II—pushed Protestants into a minority status that they have not recovered from. Although Catholicism now seems as American as apple pie, several paranoid fringe organizations—such as the Confederation for Immigrant Selection founded by Mark K. Stein—were started in the 1950s because of fear from the communist and Catholic menace to traditional America.

Fact: Catholicism never became the largest religion in the United States, but the majority of all immigrants in most years have been Catholic. Also, widespread anti-Catholicism did not diminish substantially until John F. Kennedy was elected America's first Catholic president in 1960.

Before World War II, immigrants were strongly opposed to conscription and the maintenance of a large American military force. In the translated words of one such immigrant, "We left our homelands because we didn't want to serve in the military like serfs." Many were disappointed when their new country created a draft to fight in the two world wars. However, the communist refugees and their coethnics formed a powerful bloc of American voters who supported the continuation of the draft after World

War II. Periodic war scares—such as during many of the Berlin blockades and the Korean Peninsula crisis—delayed nascent movements to end the draft.

Another group that supported the draft was the Confederation for Immigrant Selection, which had a wing of supporters dedicated to reviving the Americanization movement that had flourished during World War I. Foreign policy hawks and refugees were never completely comfortable working with the radicals at the Confederation to push for the continuation of a draft. However, they did so anyway because they thought it necessary to show the American public that Old Stock Americans also supported the draft and other efforts at enhancing American military preparedness.

Fact: The draft was continued after World War II for other reasons.

Up until World War II, about one-third to one-half of all immigrants to the United States stayed temporarily before returning home. Many came for several years to work and then returned home with their new skills and money to start businesses. In this way, much of southern China, Italy, and Mexico developed their economies quite substantially. The communist refugees bucked that trend because their countries were occupied by a foreign power, so they couldn't return. But new waves of immigrants from Mexico, Central America, and the Caribbean went to the other extreme: about 80 percent of them returned after working for a short time in the United States.

Economists later found that economic and democratic development was fastest in regions that had sent the most temporary immigrants to the United States, on both the national and subnational scales.[24] Although tens of millions of Mexican, Central American, and Caribbean immigrants eventually settled permanently in the United States by the end of the century, the flow back and forth was far more substantial and offered a taste of how American immigration would evolve in the late 20th century.

Fact: Return migration was a well-known component of immigration before Congress closed the borders in the 1920s and boosted border security in the 1980s. It continues to this day but at a lower rate.

The three most contentious and dramatic post-World War II events in the United States were the civil rights movement, the Vietnam War, and the so-called Failed Society. Millions of black Americans moved to northern cities in the 20th century, but the flow was likely lower than it would otherwise have been if tens of millions of immigrants had not also arrived from Europe, Asia, and the Americas during that period. However, a small but steady stream of black African and Caribbean immigrants, some of the former from apartheid South Africa, did form a visible minority in northern cities, and they were generally aghast at the treatment they received in states still governed by Jim Crow laws.

It is important not to overstate the influence of black immigrants on the civil rights movement, as all of the major activists and organizers were native-born Americans and only a few were second generation. Compared with all other social movements, the civil rights movement is rightly regarded by historians as the 20th-century social movement most controlled and run by Americans whose ancestors had been here for a very long time.

Jim Crow segregation was overturned by a combination of legislative actions, constitutional amendments, and court rulings during the late 1960s. At the same time, American military intervention in Vietnam was faltering.

The draft was always an unstable institution in the United States, which was, at its core, a fundamentally nonmilitarized society. Waves of immigrants fleeing, in part, the rigors of military conscription in Europe had left their mark on American society. The political alliance of Old Stock Americans—who wanted military service to speed assimilation as a substitute for immigration restrictions—and the newer immigrants—who supported a strong national defense to oppose communism—faltered in the face of a new Americanized generation born in the postwar baby boom.

The boomers didn't share their parents' more militaristic values. Consequently, the American military setback in Vietnam and the perception that communism was generally on the retreat demilitarized their policy outlook. Communist failures in Cuba and China and chronic instability in Eastern Europe—the last fueled by the "Free Governments in Exile" movement in the United States, whereby refugees operated fake governments supported by the U.S. government to undermine communist regimes—made the Cold War seem less urgent. So why were so many Americans dying in a war in Southeast Asia?

Fact: The communist revolutions succeeded in China and Cuba, and communism was generally advancing around the world.

The 1971 Arab oil embargo exposed problems with the U.S. economy, such as growing inflation, that had been brewing for some time. Immigration subsequently slowed dramatically during the mid-1970s. More important, however, the recession and the growing protest movement at home prompted the United States to pull its troops out of Vietnam by 1973; Chinese Nationalist troops took their place just as the United States had taken France's place a decade and a half earlier. Chinese troops occupying North Vietnam fought a brutal insurgency until the fall of the Soviet Union.

Fact: The oil crisis was in 1973. The United States did pull out of Vietnam in 1973 but was not replaced by Chinese Nationalists, who were limited to the island of Taiwan.

The third big event in American society at this time was the so-called Failed Society. Beginning in the mid-1960s at the height of the postwar economic expansion, some progressive Democrats began to push forward arguments for restarting the stillborn New Deal as a means to help poorer Americans. They called their movement the Great Society—a moniker that would not last. Compared with previous efforts, Great Society proponents did not want to focus on helping poor white Old Stock Americans and blacks but wanted to broaden aid to all Americans.

Senator Lyndon Johnson (D-TX) led the conservative Democratic opposition to the Great Society. In a famous television interview describing his opposition to the program, he argued that expanded welfare and government intervention to help the poor would instead be consumed by immigrants who would then come here for government benefits rather than for the promise that America held. He described such a dystopia as the "Failed Society," and the nickname stuck until the policy experiment ended in 1970 with few federal legal changes but much acrimony. States then experimented with welfare programs on their own, but those petered out by the 1980s as the costs proved prohibitive and the benefits elusive.

Fact: The immigrant population reached its nadir in the early 1960s, which was a major reason that President Johnson could push through the Great Society programs, because there was no worry that immigrants would come just to receive welfare. In 1965, shortly after creating the Great Society, Congress liberalized immigration policy slightly, a change that resulted in more legal immigration from Asia, Africa, and, eventually, the Americas.

Recession, Retrenchment, and Victory: 1973–2000

The slow economic growth of the mid-1970s set off a depressing time in American history. Rising crime and terrorism from leftist radicals and Puerto Rican separatists kept everybody on edge. American policy setbacks and failures—such as the ignominious withdrawal of American troops from Vietnam and the Iranian

Revolution—depressed many Americans around the time of the bicentennial.

The growing stream of Vietnamese and Iranian immigrants, especially those with skills and money, reminded many Americans of those foreign-policy failures, especially in the California cities where they settled. There, the Republican governor Ronald Reagan led a conservative revival that blended pro-immigration themes with traditional American free-market capitalism, anticommunism, and traditional social values that bridged Catholic and Protestant voters. He rode that successful blend of ideas, combined with worries about recent American foreign-policy setbacks, into presidential election victories in 1980 and 1984. He celebrated his 1980 election with a nod to the new census estimates that the United States had a record population of 450 million, about 35 percent of whom were foreign-born.

Fact: The population of the United States was about 227 million in 1980, and 6.2 percent of the population were immigrants.

The 1980s were a boom time for the United States. Renewed economic growth, partly fueled by modest tax cuts at the beginning of the Reagan administration, incentivized immigration from China, India, the Middle East, and South America. For the first time, immigrants from Sub-Saharan Africa also made up more than 10 percent of new arrivals in 1983.

The end of the draft during the Vietnam era prompted the U.S. military to focus more on capital-intensive defense strategies than on the labor-intensive ones enabled by the country's huge and growing population. A Cold War arms race was then followed by American military interventions on three continents to halt nascent communist revolutions and coups. President Reagan boosted American foreign intervention into high gear with mixed results.

Reagan's hyperinterventionism and arms buildup were followed by a gradual winding down of tensions, new arms control treaties, and the Soviet realization by 1990 that they could not compete against a country of more than 550 million capitalists with the highest standard of living on the planet. The fall of the Berlin Wall signaled the end of confinement for hundreds of millions of people trapped in Eastern Europe and the Soviet Union.

Tens of millions fled the poverty of communism, most going to the United States, while the fall of the Soviet Union sent more waves of ethnic and religious minorities, along with some Russians, who settled mostly in the New York City area. Those immigrants pushed its population over the 30 million mark and turned the Big Apple into the first officially designated "megacity," followed by Los Angeles in 2010.

Fact: In 1990, the United States had about 249 million residents, about 7.3 million of whom lived in New York City.

The 1990s were another boom time in America. The peace dividend kicked in after a brief American military engagement in the Middle East to halt the Iraqi intervention in the Iranian

Civil War. After the Islamic Revolution of 1979, six million disproportionately educated and well-off Iranians fled to the United States, taking everything with them (except, in many cases, their religion), which caused a predictable internal political collapse in Iran.

Fact: Iran did not have a civil war, Iraq invaded the country in 1980, and many fewer Iranians immigrated to the United States.

The New Century: 2001–Present

The American population reached 700 million in 2000. The postwar baby boom did not end so much as taper off slightly and then recover by 1990. The economic boom also attracted a steady stream of immigrants, but one that showed signs of faltering as economic growth took huge bites out of poverty in Mexico, China, India, and the newly freed European countries. Return migrants from the United States took investments and know-how back home, reforming governments and Americanizing their cultures. In 2000, U.S. GDP per capita hit $50,000, accounting for about 40 percent of global economic output.

Fact: The United States' population was 282 million in 2000, GDP per capita was about $36,000, and U.S. GDP accounted for only 27 percent of global output.

Islamic terrorism on U.S. soil—some of which was carried out by recent immigrants and visitors from the Middle East—threw a profound wrench into this optimistic era. It also shocked the long-settled American Muslim community that had immigrated in dribs and drabs over the past century when the attacks rekindled a long-dormant American nativist movement.

Constitutional amendments were proposed in many states after one of the largest attacks in New York in 2002; proponents argued that modern immigrants differed from those in the past and that they were unable to assimilate nearly as well. A bill banning Muslim immigrants—justified on the grounds that their religion was a uniquely violent ideology that intended to overthrow the American government—attracted lots of support in Congress before Speaker Paul Ryan (R-WI) came out in opposition.

On the federal level, a conservative constitutional amendment that would have allowed Congress unlimited authority to restrict the movement of people made it further than any of the proposed legislation, but it has still not been approved by enough state legislatures to become law, despite persistent efforts by American nativists.

By 2018, the U.S. population reached 800 million, but a majority of the growth since 2000 was from births, not new arrivals. Immigration from China, Europe, and Latin America was near net zero, with only India and Sub-Saharan Africa as likely sources of future immigration. Currently, Europe, Australia, and other developed nations are major U.S. competitors for the waning global supply of immigrants.

Fact: The U.S. population was about 325 million in 2018.

Conclusion

A United States that never closed its borders would be very different from the one we know. Rapid population and economic growth as well as a steady stream of return migration would have raised global economic growth substantially. More speculative are the cultural, domestic policy, and foreign policy debates that might have flared up in such a world.

On the basis of some social science research, I speculate that the United States would have had a smaller welfare state and less government intervention in the economy. The reason is that "immigrants will come here and consume all of the government benefits" serves as an effective political argument in diverse societies that do not generally support government programs to aid people different from themselves.

Less positively, I speculate that the United States would have been more involved in foreign affairs and may have had more military interventions, to everybody's detriment, made possible by closer American cultural and immigrant ties with many more countries around the world during the Cold War. Little social science supports this speculation. However, anecdotes exist—such as Cuban Americans keeping up the pressure on communist Cuba. Since I couldn't write a utopian fantasy, this is the policy I thought was most likely to suffer in such a world during the Cold War.

Americans have been concerned about immigration since the Founding, but immigrants and their children have always assimilated more quickly than nativists have assumed. One of the arguments for immigration liberalization today is our success at turning the huddled masses and their descendants into new Americans and the ways that they have in turn beneficially transformed American identity. Despite the problems in modern America, we're still good at that, and we should specialize in our national comparative advantage.

11

Foreign Policy and National Defense

John Glaser

Americans don't like to think of their country as militaristic. Most believe in an America that uses military force only occasionally, and even then, righteously and as a last resort to extinguish threats to the homeland or to crush the enemies of progress. But the common perception is largely imaginary. We are, indeed, an exceptional nation—exceptionally bellicose.

Yet we don't have to be. America's extraordinarily interventionist approach to the world isn't necessary to secure the national defense or a peaceful global order, which indeed it often undermines. A radically different foreign policy that eschews military intervention not directly tied to defending U.S. territory from external attack is not only possible but appropriate given our circumstances. Moreover, it would be consistent with libertarian values by cutting wasteful spending, shrinking a bloated and rights-abusing military and national security apparatus, and limiting the exercise of force and coercion.

The outsize role of U.S. military intervention in the international system has its origins in the end of World War II. By 1945, the great powers in Europe and Asia were devastated from the battle against Nazi Germany, Fascist Italy, and Imperial Japan. Compared with our allied victors, America was largely untouched by the ruin and therefore possessed immense relative power. The United States accounted for roughly half the world's wealth and only 5 percent of the world's population. Our advanced industrial base meant we had an enormous military capacity and a technological edge. For a time, we also had a monopoly on nuclear weapons.

Power held tends to be power wielded. Unlike after previous wars, the United States never fully demobilized following World War II. Memories of failed efforts in the interwar period to reform the international system, to establish international forums like the League of Nations, and to regulate relations between states to avoid destructive conflagrations like World War I spurred U.S. policymakers to build an international order with American military predominance as its anchor. The Soviet Union's perceived postwar gains in Eurasia further pushed Washington to go on the offense.

Washington built up a colossal military-industrial complex, extended security commitments to scores of allies and client states, deployed a permanent globe-straddling overseas military presence, and relied on the frequent threat and use of force in pursuit of a wide range of perceived national interests, not merely to protect America's physical security. Washington now defined U.S. national interests so broadly that virtually no region of the world was considered nonvital.

No longer would we canonize George Washington's warning against entangling alliances or extol the counsel of John Quincy Adams that America "goes not abroad, in search of monsters to destroy." Now, policymakers decided, America had to go abroad, hunt monsters, and actively entangle itself in the internal affairs of other nations.

American activism in this period was truly without parallel. Throughout the bipolar Cold War rivalry, writes Kenneth Waltz, "the military forces of the United States and the Soviet Union remained in rough balance," but "the interests we identified with our own were even more widely embracing than those of the Soviet Union," and "in the roughly thirty years following 1946, the United States used military means in one way or another to intervene in the affairs of other countries about twice as often as did the Soviet Union."[1]

From 1946 to 2000, the United States meddled in foreign elections more than 80 times, often not on the side of the democrats.[2] That number does not include major covert regime change operations to overthrow democratically elected governments and impose dictatorships in their place, like in Guatemala, Iran, Chile, and beyond. In this new post–World War II era of America's hyper-interventionist foreign policy, according to the RAND Corporation, "there was only one brief period—the four years immediately after U.S. withdrawal from Vietnam—during which the United States did not engage in any interventions abroad."[3]

When the Soviet Union collapsed in 1989, thus dissolving Washington's primary geopolitical threat, one might have expected the United States to scale back its military commitments and its penchant for fighting wars for the sake of peripheral interests. Instead, interventionism rapidly accelerated.

The United States has engaged in more military interventions in the past 30 years than it had in the preceding 190 years altogether.[4] In 2017, U.S. special operations forces were deployed to 149 countries.[5] Washington maintains a startling 800 military bases in more than 70 countries abroad.[6] We export more arms to foreign governments than any other nation in the world, often to the detriment of democracy and human rights.[7] We have spent roughly $15 trillion on the military since 1990, an enormous price tag that far exceeds what any other country has spent.[8]

This is not an environment conducive to liberty and limited government, either at home or abroad.

War and government power are intimately connected. War, as writer Randolph Bourne famously put it, is the health of the state.[9] During times of war, the state centralizes power, raises taxes, proliferates bureaucracies, violates civil liberties, and usurps more control over the economy.

America's earliest experiences with foreign conflict attest to that fact. In the Quasi-War with France in 1798, Congress passed and President John Adams signed the Alien and Sedition Acts, which effectively criminalized free speech and empowered the president to deport noncitizens he deemed dangerous. Benjamin Franklin Bache, a journalist and the grandson of the famous Founding Father, was arrested for accusing the Adams administration of nepotism and monarchical ambition. Matthew Lyon, a member of Congress from Vermont, was indicted, fined, and sentenced to jail for writing an essay ridiculing the White House for its "pomp, foolish adulation, and selfish avarice."[10]

A little over a century later, in the jingoist zeal of World War I, President Woodrow Wilson formally asked Congress to enact a law targeting citizens "who have sought to bring the authority and good name of our Government into contempt."[11] In 1917, Congress obliged, passing the Espionage Act, later amended by the Sedition Act, which prohibited "disloyal, profane, scurrilous, or abusive language" about the U.S. government, the flag, or the armed forces—effectively making it illegal to criticize the war.

The law empowered the Post Office Department to withhold mailing privileges from publications that scrutinized the war effort. At least 75 different publications were effectively banned under this authority.[12] Eugene V. Debs, the well-known political activist whom President Wilson called a "traitor to his country," was imprisoned for speaking out against the military draft. One woman, Rose Pastor Stokes, was tried, convicted, and sentenced to 10 years in prison for writing a letter to the editor of the *Kansas City Star* that said the government was allied with the war profiteers. She later successfully appealed, but more than 8,000 Americans faced imprisonment, deportation, and other forms of official repression during the war.[13]

War not only spurs the growth of government power to the detriment of individual liberty, it also tends to generate a public fervor for state worship, in-group superiority complexes, fear of "the other," and a kind of nationalism that is slavishly unquestioning of authority.

In April 1918, a mob in St. Louis, Missouri, attacked a German American named Robert Prager when he tried to enlist in the navy. They wrapped him in the American flag and lynched him. The jury ultimately found the mob leaders not guilty, labeling it a case of "patriotic murder."[14] Following the Japanese attack on Pearl Harbor in 1941, wartime exigencies also justified the internment of 120,000 people of Japanese ancestry, most of whom were U.S. citizens, an affront to liberty that could only be perpetrated in a time of war.

During the most intense years of the Vietnam War, Presidents Lyndon Johnson and Richard Nixon directed the Central Intelligence Agency to conduct illegal domestic surveillance and suppression tactics against a range of civil society groups and activists, particularly those that vocally opposed the war. Martin Luther King Jr.—who described the war as a perverse and cynical evil and pronounced his "own government" as "the greatest purveyor of violence in the world"—was among those domestic activists whose civil liberties were defiled by a rapacious wartime surveillance regime.

More recently, the government engaged in egregious wartime civil liberty abuses in the aftermath of the terrorist attacks on September 11, 2001. The Bush administration not only established a system of torture, rendition, and indefinite detention without trial for terrorist suspects but also secretly engaged in warrantless surveillance. The National Security Agency unlawfully collected the electronic communications of countless Americans, leading a DC District Court judge to exclaim in a ruling on the program, "I cannot imagine a more 'indiscriminate' and 'arbitrary

invasion' than this systematic and high-tech collection and reten-
tion of personal data on virtually every single citizen."[15] He added
that he had little doubt the agency's program violated the Fourth
Amendment, but the case was later dismissed because the plaintiff failed to establish standing.

As in past wars, executive power expanded in the post-9/11 years.
Congress passed two authorizations for the use of military force,
in 2001 and again in 2002. Both were extremely broad and failed
to impose serious limits on presidential war. Those authorities
were intended to combat specific entities, like the terrorist group
that perpetrated the 9/11 attacks and the Iraqi regime of Saddam
Hussein. The latter was obliterated in 2003 and the former has
been substantially exhausted and hardly poses enough of a threat
to justify a permanent war footing. Nevertheless, presidents continue to use those authorities as the legal basis for military action
in at least 14 countries.[16]

It's not just active wars that tend to increase repression at home.
A militarism below the threshold of actual warfare can shape
society, culture, and governance in ways that diminish liberty
and pervert domestic life. President Dwight Eisenhower warned
in his 1961 farewell address about the pernicious "acquisition of
unwarranted influence" in the "counsels of government . . . by
the military-industrial complex." In the following decades, Ike's
prophecy of "the disastrous rise of misplaced power" came true.
Defense corporations shrewdly dispersed their military manufacturing across many states and districts, creating constituents
disproportionately dependent on high levels of military spending. They lobbied Congress to keep defense budgets unnecessarily

high and have been so effective that high military spending is politically synonymous with patriotic duty.

Federal spending on the armed forces is so gratuitous that Congress passed a law in 1990 permitting the Department of Defense to transfer "excess" military equipment to local law enforcement. In other words, Congress was allocating so much money to the Pentagon that even the most activist military in the world had more stuff than it knew what to do with. The transfer program led to a rapid militarization of local police forces across the country, where cops are fitted with gear more appropriate for soldiers in the battle for Fallujah than for traffic stops on Main Street.

This program has had baleful effects on civil liberties and domestic tranquility, particularly in how it has intensified enforcement of the drug war. Law enforcement agencies conduct about 20,000 SWAT team raids into residential homes every year, about 20 times the number in 1980, when the overall crime rate was 40 percent higher than it is now. The vast majority of these raids are intended to execute a search warrant related to illicit drugs, but forced-entry SWAT raids find drugs only about 25 percent of the time.[17]

The foregoing describes the second-order effects that a state of war can have on government power and domestic liberty. But nothing is more anti-liberty than actual warfare. War itself is the antithesis of peace, and liberty is impossible without peace. The prevailing view in Washington is that U.S. foreign policy since 1945 has fortified global stability and freedom. But those on the receiving end of U.S. violence would probably have a very different view.

In the Korean War, for which the Truman administration refused to seek congressional authority as required by the Constitution, U.S. forces carpet-bombed much of the North, including with 32,000 tons of napalm, often deliberately leveling civilian as well as military targets. Air Force General Curtis LeMay, head of the Strategic Air Command during the Korean War, later nonchalantly admitted, "Over a period of three years or so, we killed off—what—20 percent of the population."[18] Even acknowledging the broader aim of the war—to halt the advance of the totalitarian communist regime in the North—doesn't excuse the slaughter. After all, the purported normative justification—protecting democracy in South Korea—was not even a war aim: the U.S.-backed South Korean regime was a dictatorship until the late 1980s.

Mass murder doesn't enhance liberty. The Vietnam War killed more than 2.5 million people for no good reason. In classified internal documents, U.S. officials conceded as early as 1964 that most of the rationale for continued U.S. involvement was to avoid the humiliation of defeat, not to halt the spread of communism or make life better for the South Vietnamese—and certainly not to protect the United States from imminent threats.[19] And yet between 1965 and 1968, the United States dropped 32 tons of bombs per hour on North Vietnam. Throughout the war, the United States dropped more munitions in Southeast Asia than it had dropped in all theaters of combat throughout the whole of World War II, adding up to about 640 Hiroshima-sized atomic bombs.[20]

The same kind of preoccupations that kept us fighting an unwinnable war in Vietnam are keeping us fighting an unwinnable war in Afghanistan. Now the longest war in U.S. history, the nation-building mission in Afghanistan has failed to quell the Taliban insurgency or to establish a viable regime in Kabul. Since 2009, almost 30,000 Afghan civilians have been killed, and more than 52,000 injured, in a futile effort that bears little on the physical security of the United States.[21]

The Bush administration's war in Iraq was an obscene, depraved act of naked aggression. Historian and former Kennedy administration adviser Arthur Schlesinger Jr. described it as a war crime and likened it to the attack on Pearl Harbor by Imperial Japan.[22] Every initial security-oriented justification for the war—including that Saddam Hussein's regime possessed weapons of mass destruction and was allied with al Qaeda—was conclusively falsified not long after the invasion, with plenty of evidence indicating that the administration had cherry-picked intelligence and misrepresented the facts to generate public support for an elective war. Post hoc justifications centered on replacing a vicious dictatorship with a vibrant democracy, an excuse so transparently ludicrous it hardly merits refutation. Tyranny still reigns in Iraq and across the region, and it receives considerable support from Washington. In the end, the war destabilized the entire Middle East, generated more jihadist terrorism, cost trillions of dollars, killed hundreds of thousands of people, injured millions, and failed miserably by every conceivable metric. U.S. military action is still being deployed in the region to manage the fallout of this colossal fiasco.

Supporters of America's activist foreign policy would criticize the above viewpoint as one-sided. These costs and mistakes, they believe, are the price we pay for being the indispensable nation, stabilizing the international system, and policing the world's problems so that other, less enlightened countries don't have to.

The reality is that this activism has not made us, or the world, freer or safer.

It is true that this period of U.S. foreign policy activism has coincided with a period of fewer interstate conflicts and greater international stability, but the causes of this Long Peace, as political scientists call it, are varied and originate from trends exogenous to Washington's designs.

Scholars point to the existence of nuclear weapons and the enhanced destructive capacity of modern conventional military power as having deterred great-power conflict in this era. Others argue that the forces of globalization, increased economic inter-dependence, and expanding wealth have given states both more to lose from war and more peaceful options for pursuing the national interest. Still others suggest that a gradual normative shift has occurred in how most of civilization sees war: as an immoral bar-barity rather than a glorified ideal. Relatedly, states may also be constrained by the legal regimes and norms embedded in inter-national institutions, which reinforce the taboo on aggression and bolster respect for territorial integrity. Other forces—like the proliferation of democratic systems and improved information flows—can also have pacifying effects.

Together, these trend lines are a far more persuasive explanation for today's lower rates of international violence than America's wanton military interventionism and its often-bumbling execu-tion of its global cop role. We could eliminate a great deal of this foreign policy activism and still enjoy relative peace and stability.

National defense is almost universally considered a necessary and legitimate function of government. Some libertarian anarchists, like Michael Huemer, argue that nongovernment forms of societal defense, like guerrilla warfare and mass nonviolent resistance, could be workable alternatives for fending off foreign attack or invasion.[23] Huemer rightly points out that having a big powerful military doesn't necessarily translate into victory in war. The United States failed against conventionally weaker networks of guerrilla resistance fighters in Vietnam and Afghanistan, for example.

However, while guerrilla warfare can raise the costs to more powerful military occupiers, the costs borne on behalf of the indigenous society in these types of conflicts are typically orders of magnitude higher. It is much better to possess enough military power to deter adversary states from contemplating attack in the first place.

Some states do have very minimal military postures and seem to be quite successful. Political scientist John Mueller provocatively posits the "Costa Rica option" for the United States. Costa Rica abolished its military in 1948, and, Mueller argues, "the United States is, not unlike Costa Rica, substantially free from security threats that require the maintenance of large numbers of military forces-in-being." Mueller suggests that a minimalist, rather than nonexistent, national military force that preserved America's nuclear arsenal could deter foreign attack while putting a leash on interventionism.[24] Cutting active-duty forces from each branch of service by roughly one-third, scaling down the Pentagon's civilian workforce by 30 percent, halving the nuclear arsenal, and reducing the number of aircraft carriers, navy destroyers, fighter jets, and other expensive weapons systems would be a modest first step toward this considerably more restrained posture.[25]

Switzerland might be a more appropriate model. Switzerland formally established neutrality in 1815 and has maintained that posture ever since. Like the United States, Switzerland benefits from protective geography, surrounded as it is by mountainous terrain that has served as an obstacle to foreign attack throughout history. The Swiss military focuses on strict defense of the territory. Switzerland spends less than 1 percent of its gross domestic product on defense and declines any membership in military alliances or multinational warfighting structures. However, the country has not let this noninterventionism translate into isolationism. Swiss foreign policy is centered on improving its own economic well-being by pursuing international trade agreements and engaging in robust diplomacy when appropriate.[26]

Broadly speaking, the United States should adopt a noninterventionist approach to foreign policy. That means withdrawing from the hundreds of military bases and outposts America has overseas. It means spending hundreds of billions of dollars less per year on the military. It means extricating ourselves from our multifarious security commitments and ongoing hostilities and returning to a constitutionally bounded conception of war powers that balances the commander in chief's responsibility to repel sudden attacks and execute wars with Congress's power to authorize military action. It means letting other countries handle local problems, from deterring hostile states to mitigating regional instability and the effects of civil conflicts. It means abandoning policies purported to export democracy and promote liberalism, whether through the proverbial barrel of a gun or shoveling money into other countries' internal politics. It also means cutting off the support we give to authoritarian regimes all over the world. Essentially, it means forsaking the fatuous idea that America is Earth's indispensable nation with a divine mission to police the world and save it from villainy and damnation.

The purpose of American foreign policy should be, simply, to protect our sovereign territory from external attack and to shield our domestic affairs from foreign machinations that might undermine our halting, imperfect, ongoing experiment in republican government. A robust and active diplomacy should maintain friendly relations with allies, engage constructively with adversaries where possible, and pursue U.S. economic interests. But military force should be reserved for extreme circumstances that threaten core security interests.

Any mandate beyond that risks doing the work of our foreign enemies for them. As John Quincy Adams put it: if America goes down the path of global dominion, "she would involve herself beyond the power of extrication, in all the wars of interest and intrigue, of individual avarice, envy, and ambition, which assume the colors and usurp the standard of freedom. The fundamental maxims of her policy would insensibly change from liberty to force. . . . She might become the dictatress of the world. She would be no longer the ruler of her own spirit."[27]

At the very least, dispensing with the superfluous, counterproductive, and downright immoral policies of the national security state would free up an enormous amount of money and labor. Over the past generation, American taxpayers have spent more on national security than the citizens of any other country. The Department of Defense is the largest employer in the world, keeping more than 3.2 million people busy.[28] Thousands of government organizations and private contractors work on programs related to counterterrorism, homeland security, and intelligence.[29] If all that money and human capital could stay in the productive sectors of the private economy, devoted to providing products and services to consumers instead of pursuing destructive foreign policy adventures and chasing threats that don't exist, we would all be better off.

Many new technologies invite opportunities for a reduced U.S. military posture. Innovations have increased the destructive capacity of modern conventional militaries in ways that arguably have pacifying effects on the international system. Because tanks, bombers, advanced artillery, and intercontinental ballistic missiles are widely dispersed among states, they raise the costs of war and generally make conquest harder. In this environment, states tend to focus more on defense than on offense. Nonoffensive weapons, like sophisticated missile defense systems, further reduce the need for active overseas military efforts to defend against perceived threats.

Evolving military technologies continue to spread rapidly in ways that make power more diffuse and erect obstacles to U.S. foreign policy activism. Improvements in robotics, artificial intelligence, 3D printing, and nanotechnology are making it easier and cheaper for small, weak states and even nonstate actors to obtain military hardware and sophisticated weapons, from jet engines to autonomous armed drones.[30] That capability could make it harder for the United States to assert its military dominance in distant regions unopposed.

But such technologies also invite opportunities for more repression and state power. Drones enabled the Obama administration to conduct air wars in numerous countries largely in secret and without oversight, because Americans were not directly on the battlefield and the technology is easy and cheap enough to deploy that voters felt no cost or risk and therefore no concern. Cyberweapons and internet technology also aggrandize state power, particularly in the realm of surveillance.

Radically rethinking the U.S. role in the world, reducing longstanding security commitments, and reversing many decades of rapid growth in the national security state may seem like an implausible list of distant fantasies in the current moment. But retrenchment is not all that rare; in fact, throughout history it is "the most common response to decline," according to political scientists Paul K. MacDonald and Joseph M. Parent.[31]

And decline—that is, decline in economic and military power relative to other states—is certainly upon us. Compared with the middle of the past century, when the United States accounted for roughly 50 percent of global economic output, today it accounts for only 15 percent, and the downward trend is likely to continue. America remains predominant in overall military power, but military capability does not reliably translate into global influence, especially in a context in which nuclear bombs, modern weaponry, the forces of nationalism, economic interdependence, and international laws and norms make war an increasingly futile method of pursuing the national interest.

The United States is remarkably insulated from external threats, and its role as the guarantor of the so-called international order is not necessary—and, indeed, is often counterproductive—to maintain global peace and stability. A narrow set of interests—confined primarily to defense of U.S. territory—should therefore determine America's military posture. Pulling away from existing security commitments and active conflicts, however, doesn't mean we should retreat into an isolationist Fortress America. Free trade, immigration, and robust international diplomacy should drive Washington's engagement with the world.

Americans have lived with excessive foreign policy activism for so long that it feels like an essential element of who we are and what we must do in the world. It is not. The logistical and practical challenges of extricating ourselves from our overseas garrisons, our entanglements in distant disputes, and our ongoing wars pale in comparison with the intellectual challenge of acknowledging that they are in fact expendable policies. Making that case is the first step in realizing a future foreign policy that is grounded in the ideas of political liberty and limited government.

Money and Banking

George Selgin

So constantly have the ideas of currency and government
been associated—so universal has been the control exercised by lawgivers over monetary systems—and so completely have men come to regard this control as a matter
of course, that scarcely any one seems to inquire what
would result were it abolished. Perhaps in no case is the
necessity of state-superintendence so generally assumed;
and in no case will the denial of that necessity cause so
much surprise. Yet must the denial be made.[1]

So wrote Herbert Spencer, the Victorian polymath, in 1851,
during a period now seen as the apotheosis of laissez-faire economic thought. Yet even then, Spencer's thesis—that legislative
interference with money and currency "is not only needless, but
injurious"—was an extremely radical one. Spencer wasn't content
to merely argue for open competition among rival private suppliers of paper currency, as he did by unfavorably comparing the

results of the Bank of England's monopoly privileges with those of Scotland's less privileged (and less regulated) banks. He also dared to challenge the most ancient of all forms of government control of money by insisting that the minting of coins itself ought to be left to the private sector.

Since Spencer wrote, studies of the Scottish "free" banking system—a remarkably unregulated and efficient yet famously stable commercial banking and currency system that flourished during the first half of the 19th century[2]—and of several past competitive coinage systems, have shown that, for all its radicalism, Spencer's critique of state interference rested on solid empirical foundations. Just as importantly, it remains as true today as it was in Spencer's day that the only way to determine whether such interference is desirable is by asking what would happen without it.

Monetary Freedom, Then

Answering that question is, however, never easy. Partly that's so because of "status quo bias"—a natural tendency to assume that what's customary is necessarily best. The problem is one of which Spencer himself was well aware. "So much so does a realized fact influence us than an imagined one," he wrote, "that had the baking and sale of bread been hitherto carried on by government-agents, probably the supply of bread by private enterprise would scarcely be conceived possible, much less advantageous."[3]

Yet it was far easier to envision a monetary system independent of state interference in 1851 than it is now. Back then, the monetary systems of all advanced nations were based on units of gold or silver or (in so-called bimetallic systems) both, and although state interference sometimes favored one metal over the other, one didn't have to suffer from status quo bias to take a precious-metal standard of some sort for granted, as Spencer himself did.

And although a handful of nations, England among them, had rudimentary central banks that enjoyed special privileges, especially when it came to issuing circulating paper notes, others (like Scotland) allowed numerous commercial banks to issue notes and otherwise compete on roughly equal, if not liberal, terms. Although they were as yet few and far between, bank clearing-houses—the agencies responsible for gathering notes and checks issued by or drawn on various banks, returning them to their sources, and arranging for the settlement of interbank dues—were themselves still private institutions. Finally, although coining was a state monopoly almost everywhere, an entirely private coinage system was thriving in California, whereas another had been snuffed out only a few decades before by authorities in England.[4]

In short, one did not have to look all that far, or to strain one's imagination, to realize how both coins and paper money might be manufactured and supplied entirely through private initiative, much as bank deposits are supplied today, except without the least hint of state interference.

Monetary Freedom, Now

Today, governments are far more heavily involved in the business of supplying and regulating money than most were in Herbert Spencer's day. Here and there, to be sure, banks enjoy certain freedoms denied them in the past. In the United States, for instance, banks can now have branches across the nation, whereas before the 1990s, many were limited to a single location only. But in many other respects, both here and elsewhere, banks are more heavily regulated than ever. Here in the United States, federally chartered ("national") banks are regulated by the Federal Reserve (the Fed), the Comptroller of the Currency, and the Federal Deposit Insurance Corporation (FDIC), while most state-chartered banks are regulated by the Fed and the FDIC as well as by state regulatory authorities. U.S. banks are also indirectly subject to international regulations, including those promulgated by the Basel Committee—the global prudential regulatory authority housed within the Bank of International Settlements.

While most forms of bank regulation limit what banks can do, ostensibly to prevent them from behaving imprudently, others actually tend to encourage imprudent behavior. Deposit insurance, which was relatively unknown before the 1930s, and which has since been adopted by most nations, falls into this category: by protecting depositors from losses, it encourages them to overlook the risks certain banks take, and even to patronize risky banks that pay higher rates on their deposits.[5]

Although the explicit coverage offered by government deposit insurance schemes is usually limited—in the United States today, individual bank accounts are covered up to a (very generous) limit of $250,000—creditors at very large or otherwise important financial institutions enjoy the equivalent of unlimited coverage, thanks to the now-prevalent view among government officials that such institutions are "too big to fail." Provided he or she keeps it at one of these institutions, a creditor with a balance well in excess of $250,000 has good reason to assume that, should the institution get into trouble, the government will rescue both it and its depositors.

Perhaps most importantly, precious-metal monetary standards have given way to fiat-money systems, in which the standard money unit is represented by nothing more substantial than an irredeemable slip of paper issued by some national central bank. Commercial banks have also stopped issuing paper money of any sort, except in three places: Scotland, Ireland, and Hong Kong. And even in those exceptional cases, note issue is very strictly regulated. All other commercial banks are limited to receiving and managing digital credit balances known, somewhat inaccurately, as "deposits," denominated and redeemable in official fiat money units.

The much-enlarged role of government in modern monetary systems makes it especially difficult to "inquire what would result" were the government to cease playing any role. Some might be tempted to suppose that ending the government's involvement now would necessarily lead to the spontaneous revival of market-based monetary arrangements of the past, including a gold (or silver) standard. But the temptation ought to be resisted. To suppose that, were they given free rein today, market forces would restore the gold standard, or cause commercial banks to start issuing their own redeemable banknotes, just because these were features of less regulated monetary systems of the past, makes about as much sense as supposing that privatizing Amtrak would bring back steam locomotives. Instead, a modern laissez-faire monetary system of the future might well have even less in common with a circa 1851 laissez-faire system than with today's heavily regulated arrangements.

But just how great those differences will be, and what precise forms they take, will depend on precisely how we go about "abolishing" the "control exercised by lawgivers" over today's system. It's easy enough to agree that doing so means doing away with both explicit and implicit deposit insurance so that all bank creditors have a reason to consider the safety of the banks they do business with. Taking that step in turn paves the way for repealing all bank regulations designed to do something other than enforce voluntary contracts between commercial banks and the persons and institutions that deal with them, including usury laws and minimum reserve, capital, and "liquidity" requirements, among other regulations.

It's also easy enough to imagine a reform that privatizes the present, Fed-operated payments and settlement system by converting today's Federal Reserve banks into so many private clearinghouses, owned and governed by their member banks, by making commercial banks' participation in the newly privatized Fed system voluntary, and by allowing banks and other financial firms to either take part in that newly privatized system or to create or join alternative private arrangements.

A privatized U.S. mint that's forced to compete with rivals in supplying banks with small change, consisting of "token" metallic coins as well as full-bodied gold and silver "bullion" coins, for those who'd rather deal in those metals, is also pretty easy to ponder, as are other private mints that compete directly with it. Finally, the advent of Bitcoin and other cryptocurrencies makes it easier than ever to imagine a competitive market not just in bank-supplied digital dollars but in blockchain-based alternatives to dollar-denominated monies.

Plus Ça Change . . .

What would such a future, free-market monetary system be like for the typical consumer? Would someone from the world today, time-traveling to take part in it, find it utterly bizarre?

Although there's no predicting the details of such a system with any degree of accuracy, if past experience is any guide, it will have enough in common with today's arrangements to make it possible for our time traveler to quickly get the hang of it. Chances are that a small number of general monetary standards, if not a single standard, will prevail in most places. The prevailing standard monetary unit might still be the U.S. dollar (see the next section). Or it might be some cryptocurrency unit. Or it might be a unit of gold, or of silver, or even of some foreign currency. Or we might see several (but probably not many) of these different standards operating in parallel, as happens already, though only to a limited extent, in some parts of the world.

In the free system of the future, almost all transacting will be done digitally, and the vast majority of payments will be made using convertible substitutes, supplied by banks or other companies, for "standard" money or monies—the counterparts of today's transferable bank deposits. Those substitutes would include transferable deposits themselves—where the transfers are mainly done using smartphone apps, debit cards having become old-fashioned, much like checkbooks today. Smartphones could also carry digital "cash" balances—the counterpart of old-fashioned banknotes—that could be transferred from one phone to another, with no need for recipients to have their own bank accounts. To enhance the acceptability of their digital cash, private issuers could establish and police cash-provider networks, not unlike the ATM networks in use today, so that consumers might confidently accept cash from any supplier belonging to a trusted network. Although coins and paper money would largely be dispensed with, a niche market for either might be supplied with private banknotes or privately manufactured token coins, rather than with the products of central banks or government mints.

Standing behind these forms of private money itself would be an intricate clearing and settlement system, by which transfers of all sorts would be electronically executed, tracked, and reconciled or, when necessary, settled by firm-to-firm transfers of designated standard monies. Those behind-the-scenes private arrangements would function much like today's partly nationalized arrangements, though (thanks to private innovation) probably more economically and expeditiously.

A Free-Market Dollar?

The hardest questions concern what to do with the U.S. dollar itself. Presently, as we've seen, that dollar is a "fiat" unit, convertible into nothing else. The stock of "base" dollars—the modern counterpart of the stock of gold coins and bullion in the 19th century—consists of the sum of Federal Reserve notes outstanding and banks' credit balances at their regional Federal Reserve banks and is regulated by the Federal Open Market Committee (FOMC), a semipublic central governing body. Will the dollar continue to serve as the nation's most basic monetary unit? If so, how will the supply of dollars be regulated, if not by a bureaucratic committee? Must there still be an FOMC, or something like it? If not, is there an obvious free-market alternative?

Concerning the first question, although a free-market monetary system would exclude all barriers to the emergence of alternative monetary standards, it wouldn't necessarily result in the mass adoption of any of those alternatives. On the contrary, so long as the established dollar standard continued to command some confidence, powerful forces would incline people, both in and beyond the United States, to go on employing it. The choice of a preferred monetary standard, like that of a computer operating system, depends heavily on the size of its established network, making it relatively hard for new upstarts to gain a foothold, let alone sweep the field.

So although alternative potential monetary standards, based on gold, one or more blockchain-based cryptocurrencies, or some foreign central bank unit, might gain adherents, the dollar would probably survive, at least for a time. Nor would it be reasonable to look forward to, let alone take steps to achieve, its rapid overthrow: whatever long-run gains such an overthrow might promise, the short-run consequences could be dire. Innocent dollar holders both in the United States and abroad might suffer a sudden decline in the value of their holdings. And even if they don't, the continued use of the dollar could mean both a high level of uncertainty about the dollar's future value and a substantial increase in the amplitude of the business cycle. Although it's true that Fed actions themselves have often contributed to booms, busts, and inflation, it hardly follows that simply doing away with the Fed will somehow make the dollar work better than ever!

If we aren't to simply abandon the dollar to some uncertain fate, how can we free it from government control? In one sense, we can't: unlike the gold dollars of yore, the paper dollar won't "manage itself." A dollar bill today costs less than 6 cents to manufacture, while a $20 bill costs just under 11 cents. The Fed can also add dollars to commercial banks' balances at practically no cost at all. Consequently, allowing a fully privatized and profit-maximizing set of Federal Reserve banks to create as many inconvertible dollars as they like would be asking for trouble.

Instead, some alternative limit—call it "the last monetary regulation"—must be placed on those banks' ability to issue dollars. Although that limit itself would have to be imposed and therefore wouldn't qualify as a "market"-based solution, when it comes to regulating the supply of dollars, it could at least serve to replace the "rule of men" with the "rule of law."

Convertibility, or a Quantity Rule?

Broadly speaking, either of two rule-based means for regulating the quantity of dollars is possible. A "convertibility rule" would make dollars once again convertible into some scarce commodity, like gold. A "quantity rule" would instead regulate their total quantity according to some definite formula. The convertibility rule owes its appeal to the fact that it has been successfully used in the past, particularly during the classical gold-standard era of 1871 to 1914.

But replicating that success won't be easy. For one thing, the classical gold standard's success rested on its having been not just a U.S. standard but an international one. The classical gold standard's international status contributed to its appeal by guaranteeing stable exchange rates and also by limiting short-run fluctuations in gold's purchasing power by reinforcing and stabilizing the world demand for that metal.

More important, the gold standard's success rested on people's confidence that banks—including central banks—would honor their convertibility commitments. That confidence, which remained more or less intact until the outbreak of World War I, was shattered afterward, especially during the 1930s, when nation after nation suspended convertibility. Subsequently, the United States alone offered to exchange dollars for gold, albeit at a reduced rate and only for foreign central banks, until the late 1960s, when it also abandoned the gold standard.

Today, thanks to that experience, people are naturally wary of central banks' convertibility pledges. Consequently, such pledges—which in recent decades have taken the form of commitments to maintain a fixed rate of exchange between one central bank currency and another—have become vulnerable to "speculative attacks." In such attacks, currency speculators, betting that the commitment will be dishonored, seek to convert as much of the central bank's currency as possible at the promised exchange rate. Because such attacks tend to exhaust a central bank's foreign exchange reserves, the prophecy that gives rise to them is often self-fulfilling.

The public's newfound tendency to distrust central banks' convertibility commitments poses an obvious problem for any modern attempt to reestablish an official gold standard. Speculators will be tempted to "test" any renewed offer by the Fed or any other central bank to convert its currency into gold at a fixed rate. And such testing could cause even a central bank with the best of intentions to renege on its offer, causing the new regime to collapse.

The risk of a successful speculative attack would of course be mitigated by equipping the central bank with gold reserves fully equal to its outstanding (currency and bank reserve balance) liabilities. In that case, the central bank would never be compelled to suspend or devalue by the prospect of running out of gold. But doing that wouldn't be as simple as it sounds.

Today, the Fed's liabilities amount to about $4.4 trillion. Even assuming a reduction to just $2 trillion—a far more aggressive "unwind" of the Fed's crisis-era asset purchases than presently appears likely—the government's gold stock, valued at gold's mid-2018 price of about $1,200 an ounce, would be worth about $314 billion, or less than one-sixth the value of the Fed's liabilities. To allow for 100 percent cover, gold's official price would have to be set at over $7,600 an ounce, which high gold parity, as Lawrence White has explained (in a somewhat different context), would imply "a large influx of gold from the rest of the world, a large loss of other U.S. wealth in exchange, and a sharp transitional U.S. inflation."[6]

Because it doesn't invite speculative attacks, a quantity rule offers a more reliable (or far less expensive) alternative for non-bureaucratic control of the dollar supply. Many alternative quantity rules are possible, but this isn't the place to argue the virtues and drawbacks of various alternatives. However, any desirable rule should satisfy at least two requirements. First, if consistently abided by, it should guarantee a reasonably stable and predictable value for the dollar, especially in the long run.[7] Second, the rule should be "hardwired" into the monetary system, as it might be by enshrining it in a constitutional amendment, or by allowing the public to trade in existing Federal Reserve dollars for new "cryptodollars" whose supply, like Bitcoin's, is regulated by a tamperproof computer algorithm.

A Level Monetary Playing Field

To argue for rules that would allow the dollar to survive in a future state of monetary freedom isn't to say that it *must* survive, much less that it should not have to compete with rival currencies. On the contrary: if monetary freedom means anything, it means that people are free to choose what sort or sorts of money they will keep on hand, or accept from others, in exchange for their labor, goods, or services. And enjoying such freedom in turn means that government regulations neither compel people to use any particular sort of currency nor prevent entrepreneurs from marketing alternatives to the dollar, whether those alternatives consist of foreign currencies, precious metals, or digital code.

To offer some specifics: there would be no such thing as "legal tender" in a free monetary system. The government and its agencies might, for the sake of convenience, specify the currency standard in which they prefer to receive tax payments and fees. But they would be expected to accept any private currency denominated in that unit and supplied by a firm that is in good standing (e.g., a bank that is a member of the local clearinghouse). To allow that option is merely to place the government on a footing similar to that of private merchants, who would likewise be allowed to choose which currencies to accept, and who would furthermore be allowed to refuse the currency of any specific issuer or issuers.

Entry into the business of supplying alternative "standard" monies (meaning monies that are not themselves claims to other monies) would be free, with legal requirements applicable to any ordinary business. Requirements would include sanctions imposed on suppliers that dishonor their contractual obligations or are found guilty of fraud, including the counterfeiting of any rival producers' goods, when that's possible. Because the principle of "caveat emptor" would apply, those contemplating using unfamiliar alternative currencies would have every reason to inform themselves about the issuers of those currencies and to read the fine print accompanying their contracts.

Nor should that circumstance change once one or more of these alternatives achieve widespread use. So long as consumers retain an incentive to shop for quality, they are likely to be well served by various product-rating services, which are no less capable of reporting on the quality and performance record of various alternative monies than they are today of reporting on the quality and performance of cellphones, automobiles, and mutual funds. Firms may also have strong incentives to investigate products issued by their rivals, and to expose their flaws, much as California's rival mints did during the 1850s.

Finally, banks and other private financial institutions should be free to manage deposits and make loans in any currency unit their customers prefer. In doing so, they will almost certainly stick to the traditional practice of matching liabilities in any one currency with loans made in the same currency so as to avoid exposing themselves to unnecessary exchange rate risk. But here again, the best guarantee that such prudent procedures will be followed consists, as usual, of the expectation that imprudently managed banks will be allowed to fail, that their shareholders will be wiped out before their creditors bear any losses, and, finally, that creditors may themselves suffer if they do business with a poorly run bank.

Freedom and Failure

Indeed, of all the forms of government interference in modern banking systems, none poses a greater barrier to the achievement of genuine freedom in banking than the various guarantees, whether explicit or implicit, aimed at protecting bank depositors from losses if their banks fail. By removing natural incentives for depositors to avoid excessively risky banks, or to seek correspondingly high interest rates from banks that make risky investments, such guarantees remove market discipline from the banking system, encouraging banks to engage in risky lending for the sake of attracting depositors who don't bear any of the risk themselves. Then, to compensate for the lack of market discipline, regulators are compelled to impose all sorts of other "prudential" regulations on banks, including minimum reserve requirements, liquidity coverage ratios, minimum capital requirements, and limitations on the sorts of loans they can make, in the hope that doing so will make up for the fact that bank depositors couldn't care less about how safe their banks are.

It follows then that if we are ever to have a less regulated banking system, we must start by doing away with those government guarantees. Reducing the power and privileges of the central bank, so that it can't simply bail out any bank it deems "too big to fail," is an obviously important step, and one that is a natural component of any plan to put central bank money creation on automatic pilot. But explicit deposit insurance, such as that provided in the United States by the Federal Deposit Insurance Corporation, must be rolled back as well. That's because such insurance now protects individual deposit balances up to $250,000, a sum equal to about half of all bank deposits (the rest of which are mainly held by "too big to fail" banks). In other words, the vast majority of bank depositors have no reason to worry that their banks may be unsafe.

To many, it seems unreasonable to place any part of the burden of bank failures on banks' creditors, and on ordinary depositors especially. Such depositors, the popular view has it, are often too unsophisticated to tell the difference between a safe bank and a dangerous one. They therefore require extra protection, in the shape of deposit insurance or, alternatively, a postal saving system or other "narrow" banking arrangement, in which their deposits are fully backed by cash or other safe assets.

But so long as depositors, or many of them, value bank safety, a free market in money will include a market for safe money, including deposits that are well secured by some combination of bank capital and safe bank assets. And it isn't difficult, after all, for bank customers to inform themselves of the relative safety of different banks, so long as they have any incentive to do so. Although it's true that an ordinary bank customer is unlikely to be informed of the quality of a bank's loans, a customer prizing safety above other advantages can look for a bank with a large

capital cushion or a portfolio heavy on cash and government securities. Provided enough such customers exist, banks wishing to
attract them will flaunt these features of their balance sheets, as
U.S. banks often did before the days of federal deposit insurance.
And here also, various consumer rating services and watchdog
publications might be expected to come to the public's aid.

That safe banks will exist for those who put safety first doesn't
mean, of course, that banks catering to "high rollers" won't also
exist. In a free and competitive economy, different firms may cater
to different sorts of consumers; banks are no exception. Some will
display their high (non-risk-adjusted) deposit rates for the sake of
attracting deposits from more risk-loving clients, whereas others
will advertise their high ratios of capital government securities
and cash to a risk-averse clientele. Will some who can't afford to
be tempted nonetheless place their life savings in the least safe
banks? The answer, alas, is almost certainly yes, just as some will
patronize casinos and horse races. In Hong Kong, where I lived
during the mid-1980s, and where there was as yet no deposit
insurance, everyone knew that the major "European-style" banks
were much safer than most of the local banks, while the local
banks often paid higher deposit rates. Yet many poorer people
preferred the local banks, presumably for the same reason that
many enjoyed patronizing mahjong parlors.

It would be foolish, therefore, to suppose that a truly free banking system of the future would be one in which banks never failed.
But it doesn't follow that free banking would itself be undesirable.
As the late Allan Meltzer famously observed: "Capitalism without
failure is like religion without sin. It doesn't work."[8] One wants

to allow for variety and innovation, to cater to the needs of different consumers and also to allow for the discovery of new and better ways of banking. But doing that means having banks fail occasionally.

If the experience of free banking systems is any guide, those failures needn't involve major losses to bank creditors—most would avoid such losses altogether. Nor would they give way to full-fledged banking crises. Instead, failures would be limited to particular banks. The reason for this is that troubled banks in a truly free-market banking system tend to close down rapidly, as private creditors abandon them, before their losses can accumulate to the point of wiping out their capital. That happens mainly because such a system has no "last resort" lenders that can keep such banks on artificial life support. Unlike many central banks, including the Fed, that have dismal records when it comes to shoring up or bailing out reckless banks that deserve to fail, private banks tend to be very good at telling unsound banks from sound banks and offering last-minute aid to the sound ones only. For that reason, a free banking system tends to quickly weed out unsound banks before they suffer losses big enough to exhaust their capital.

A Future without Fractional Reserves?

Although deregulated banks catering to risk-averse customers might do so in part by keeping larger-than-usual cash cushions, they would more likely do so by holding government securities and other assets that, although still relatively safe, would at least earn some interest.

But even if some free banks succeeded in marketing 100-percent-reserve accounts, such accounts would be exceedingly unlikely to sweep the board. On the one hand, there would be no rules to prohibit voluntary acts of fractional-reserve banking among consenting adults in a free society. Despite what Austrian economist Murray Rothbard and some of his followers claim, there's nothing inherently fraudulent about fractional-reserve banking, the legal basis for which derives from ancient law.[9] Experience suggests, moreover, that whenever banks have been relatively unhindered by regulations and bank depositors have been unprotected by guarantees, fractional-reserve banking has thrived.

On the other hand, 100-percent-reserve banks have been rare historically and have tended to thrive only where regulations artificially favored them, either by granting them subsidies or by outlawing fractional-reserve rivals. Indeed, until the advent of government deposit insurance, regulations tended to hamper rather than encourage fractional-reserve banking. Thus, although many governments imposed minimum reserve requirements on banks, so far as the record indicates, none have ever insisted on a *maximum* reserve requirement.

Nor, finally, would the survival of fractional-reserve banking depend in any way on that of the dollar. Just as fractional-reserve banking systems have grown on the foundation of all sorts of past monetary standards, whether fiat or metallic, so too might one flourish on the basis of any future standard. Although some fans of Bitcoin seem to think otherwise, there is also no reason to suppose that the spread of crypocurrencies would prove fatal to fractional-reserve banking, as banks might play the same role in lending and borrowing cryptocurrency-denominated funds, and in creating close cryptocurrency substitutes, as they played in specie-based monetary systems of the past and as they play in today's world of fiat monies.

Were the Bitcoin unit to become widely adopted as a unit of account, prices would be expressed in it and contracts written in it. Those contracts would include debt contracts, specifying that a loan of X units of Bitcoin today is to be repaid in $X + Y$ units at some future date. Such debt contracts could take many forms, including bank deposit contracts that allow deposit holders to redeem any part of their Bitcoin credit balances on demand while allowing them to earn interest (again, in Bitcoin) on those balances so long as they retain them.

In short, in a free economy, so long as opportunities exist for profitable lending and borrowing, there will be banks and fractionally backed bank money, and that will be so regardless of the basic form of money people employ.

Other Aspects of Future Monetary Freedom

But perhaps I'm dwelling too much on old-fashioned banking. The truth is that a truly free monetary system of the future might be one in which the banks and means of payments we're familiar with today no longer play such an important role. It's quite possible, for example, that not long from now, if regulators allow it, most of us will pay for things using our cellphones, rather than debit cards (let alone cash or checks), and that wallets (I mean, the nonelectronic kind) will become curiosities and eventually collector's items, like so many slide rules. And in a truly free monetary system, firms like Walmart and Amazon, to name just two, that presently play only a small part in the payments business would take on a much larger one. Who knows?

Only one thing can be said with confidence regarding future monetary innovations: there will be more of them, and better ones, in an open and competitive monetary and banking system than there ever could be in the heavily centralized and regulated system of today. We know that not just because common sense leads us to think so, but because the freest money and banking systems of the past, like the Scottish system, were also the most innovative. As banking consultant Eric Grover observed a while back, those crafty Scottish bankers of long ago "invented branch banking, interest-bearing savings accounts, overdrafts, lines of credit, and two-sided and multicolor banknotes,"[10] among other things—all while achieving a record for safety that any bank regulator today might envy. If Scottish bankers could do all those things centuries ago, who can say what novel improvements today's financial market entrepreneurs might come up with, if only we let them?

But as impossible as it is to foresee the technical innovations that a future free monetary regime would bring forth, it's also important to recognize that such innovations will take hold only to the extent that people voluntarily embrace them: unlike government regulatory agencies, private financial firms cannot force new arrangements on an unwilling public. For that reason, it's also likely that a free monetary system of the not-too-distant future would continue to retain many of the features of today's arrangements. That system would, in all likelihood, comprise one or at most a small number of prevailing "standard" monies;

it would also have numerous competing issuers of convenient substitutes for those standard monies, where the substitutes consist of instantly redeemable and readily transferable IOUs denominated in the basic money units.

Of course, the specifics would differ. Digital or commodity standard monies might circulate alongside, or replace, "fiat" standard money; "banks" (using that term broadly to refer to firms supplying convenient substitutes for standard money), instead of operating brick-and-mortar facilities, might offer online services only; and transfers in bank-supplied money might be affected using cellphones instead of debit cards or checks.

But apart from such superficial differences, the everyday experience of making payments would not be fundamentally different from what it is now. The real differences would consist not so much in how money would work, but in its overall convenience and dependability. And in those respects, as Herbert Spencer long ago insisted, the change would almost certainly be for the good.

Cryptocurrencies

Diego Zuluaga

Imagine that you had to hire a translator every time you wanted to speak to someone. At home, you would need one to interact with your parents and roommates. Every school, college, and workplace; every hospital, post office, and bank; every store and every household would require ready access to a translator to be able to function.

In such a world, even the most mundane interactions would be costly and cumbersome. Given the scarcity of translators, conversations, meetings, and social gatherings would require planning well in advance to ensure that a professional was available to make dialogue possible. Socializing among a small number of people would be expensive, resulting in forgone fruitful exchanges and potential friendships.

In their position as crucial brokers of social life, translators would have considerable market power. Such power would bring with it many risks. One such risk is the abuse of monopoly—the extraction of rents from customers, leading to still fewer interactions. Another is fraud: you can imagine how an unscrupulous translator might collude with a merchant to fleece an unwitting customer. Yet another risk is that translator mistakes would result in miscommunication, potentially causing offense or economic loss to the parties affected.

The need for translators would also create new opportunities for government control. Repressive regimes could undermine resistance by monitoring and censoring translators and by requiring them to report on private interactions. Authorities could more subtly restrict the freedom of translators by mandating that they hold a government license. The threat of losing that accreditation would be enough to elicit conformity from a great many translators.

We Live in a World of Intermediaries

You may find the foregoing sketch ridiculous, but it merely extends to all facets of economic and social life an already widespread phenomenon: the need for intermediaries to engage in many day-to-day activities.

If you wish to find out about today's weather, you're likely to ask Alexa or Google. For transportation, you may rely on Uber or Lyft. Perhaps you use PayPal or Venmo for expenses. Sometimes, the intermediary is not a firm but a person—try to buy a house without a real estate agent or to sue for compensation without a lawyer. Both are licensed intermediaries and can command high fees for their services.

Many of our intermediaries are highly efficient. For example, before the advent of search engines, people seeking information had to consult individual sources such as encyclopedias, address books, and other guides. They risked finding outdated, incomplete, or biased information. Search engines such as Google have enabled access to hundreds of thousands of independent references in one place, with search results updated as new information comes online.

Credit card networks and mobile payment apps have made transferring funds a cheaper, faster, and more reliable experience for consumers. Ridesharing platforms have created flexible employment opportunities for drivers and affordable transportation options for passengers. Financial technology firms help borrowers manage their finances and sort through loan options. Social media platforms make interaction with faraway relatives, friends, and like-minded people much easier.

But every intermediary is also a potential weak link. Banks and other financial firms spend billions of dollars fighting cyberattacks and other forms of fraud. Ridesharing apps are often accused of setting fees too high. Many people increasingly worry about social media's role in creating ideological echo chambers and spreading inflammatory false news.

What's more, every intermediary is vulnerable to government intrusion. Banks, whether they like it or not, must collect copious information from their customers, even though much of it is irrelevant to their business. Social media platforms figured among the private organizations that, some years ago, were revealed to have facilitated global surveillance of private individuals in the name of national security. Today, these platforms face growing demands to police their content more forcefully on behalf of public authorities.

Enter Blockchains

Intermediaries help make modern economic life possible. But some people believe that technology can deliver a world without intermediaries, eliminating risks to individuals while continuing to facilitate productive exchange. The world these people envisage is one of fully decentralized networks: communities that no user controls but that are designed to encourage all users to behave in a constructive way, because it is in their self-interest to do so.

Until recently, decentralized networks existed mostly in the minds of their supporters. But in 2008, someone writing under the pseudonym of Satoshi Nakamoto proposed "a peer-to-peer electronic cash system."[1] Bitcoin, the network Nakamoto had outlined, went live in January 2009. Embedded in the code of the first batch of Bitcoin transactions was a headline from the lead story in the London *Times* on January 3, 2009: "Chancellor on Brink of Second Bailout for Banks." At a time when the global financial system appeared close to collapse, Nakamoto was hinting at the future he was hoping to help build: a future without banks.

Bitcoin is a payment system that no individual can control. Users wishing to transfer funds to other users need only know the recipient's address. Encryption makes it possible to verify a user's identity without gaining access to his or her bitcoins.[2] That makes the network both transparent and secure. Transactions are recorded on a shared ledger that any user can update, known as the Bitcoin blockchain. But no central authority puts through transactions. Instead, other users compete to validate transactions in exchange for a fee, including newly created bitcoins. The result is a payment system that works, even though no single person "runs" it. Everybody does.

Bitcoin has existed for 10 years. During that time, the price of a bitcoin has reached vertiginous heights ($17,060 in December 2017) and has seen precipitous drops. It stands at $7,808 at the time of publication. But those who view the Bitcoin price as a measure of the success of the underlying technology are missing the point. Bitcoin was designed as a payment system, not a vehicle for speculation. The token whose price has fluctuated so much in recent years is the means by which Bitcoin creates value for users. But Nakamoto never intended the goal of the network to be the maximization of the bitcoin price.

The birth of Bitcoin has gradually spawned hundreds of other decentralized networks. Reading Nakamoto's original paper, many realized that his prescriptions could be applied to uses far beyond payments. One such inspired reader was Vitalik Buterin, a Russian-Canadian prodigy who in 2014 led in the creation of Ethereum, a platform he has described as "a 'world computer': a place where anyone can upload and run programs that are guaranteed to be executed exactly as written on a highly robust . . . network consisting of thousands of computers around the world."[3] Upward of 1,800 Ethereum-compatible programs have since been launched.

Why Libertarians Like Decentralization

Libertarians favor decentralization for two reasons.

It Can Enable People to Opt Out of the State

It's well-known that libertarians are wary of the power of government. They fear that a state monopoly on violence will inevitably be abused by those with the authority to use it. If such a monopoly is at all to be tolerated, the ability of government to exercise it should have constraints. The U.S. Constitution is one of the more successful historical examples of free societies' attempt to limit the power of public officials.

In societies lacking the constitutional protections that allow individuals to preserve their freedom, decentralized networks can help people escape the yoke of tyranny. For example, Venezuelans in recent years have increasingly resorted to Bitcoin to avoid both the rapidly depreciating currency issued by their national central bank and the capital controls that trap people's savings inside Venezuela's borders.[4]

It Promises to Reduce Corporate Power

But the ability to opt out of the state isn't the only reason fans of freedom are bullish on decentralization. Libertarians worry about government more than about private institutions because of the government's privileged position. No competing entity exists to check the power of the state and to which dissatisfied citizens can turn for better service. Government's monopoly status makes it more prone to inefficiency, abuse, and stagnation.

Yet libertarians' concern with government should not be taken to mean that they are necessarily sanguine about concentrations of power beyond the institutions of government. More than 150 years ago, John Stuart Mill, writing about the perils of the "tyranny of the majority," warned:

> Society can and does execute its own mandates; and if it
> issues wrong mandates instead of right, or any mandates

at all in things with which it ought not to meddle, it practices a social tyranny more formidable than many kinds of political oppression, since, though not usually upheld by such extreme penalties, it leaves fewer means of escape, penetrating much more deeply into the details of life, and enslaving the soul itself.[5]

Although Mill's admonition targeted the "tyranny of the prevailing opinion and feeling" in society, it applies to any situation where people have the ability, and the incentive, to impose their views on others against their will. Corporations—organized groups of people pursuing common aims—may certainly find themselves in a position of temporary power from which to attempt to coerce individuals.

Whether corporations ever have an *incentive* to abuse this power is debatable. Competition normally provides a strong check on corporate fraud and abuse, since disgruntled customers, suppliers, and workers can readily switch to alternatives. But in certain circumstances, corporations may be able to exploit their large size and counterparties' imperfect information to the corporations' advantage. They may attempt to co-opt the government against the public interest. Or the government might target large corporations to exploit individuals, knowing that the firms have too much to lose by refusing to acquiesce.

Market economies typically have institutional mechanisms to guard against these various forms of abuse: antitrust laws aim to protect against the harmful use of corporate power; gift and emoluments statutes seek to prevent the bribery of public officials;

and constitutional protections, such as the Fourth Amendment to the U.S. Constitution, are meant to shield citizens from unauthorized surveillance. Yet these protections aren't foolproof, with many people arguing that monopoly, graft, and the closeness of government and corporate leaders remain problems.

By removing the need for a go-between, decentralized networks also eliminate the chance that intermediaries might engage, or be forced to engage, in the abuse of individuals. Libertarians thus believe that decentralization can make people freer, more autonomous, and better able to preserve their freedom.

Do Decentralized Networks Spell Doom for Intermediaries?

Not only do intermediaries feature prominently in any modern economy, but their role has grown with the internet, which has shifted the focus among many entrepreneurs from increasing production to using output more efficiently. Airbnb, Facebook, Google, PayPal, Uber, and YouTube are but the most valuable firms in an increasingly crowded field.

In light of such evidence, is it sensible to expect the next wave of innovation to render intermediaries redundant, as economic activity gradually moves to decentralized platforms? Some libertarians and many cryptocurrency enthusiasts (two groups that frequently overlap) seem to think so, and they look forward to a disintermediated future. But such a future cannot materialize unless the bulk of the population—who are neither libertarian nor enthusiastic about (when not actively averse to) cryptocurrencies—move to decentralized networks.

There are reasons to believe they will be reluctant to do so. Decentralized networks offer users autonomy and privacy, two qualities that libertarians rate highly. But the average person places greater emphasis on factors such as cost, convenience, and accountability. On all of these counts, decentralized networks currently underperform relative to intermediaries, and they're unlikely to dramatically improve their performance anytime soon.

Decentralization Is Costly

Proponents of decentralization are fond of pointing out the costs of running economic activity through intermediaries. These costs are both explicit, in the form of fees to cover the intermediaries' operating and financial expenses, and implicit, such as the risk of failure, manipulation, and abuse. For example, the intermediation costs of financial institutions—commercial banks, asset managers, and insurers—are 1.5 percent of total assets and have remained quite stable over the years.[6]

To those must be added the cost of uncertain events, such as credit crunches, solvency crises, and government bailouts. During the last financial crisis, the U.S. government committed $700 billion (5 percent of gross domestic product at the time) to buy mortgage-backed securities from banks.

The 2008 crash galvanized supporters of decentralized networks. But removing the intermediary is not cost-free. As mentioned earlier, instead of having a central counterparty validating transactions, the users compete to perform this task on networks such as Bitcoin. To win, these users must solve a mathematical problem. They attempt to do so by using copious amounts of computing power. In other words, running a decentralized network is very electricity intensive, at least for the time being. How intensive is it? A 2018 study calculated that Bitcoin's annual electricity requirements, at 67.2 terawatt-hours, equal those of medium-sized economies such as Ireland and the Czech Republic.[7]

That may seem outrageous. Indeed, it takes two-and-a-half times as much electricity to process a single Bitcoin transaction as it does to process 100,000 transactions on the Visa card network, making the leading decentralized payments system 250,000 times less energy efficient—on a per-transaction basis—than the leading intermediated network.[8] On a dollar basis, Bitcoin doesn't underperform quite so woefully, because the average Bitcoin transaction has a much higher value than the average Visa transaction.[9] In fact, Bitcoin currently processes $1.7 trillion in transaction volume per year to Visa's $11.2 trillion.[10]

Yet Bitcoin currently consumes more than $7 billion worth of electricity each year. If we include the cost of the computer hardware to validate transactions, the annual running costs of this decentralized network are $10 billion to $12 billion.[11] By comparison, Visa's operating costs for 2018 were $7.8 billion. Thus, dollar for dollar, Bitcoin is not hundreds of thousands of times less efficient than the largest intermediary. But it's still between 8 and 10 times less efficient—not a great starting place for a challenger.

Decentralization Is Inconvenient

Today, if you wish to operate on a decentralized network—say Bitcoin—you can do so in two ways. The first is the intermediary-free way. Start by buying bitcoins from a neighbor whom you can pay in cash, store your private key (which gives access to your bitcoins) in a safe electronic or physical place, and then learn some computer code. You can then begin using the Bitcoin network. Avoiding intermediaries completely is still possible on Bitcoin, but it can be quite a nuisance to the uninitiated.

The second way is to set up an account on a cryptocurrency exchange, such as Coinbase or Kraken, to which you must provide your personal information, including your Social Security number and bank details. This way of holding cryptocurrency is far easier and more secure for the user, but it doesn't avoid intermediaries. Insisting on the maximum possible disintermediation complicates the prospects for widespread adoption of decentralized technology, since the intermediaries—such as exchanges—facilitate access for retail customers.

Decentralization Is Intolerant of Mistakes and Complicates Accountability

A useful trait of most intermediaries is that they typically have the power (sometimes even the legal obligation) to reverse erroneous and fraudulent transactions. Given imperfect customers with fat fingers and a surprising propensity to fall for obvious scams, the ability to provide redress increases trust in intermediaries.

It's another reason why those not ideologically predisposed to decentralized technology may prove reluctant to shift their custom to decentralized networks. Correcting mistakes and righting wrongs involve discretion. Intermediaries can use their discretion because they control the network; furthermore, they have an incentive to use such discretion fairly but sparingly, so as to maintain a good reputation in the eyes of customers, who like certainty but are wary of irreversible mistakes.

By contrast, discretion isn't easy to code into the software protocols that govern decentralized networks. The reason is discretion means doing something that contradicts standard procedure. If you book your plane tickets for the wrong date by mistake, normally you would have to pay for new ones. But if you notice early enough, an intermediary such as eDreams may (as a matter of mercy or of policy) cancel the transaction at no or low cost. Who would you turn to for help if you had instead booked your tickets on a decentralized marketplace?

The main differentiating characteristic of decentralized systems compared with centralized ones is both a strength and a weakness. Policies with respect to all foreseeable future events on the network must be specified in advance, leading to perfect predictability, which increases trust. Yet invariably, the network's designers—no matter how expert and prescient—will fail to code for some future developments. In those circumstances, decentralized networks will struggle to offer users a satisfactory response, decreasing the users' willingness to join.

Where Can Decentralized Networks Make an Impact?

Pointing out the weaknesses of disintermediated platforms is not to suggest that decentralization will fail. To learn where Bitcoin and similar networks will likely play an increasing role, start by asking, where are intermediaries currently doing a comparably lousy job?

International payments are one such area. Typically, a money transfer takes three to five days to arrive in a foreign account. Fees range between 3 percent and 10 percent of the transaction amount. What's more, the incumbent payment system is regressive because low-income immigrants use costly remittances to send money home and because they typically transfer smaller amounts, for which the percentage fees are higher. Bitcoin can easily reduce the cost of international payments, although the slow speed at which transactions are processed and the volatility of the bitcoin price discourage take-up.

Other decentralized networks, however, promise to achieve low-cost money transfers without the pitfalls of Bitcoin. Ripple, for example, uses the cryptocurrency XRP to avoid the slow and expensive bank transfer system, which requires the sender's money to go from his or her bank to a correspondent bank; from there to the central bank of the sender's country; from that central bank to the central bank of the recipient's country; and from there to the local correspondent bank, before finally landing in the recipient's bank account. That amounts to five discrete transactions! Instead, Ripple converts the sender's (say) U.S. dollar funds into XRPs, processes the transfer on the XRP blockchain, and then converts the XRPs into (say) Philippine pesos for the recipient. Ripple bears all the exchange rate risk, for which it charges users a fee. Still, the company claims to be able to lower the cost of international payments by up to 60 percent.[12]

Decentralized networks will also put pressure on poorly performing governments. As regulators, legislators, and adjudicators with near-monopoly powers, governments determine whether economic activity flourishes or perishes within their jurisdiction. Many countries in Africa and Latin America—whether through corruption, neglect, or path dependency—have struggled to grow. But decentralized networks could put an end to this poverty trap.

Consider property titles. In developing countries, people often have difficulty proving ownership of the land they've lived on and worked for decades. Official property registries are inefficient and corrupt. Yet proof of title is often essential to obtain affordable credit, for which the land acts as loan collateral. Hernando de Soto has championed the formalization of property rights as a development tool and thinks blockchains are a cheap, reliable, and tamperproof means of record keeping.[13]

Companies are testing the use of decentralized ledgers like the Bitcoin blockchain for their own internal processes: technology giant IBM, shipping behemoth Maersk, and e-commerce leader Amazon are some examples. As already mentioned, decentralized networks can be weapons against monetary mismanagement and tyranny, from Venezuela to China. Wherever intermediaries—whether governments or firms—are failing, decentralized networks will challenge them, forcing the intermediaries to improve or face extinction.

Intermediaries Are Dead; Long Live Intermediaries!

Decentralized networks have shortcomings. All new technologies do, including those—such as the internal-combustion engine and the internet—that end up proving revolutionary. The high cost, inconvenience, and inflexibility of decentralized systems are important weaknesses, but ones that can be easily overcome with intermediation.

For example, a promising avenue to reduce Bitcoin's per-transaction electricity use is to have intermediaries—banks, credit card networks, even large merchants such as Amazon—process transactions on their own books during the trading day and settle the net amount on the Bitcoin blockchain at the end of the day. That approach would remove billions of individual transactions, some of which would offset each other, from Bitcoin's decentralized system, thereby dramatically reducing its computing power requirements. It would make Bitcoin useful even to people wishing to transfer small amounts.

Of course, this model would involve some intermediation and carrying risk on an intermediary's account for a period, which would create a point of failure and require users to pay the intermediary a fee. But users would gain in the form of much lower costs, greater convenience, and the opportunity to reverse transactions in exceptional circumstances. All of those improvements would make dealing with decentralized networks more attractive to the typical retail customer. Those libertarians and crypto enthusiasts who value autonomy and privacy above all else would still be able to avoid intermediaries as much as possible, but they would have to sacrifice affordability, speed, convenience, and accountability to enjoy more of the other two values.

Decentralized networks in their present incarnation are often likened to the internet in the early 1990s. At that time, the internet's staunchest proponents envisaged a future of peer-to-peer interaction, with a great deal of personal freedom and minimal government interference. The 1996 "Declaration of the Independence of Cyberspace" succinctly captured this vision:

> We are creating a world that all may enter without privilege or prejudice accorded by race, economic power, military force, or station of birth.

> We are creating a world where anyone, anywhere may express his or her beliefs, no matter how singular, without fear of being coerced into silence or conformity.

> Your [governments of the world] legal concepts of property, expression, identity, movement, and context do not apply to us. They are all based on matter, and there is no matter here.[14]

A quarter century later, the internet is dominated by large information, social media, and retail platforms. It's quite a different place from the one the early cyberspace pioneers imagined, with a greater commercial focus, corporate presence, and government meddling than many of them would have liked. Yet today's internet has also made productive exchange—whether economic or social—more accessible, affordable, diverse, and pleasant than it was before the advent of the technology. To the average person, those achievements may well be worth the downsides.

Libertarians are right to welcome decentralized technology in their quest to increase and protect individual autonomy. But those who believe that decentralization will enable societies to supersede the threat of government overreach and other concentrations of power must not let their guard down. A decentralized world is one in which intermediaries will continue to play a large role. That means the fight for individual liberty will continue even as technology expands the opportunities for peer-to-peer relationships.

14

Digital Expression
Will Duffield

You, as a contemporary American, enjoy robust speech rights. The government may not stop you from criticizing its policies or mocking its agents, and artists of all stripes may express themselves without fear of state censorship. This is freedom of speech as freedom from interference—"Congress shall make no law"—and Americans enjoy more of it than the citizens of any country at any time in history. Nevertheless, something we might call the liberal vision of free speech—a positive understanding of maximal individual expressive capacity—remains imperfectly fulfilled.

A generation ago, the American publishing environment—and, consequently, the expressive capacity of most Americans—looked very different. Before the widespread adoption of the internet, the press looked less like a set of universally accessible technologies and more like a privileged class. For most Americans, the opportunity to speak to a wide audience was limited. Media publication and distribution tools were still quite expensive or labor intensive. Listeners had limited means of searching for speakers they wished to hear. Sure, you could pump out mimeographed zines in your basement and pass them out on street corners (and many did), but technological limits placed practical restrictions on who could speak and how far their speech could travel. In turn, these natural limits created opportunities for state action that served to further fetter speech.

The advent of radio and television in the first half of the 20th century brought a wider array of speakers into American homes, but both new media forms required expensive infrastructure and the exclusive use of certain broadcast frequencies. This centralization empowered gatekeepers—from Walter Cronkite to your local newspaper editor—to decide which perspectives received wide circulation.

The internet changed all of that, throwing open the floodgates to a deluge of speech. The early internet contained few gatekeepers, although it required a fair amount of specialized knowledge to host and operate your own website. Forums, message boards, chat services, and eventually social media emerged to host a diverse cacophony of voices, allowing everyday Americans to communicate in one-to-one, one-to-many, and, for the first time, many-to-many formats, instantaneously and at a low price.

This internet speech ecosystem came with its own set of new gatekeepers. Social media platforms enlisted content moderators to keep their digital forums consumer friendly; speech middlemen deeper in the internet stack—such as Cloudflare, a content delivery network that sits between Web users and the servers of websites they visit—realized that they possessed incredible power over who could maintain a presence on the Web.[1]

With the doors (mostly) thrown open to speech, internet payment processing became a new locus of gatekeeping. Although it might have become harder to prevent given speakers from publishing their thoughts, if it could be made difficult for their fans and supporters to fund their expressive activities, the amount of time they could realistically devote to speaking would be limited. This factor has increasingly challenged speakers who toe the legal limits of free expression.

These new chokepoints—regardless of whether they are "architected" or "natural"—may be inclined to limit expression and can be influenced, or even captured, by illiberal advocacy organizations and foreign states. Some of these constraints are acceptable and unavoidable. Not every node in every network must host every sort of speech. However, understood as an ecosystem, an internet that is friendly to free expression ought to provide some means of allowing consenting speakers and listeners to interact with one another, ideally without great expense or specialized knowledge.

Predicting the future of speech is difficult. Unlike many other policy areas, freedom of expression vis-à-vis the state does not guarantee speakers an audience, or, more importantly, access to the communicative tools necessary to reach receptive listeners. Much of what we think of when we envisage a regime of expressive freedom relies on a tolerant, liberal culture willing to give dissenting voices a hearing. That being said, the technological innovations discussed in this chapter will help individuals to more easily express themselves and will limit the effective impact of both illiberal cultural turns and state exploitation of chokepoints in systems otherwise legally supportive of free speech.

The following sections examine how state censorship laundered through private platforms and the erosion of intermediary liability protections will spur the decentralization of internet forums. In turn, this development will recenter speech freedom disputes on the individual speaker while exacerbating the internet-borne challenge to authority.

Internet Speech as an Ecosystem

As a speech delivery mechanism, the internet is far more complex than its predecessors. Whenever you speak over the internet, whether publishing state secrets or sending a photo of your cat, you use the services of countless intermediaries that you share with billions of other speakers. From the physical device you use to tap out your message, and the wires or antennas through which your speech travels, to the multitude of programs and protocols that govern interactions between various layers of the internet, hundreds of hands help your speech reach its intended audience. Compared with the process of publishing a handbill, internet speech requires the participation of a wider array of intermediaries. Whereas these interreliant middlemen mostly serve to increase the range and velocity of speech, many have the capability to act as gatekeepers, refusing disfavored speakers the use of their services.

Not all intermediaries act as gatekeepers; generally, the more important the intermediary, the less gatekeeping it does. Physical infrastructure providers like AT&T or the providers of low stack functions like internet protocol address assignation rarely engage in gatekeeping. Furthermore, not all gatekeeping limits the public's publishing capacity, and some gatekeeping functions, such as spam filtering, are universally appreciated and infrequently implicated in freedom-of-speech concerns.

Nevertheless, because internet speech depends on this battery of middlemen, gatekeeping authority can be used to suppress speech. Sometimes, this is done for purely private reasons. Forums dedicated to specific functions exclude off-topic submissions. Advertising-funded video hosting platforms like YouTube exclude content that concerns advertisers. From Dove soap to Hasbro, no one likes their adverts to run in front of ISIS videos. Community formation and maintenance will always require some gatekeeping. Private speakers can usually find alternatives to social media platforms that have rule sets they find too restrictive, although those substitutes may not provide their speech with as wide an audience as larger platforms.

State interference with this ecosystem of speech facilitators is particularly concerning. Because states may coerce intermediaries to refrain from carrying disfavored speech, their prohibitions are totalizing and offer few avenues for exit. A few private platforms may gravitate toward common rule sets or embrace cartel-like cross-platform speech compacts; however, without a means of preventing defection, the power to completely exclude evades these arrangements.

Government regulation of internet speech takes many forms. Formally, states may prohibit the publication of certain words or phrases, targeting either the speaker, intermediaries, or both. They may increase the cost of participation in this ecosystem by imposing costly regulations on intermediaries or by taxing social media users directly.[2]

Increasingly, Western governments have preferred tinkering with intermediary liability—the extent to which platforms are held legally responsible for their users' speech—to regulate speech indirectly. Germany's NetzDG (Network Enforcement Act) and the United States' FOSTA (Fight Online Sex Trafficking Act) render platforms liable for certain forms of user-generated content, requiring private firms to make legal judgments on the fly.[3] Regulation can also tip the scales in favor of takedowns by shortening private content moderation windows or by mandating preemptive filtering rather than post hoc complaint and review procedures.

Less explicit regulation is accomplished through "jawboning," when governments alter private behavior through threats of regulation or legal sanction. Jawboning efforts may exhort current gatekeepers to shift the focus of their efforts, like the European Commission's hate speech Code of Conduct, a voluntary agreement presented as an alternative to regulation that privileges the removal of hate speech. The Code of Conduct not only requires platforms to prioritize the removal of hate speech over other goals, it also standardizes their definitions of "hate speech."[4]

Definitional uniformity prevents the speech ecosystem from finding even a seedy outlet for controversial or disfavored speakers. Given that most platforms are international, a definitional concession in one part of the world may affect the speech capacity of internet users worldwide. As platforms race to engage network effects by connecting ever-greater numbers of people, they risk combining the particular prohibitions of many different states and societies into a regulatory whole that is even more restrictive than the sum of its parts. As the second half of the globe's population comes online, the diversity of viewpoints and local taboos will increase, at least at first. In the long term, speech norms are likely to converge somewhat, though the maturation of translation software will exacerbate tensions in intercultural moderation.[5]

Jawboning may also impel intermediaries that have thus far refrained from exercising gatekeeping authority to begin doing so. Financial services, particularly payment processing, are increasingly being dragooned into policing speech. Beyond their use by state censors, payment processing chokepoints also serve as beacons for cultural conflict. These chokepoints provide a means of effectively politicizing commercial relationships made legible and public by their presence on the Web. Digital payments give speakers access to a far wider set of potential supporters, but the relationships between specific speakers and the services upon which they rely are made explicit by payment plug-ins, searchable fundraising platforms, and metadata.

Other commercial aspects of the speech ecosystem—from the provision of domain names to cloud storage—are similarly legible, though historically less politicized. And both state actors and private activists are likely to become more sophisticated in their selection of pressure points as time goes on.[6] Internet speech is, for the moment, reliant on this chokepoint-ridden ecosystem. Current regulation, formal and informal, public and private, uses these chokepoints to limit the distribution of disfavored speech. As such, most near-future speech conflicts will occur under a regime of confusingly muddled public and private governance. In the long run and in an increasingly global speech ecosystem, expansive expressive capacity will only be secured through decentralization.

Decentralization

On one front, speech-enhancing technologies continue to advance within the platform paradigm, offering users novel ways to communicate with one another. VRChat offers new forms of gesture-based speech, the benefits of which have already been seen.[7] However, as long as these applications are centrally distributed and administered via the Oculus or SteamVR stores, they can be bound by regulation and jawboning just as older platforms have been.

Free, encrypted, cross-platform messaging apps allow groups of people to communicate privately, establishing their own standards for group admission and acceptable speech. This development allows individuals to exit public platforms, avoiding their vulnerability to government jawboning and market-driven moderation demands in exchange for fewer opportunities for discovery. Within such closed chat networks, it is harder for speakers and listeners to find one another. As well, though these networks are encrypted to varying degrees, they still run on centralized infrastructure. They are operated by governors incapable of restraining themselves and therefore are ultimately incapable of resisting pressure to "do something" about disfavored speech.

Eschewing reliance on market forces or protective legal regimes, a structurally decentralized internet would resist state regulation and the ever-shifting tides of public opinion by eliminating chokepoints that allow single actors to limit a speaker's use of the system as a whole. From the physical antennas and receivers to the provision of microblogging services, an idealized decentralized internet would replace capture-subject intermediaries with open and secure protocols that are accessible to everyone.

Rather than being the property of a single institution, protocols need not be owned by anyone and may be used by any two parties willing to adopt the same standards. In practice, nonprofits make most decisions concerning the management of widely used protocols. Existing protocols have largely resisted state jawboning because, unlike edge publishing platforms, they are viewed as common infrastructure.

Much of the modern internet is built on top of open-source protocols; HTTP delivers our webpages, while POP3 and IMAP carry our email. But when we use the internet to interact with the rest of the world, when we buy, bank, and speak, we do so through layers of platforms. Even our email, carried by open protocols, is most often accessed via centralized webmail platforms.[8]

Although the widespread adoption of decentralized protocols to manage social identity, payments, and publishing would dramatically enhance the expressive capacity of individuals, decentralized alternatives to platforms have always struggled to gain a broad base of users. Platforms trade control for convenience. The platform takes care of setup, security, and conflict resolution, often at the expense of free speech. Decentralized services require much more of users. They may be asked to shoulder some of the load of network management or, at the very least, to take responsibility for their own security, keeping track of public and private keys rather than relying on passwords stored on platforms.

Traditionally, decentralized internet proposals, and the open-source software community more generally, have found it hard to effectively compensate those responsible for operating and improving free software. In an open ecosystem, it is difficult to stop free riders from using services without contributing to their upkeep.

Blockchain technology—a form of peer-to-peer network popularized by Bitcoin as a means of recording transactions and preventing the double-spend problem—offers a framework for remunerating network facilitators without establishing an authority capable of controlling network traffic flows. A blockchain is "an open, distributed ledger that can record transactions between two parties efficiently and in a verifiable and permanent way."[9]

Within the Bitcoin network, miners lend their computers' processing power to the network, solving incredibly difficult equations to verify the integrity of each new block of stored transactions. In turn, the network compensates them with newly created Bitcoins, distributed in a pseudorandom fashion to miners, based on the amount of work they do for the network. While the Bitcoin network prioritizes the stable creation of money, other blockchains may provide public ledgers that offer decentralized speech, social, and identity-verification services.

The InterPlanetary File System (IPFS) and the Filecoin token offer a glimpse of how blockchain-driven decentralization can radically expand and secure the individual's publishing ability. IPFS allows a file to be stored, in whole or in part, across multiple locations. An Ethereum blockchain maintains a public ledger of the file's locations. You can access any version of the file recorded on the ledger, and IPFS directs you to the nearest copy. In the event of a denial-of-service attack, or the seizure of a server holding one copy of the file, IPFS will simply direct a searcher to another copy of the file.

This system works well in principle, but it doesn't create much incentive to offer storage space to the IPFS network. That's where Filecoin comes in. Sitting on top of the IPFS network, Filecoin is a cryptocurrency used to purchase storage space on the IPFS network and remunerate users who allow IPFS files to be stored on their hard drives.[10]

The location, or locations, of a file stored via IPFS are invisible to the end user. The identity of the host is likewise unknown, and the host himself is unaware of the contents of the file fragments he stores in the unused parts of his hard drive. As such, the application of any sort of censorial pressure, by either states or civil society groups, will be extremely difficult. Discovering the physical location from which a file is hosted presents a real challenge for state authorities. Even in the event of an initial takedown of one copy of a file, it can be immediately and seamlessly rehosted elsewhere without compromising its ability to be discovered via search.

The IPFS system may feel utopian, but it has already proved its worth as a means of censorship resistance. When Turkey blocked its citizens' access to Wikipedia in 2017, a version of the site was hosted via IPFS. Turkey could identify and bar connections to Wikipedia's servers, but it could not prevent Turks from accessing copies of the site indexed through the IPFS system.[11] Although this example serves as a valuable proof of concept, the establishment of a functional ecosystem of decentralized speech protocols will face many challenges.

The timelines of both ratcheting censorial pressure and the development of user-friendly, decentralized publishing tools will determine the makeup of the community of users that composes the decentralized Web. Early adopters—who will do the most to shape its architecture and norms—are unlikely to be ordinary in either outlook or technical competence. A singular mass exodus from the platform internet is improbable; instead, specific groups of users, often from preexisting communities, will find cause to look for the exits.

Adoption will likely be piecemeal, in response to specific content moderation controversies. This response may be driven by either state or private action. The passage of FOSTA—a law that renders platforms responsible for prostitution and sex trafficking—drove sex workers to establish their own instance of Mastodon, a decentralized Twitter clone.[12] Fearing private bias in Twitter's content moderation, right-wing Twitter users have jumped ship for Gab, a more liberally governed microblogging platform. While Gab is not decentralized, its pillorying as a den of far-right villainy illustrates how the first mover problem could hobble decentralized speech protocols.

If decentralized communication networks are initially viewed as subversive or dangerous, home to speech exiled from respectable platforms, their users may suffer reputational harm, slowing adoption. These concerns may also form the basis for regulation that could strangle decentralized innovations in the crib: think licensure of, or the imposition of liability upon, network participants. Once these services are adopted widely, such regulation would become politically infeasible and practically unenforceable.

Regulating niche hobbyists and drug sellers off the internet, however, is unlikely to provoke much backlash. The cryptocurrency community has already done a great deal to normalize the use of blockchain technology, but beyond their contestation of state monopolies on the creation of money, most blockchain uses have not raised politically salient concerns.

To prevent censors from simply moving their efforts lower on the internet protocol stack or using physical chokepoints to cut off messages between decentralized network nodes, at least some of our physical internet infrastructure must be decentralized. Rather than connecting to other machines using fiber-optic cables owned by a singular utility, or via wireless infrastructure managed by a few cell service providers, users of a truly decentralized internet will avoid these chokepoints by using large-scale mesh networks. In the past, when internet connectivity was limited to desktop computers, the possibilities of mesh networks were limited. A few local routers could be connected to one another, but broad coverage was difficult to achieve.

Today, the ubiquity of internet-connected handsets and the internet of things makes large-scale mesh networks feasible.[13] In the future, you will receive internet access through your neighbor's thermostat, or one of countless other internet-connected devices. Should one device fail, or should your neighbors dislike the manifestos you publish via their thermostats and cut you off, your traffic can be routed elsewhere. This web of devices may, in turn, connect to either traditional cable networks or novel wireless networks made up of drones, balloons, gliders, and satellites.

While past satellite internet systems relied on larger ground-based gateways and faced expensive launch constraints, the falling cost of orbital delivery services and the miniaturization of satellite receivers are opening the skies to communications infrastructure like never before. It is now possible to send a message to a satellite and, using Bitcoin, pay for it to be broadcast back to Earth.[14] Though these data are broadcast, and therefore can technically be received by anyone, encrypting them ensures that only recipients with the correct keys can decrypt the encoded messages. The protocols that receive, process, and retransmit this message are content agnostic. Such a system could also host Mastodon instances or other decentralized publishing applications.

Unfortunately, taking advantage of this cutting-edge means of publication is technically demanding at present; even configuring a computer to receive this type of message is beyond the capabilities of the average internet user. That is to be expected; it will take time to make this suite of technologies user friendly. The internet was once wholly the domain of hobbyists. Demand for expressive freedom will drive adoption to some extent, but such a system of satellites, mesh networks, and decentralized software will also offer privacy benefits and expanded coverage, especially when compared with legacy infrastructure.

Although early adoption may be piecemeal, even partial adoption will greatly benefit the users who have cause to opt in to this kind of system. In time, as these technologies mature and their benefits are better appreciated, more users will join, in some cases without realizing they are doing so. When the next TikTok or Discord is natively decentralized, simultaneously used and hosted by hundreds of millions of people, the distributed anti-fragility of these communication tools will render the individual's expressive potential truly secure.

Refocusing on the Individual

With interpersonal communication thus shielded against the vagaries of law and custom, state censors and media critics will find themselves forced to refocus on individual speakers rather than the communication systems that give them voice. Internet users—either liberated or estranged from the governance of platform content moderators—will establish new, individualized means of tracking reputation and filtering out unwanted content.

Secure, decentralized, publishing protocols will not obviate the demands of censors. Speech will still be seen to cause distinct harms; some speech and media, like libel and nonconsensual pornography, will rightly remain illegal. The presence of irrepressible communication tools will force censors to refocus their efforts on individual speakers, rather than attempting to suppress undesirable speech by press-ganging intermediaries into playing censor.

This approach will spur greater focus on the tensions between individual anonymity and accountability. If instead of relying on platform governance to suppress disfavored speech, state authorities must identify and punish bad actors, software that provides for anonymous communication will face increased political scrutiny. Identity verification will gain newfound importance, as will mechanisms for tracking reputation. Even as the decentralized internet becomes more user friendly, these challenges will be, to some extent, baked into the medium. In rejecting centralized administration capable of succumbing to censorial state or social pressure, a greater onus will fall on users to ensure that they receive only the information they desire and that their sources are trustworthy.

Instead of relying on platforms to provide human or algorithmic moderation and curation, users will assemble their own sets of reputation trackers, block lists, and content curation algorithms. Many internet users approach algorithmic filtering with skepticism, largely because of the opaque nature of platform recommendation algorithms. In the hands of individuals, curation algorithms would lose their totalizing impact and could be adjusted over time to prevent either over- or undermoderation. In a decentralized environment, most users will adopt some combination of these tools to manage their social experience. Different tools will appeal to different moderation demands without affecting the internet experiences of those with different preferences.

Collaborative Twitter block lists offer one example of how these tools might function, but, freed from platform-based API (application programming interface) restrictions, many individualized moderation plug-ins will offer more fine-tuned content discrimination options.[15] Imagine deciding to see only family members' vacation photos while entirely avoiding their political rants or modifying your social feed with an algorithm that draws on past interactions to prescreen harassment without expunging the jovial use of foul language by a friend. This style of moderation will not satisfy proponents of militant democracy concerned with their neighbors' information consumption habits, but it will effectively address the concerns of everyday internet users. For users who desire a highly curated experience, the decentralized internet might look a lot like current social media platforms.

Platform-style governance disputes will not disappear entirely, but their stakes will be lowered by reduced exit costs. Not all nodes within a decentralized internet will choose to accept connections from all other nodes. The precise architecture of decentralized services will surely be a subject of continuing debate among users and stakeholders. In cases of intractable disagreement among stakeholders, the same digital protocol could be replicated under a new governance structure, or, in certain blockchain disputes, "forked" from the existing protocol with limited impact on the experience of users on either side of the conflict.

States will make use of decentralized publishing tools as well, often for malicious purposes. Just as some condemn encrypted messaging for its utility to criminal elements, some liberals may regret the loss of Mark Zuckerberg's ability to limit the voice of Myanmar's generals. The broader effects of widespread, censorship-resistant publishing tools may place new stresses on even liberal political regimes.

Current social media platforms certainly appear to be a boon to dissidents across the political spectrum. However, liberals should take solace in the fact that these innovations will merely reveal existing, albeit suppressed, discontent. Novel publishing tools do not drive otherwise satisfied citizens to hoist the black flag and turn against their governments. Instead, they provide for the perfection of liberal democracy, allowing governors to truly engage with, and respond to, the full spectrum of public sentiment, unfiltered by gatekeepers and censors both public and private.

15

Technology

Matthew Feeney

Unless you're an early riser, you woke up today shortly after your phone's alarm rang. You rolled over, unplugged the phone from its charger, used your face or fingerprint to unlock it, and began your morning digital routine. You checked your email and texts, Facebook and Instagram notifications, and the status of your recent Amazon order. You looked up the weather forecast and skimmed headlines.

You then got out of bed, took a shower, brushed your teeth, made breakfast, and got dressed. Maybe you listened to a podcast or the news. At the Metro, you swiped your card to pass through the turnstile or used a debit card to buy a ticket. Perhaps you took an Uber. You walked into your office, powered up your computer, and began surfing the Web.

Even if this doesn't describe your morning, you undoubtedly have friends, family members, and colleagues whose mornings were similar. It's a routine of activities that would be familiar to our ancestors: reading, commuting, communicating, and socializing.

A century ago, they'd have begun their workdays reading newspapers; catching a tram, train, or a bus to work; and gossiping with family and colleagues. Many of our more distant ancestors may have been unable to read, but they undoubtedly engaged in plenty of workplace and family socialization. They also ate breakfast and worried about the weather.

Although our modern morning routine is similar to that of our ancestors, it's also a routine that our ancestors wouldn't have recognized, guided in large part by devices that fit comfortably in our hands and provide us access to billions of people, as well as countless apps and services. Connectivity and access to information are a ubiquitous feature of modern life and a direct result of technological innovations.

Such innovations have revolutionized far more than our mornings. Medicine, warfare, factory production, air travel, construction, and farming have all undergone dramatic changes in the past 100 years thanks to advances in technology. In the historical equivalent of a blink of an eye, we've gone from a world where access to electricity, stoves, cars, telephones, and refrigerators was reserved for a wealthy minority to one where almost everyone in the United States now has access to these goods.

Today, more than 90 percent of U.S. households have a stove, car, fridge, air conditioning, microwave, and cellphone.[1] This technological revolution hasn't been reserved to the global rich. Residents of countries where poverty was the norm a hundred years ago have not only experienced massive increases in wealth over the past century, but they've also increased their access to the internet, cellphones, cars, refrigerators, and other common household goods.

It's hard to think of a field of human endeavor that hasn't been irreversibly changed for the better thanks to the past century of technological change. Nothing quite like it has ever been seen before.

And there's more to come. Drones, driverless cars, private space flight, artificial intelligence (AI), gene editing, 3D printing, supersonic flight, the internet of things, cryptocurrencies, and nanotechnology are poised to help make the world a safer, healthier, and more prosperous place to live.

Sadly, governments have erected barriers to many of these innovations, hampering progress and limiting access to new products. Those barriers are motivated by different impulses and concerns. Market incumbents seeking to avoid competition by engaging in lobbying and cronyism certainly deserve some of the blame, but it's an attitude toward governance rather than firms that is mostly responsible.

Too often, regulators have embraced the "precautionary principle," the notion that the release of new products should be slowed down or outright prohibited when their health or safety effects are uncertain. This attitude is keeping life-changing technologies trapped within the minds of entrepreneurs and technologists or in garages, flight hangers, and laboratories. In addition, government policies not ostensibly related to technology can nonetheless have a negative effect on technology policy. Laws and regulations governing immigration and government transparency are only some examples. After all, technologists, engineers, and entrepreneurs will have the best chance of building new technologies if they can hire the best-educated talent while working with the most accurate data.

A libertarian approach to emerging technologies embraces a presumption of freedom. It's one that acknowledges that emerging technologies are associated with uncertainties, risks, and costs, but it also holds that the benefits of innovation, creative destruction, and discovery far outweigh the costs. Such an approach would be a dramatic shift from the current regulatory environment, in which technologists are too often put in the position of asking for permission rather than forgiveness.

The Regulatory Landscape

Tackling "technology policy" can be a tricky business. Technology policy affects almost every part of our lives and is not as narrowly defined as foreign policy, housing policy, or education policy. In that sense, "technology policy" is a term that is as ambiguous as "economic policy." Like the economy, technologies are not governed or regulated by one agency or department. Rather, a plethora of departments and alphabet soup agencies govern emerging technologies.

The FAA (Federal Aviation Administration), FDA (Food and Drug Administration), NHTSA (National Highway Traffic Safety Administration), and many others have been involved in regulatory battles associated with new and emerging technologies. Other government agencies and departments can have a major impact on how we use technology, even if they don't directly regulate technologies. The Departments of Defense and Justice are perhaps the most obvious examples.

Although these regulatory agencies have different mandates, cultures, staffs, and histories, it's fair to say that they each embrace a version of the precautionary principle, which holds that if the effects of a product are unknown or disputed, then that product shouldn't make it to market. In a libertarian world, none of these regulatory agencies would exist. That regulators embrace the precautionary principle is not new or surprising, but that doesn't make it any less regrettable.

Cautious approaches to new technology can yield absurd results. In 1865, the British Parliament passed the Locomotive Act of 1865, which mandated—among other things—that a man with a red flag walk ahead of each self-propelled vehicle. After all, steam engine–powered vehicles were dangerous.

More recently, we've seen the FAA ground commercial drones, prompting Amazon to test its delivery drones abroad.[2] The FAA has also grounded the flight-sharing company FlyteNow.[3] In November 2013, the FDA sent personal genome company 23andMe a curtailment letter, ordering it to stop selling its genotype screening test, which can inform customers about their inherited likelihood of certain diseases and conditions.[4] According to the FDA's letter, 23andMe had violated the Federal Food, Drug, and Cosmetic Act. The FDA claimed that 23andMe's genome kit qualified as a medical "device" and was therefore subject to marketing approval and clearance, which 23andMe did not have.

Unfortunately for innovators working on aerial technology and medical devices, their products are, as Mercatus Center senior research fellow Adam Thierer puts it, "born captive" rather than "born free."[5]

When Uber and Airbnb arrived on the scene, no "Sharing Economy Agency" or "Gig Economy Commission" existed.

Shortly after the publication of the Bitcoin white paper,[6] computers were mining Bitcoins without the approval of a "Cryptocurrency Oversight Board." Both Uber and Bitcoin were "born free."

The same can't be said for drones. The FAA has been around since the late 1950s. It's an established fixture of the federal government's regulatory landscape. Flying machines—whether airplanes, helicopters, or model airplanes—are all subject to FAA rules and regulations. Emerging aerial technologies are "born captive" in a regulatory compound rife with fences, guards, and watchtowers. The FAA is keen on grounding new and emerging technologies, with the National Academies of Sciences characterizing the FAA's culture as one "with a near-zero tolerance for risk."[7] That outlook is a particular shame given the United States' history of flight innovation, much of which came at the expense of risk and uncertainty.

The history of human flight is replete with broken bones and deadly accidents. The life expectancy for the first U.S. mail pilots was 900 flying hours.[8] In 1919, one mail pilot died for every 115,325 miles flown.[9] Today, flying is not nearly so dangerous. According to the Bureau of Labor Statistics, air transportation workers had a fatal injury rate of 3.8 per 100,000 full-time-equivalent workers in 2017.[10] That rate is more than five times lower than for farming, fishing, and forestry occupations.[11]

A libertarian approach to technology hardly encourages the deaths of those operating new machines. But it does accept the reality that new technologies can sometime be dangerous.

When cars first rolled off assembly lines, they were much more dangerous than they are today. Seat belts and airbags were not mandated until relatively recently, and they would have undoubtedly saved some lives if they had been installed in cars earlier. But no one is going to seriously suggest that a government agency should have put the development of the car on hold until manufacturers could achieve the level of safety we enjoy today. Indeed, it's only by trial and error that manufacturers learn what safety features should be required.

Airplanes and cars are heavily regulated. They were once born free but today are decidedly born captive. In a libertarian world of permissionless innovation, entrepreneurs and inventors would be free to innovate and create without having to seek approval from the State. Such an approach is not without costs, but we can be confident that the benefits will far outweigh those costs.

When weighing costs and benefits, we should be leery of the human tendency to fixate on negative headlines and take for granted positive developments. In a libertarian world, we should expect bad news to continue to dominate headlines. That would hardly be surprising; pessimism is a critical part of human software. And, of course, bad news (crashes, deaths, etc.) takes place over short periods, whereas good news (e.g., decreases in poverty and crime rates) tends to occur over decades.

Newspapers across the world could have run with the headline "Number of People in Extreme Poverty Fell by 137,000 since Yesterday" every day for the past 25 years.[12] Despite the plethora of data showing how the world has become safer, healthier, and richer, doom-and-gloom pessimism dominates headlines as well as countless dinner-table conversations across the country.

In anticipation, it's worth considering the risks and opportunities associated with emerging technologies.

Risks and Opportunities

The government is constantly developing new technologies designed to further intrude on our private lives and improve its weapons. Technological innovations can improve our lives, but we should guard against government's use of technology that results in eliminating privacy and developing robots capable of identifying and killing targets.

Government has a long reach, but fortunately it cannot outlaw mathematics. Consequently, end-to-end encrypted communication remains available to the public, although governments could take misguided steps to shut businesses that market themselves as privacy-friendly. The proliferation of body cameras, drones, and law-enforcement AI is a trend that should not go unchecked. Technological innovation could lead to a world in which football-sized blimps surveil entire cities and cameras outfitted with facial recognition software become a regular sight.

In such a world, there would be less liberty. Fortunately, government can impose restrictions on law enforcement's use of such technology that needn't stifle private innovation. At the very least, officials at the federal, state, and local levels should be required to disclose plans for using surveillance technologies before deploying such tools.

The widespread use of surveillance technologies is not the only cause for tech-related pessimism. It's easy to feel tempted by despair when considering the perceived lack of technological advances in the years since man first walked on the moon. As Silicon Valley investor and entrepreneur Peter Thiel put it, we wanted flying cars, and we got 140 characters.[13]

Anyone who saw Stanley Kubrick's classic movie *2001: A Space Odyssey* on its release in April 1968 could perhaps be forgiven for thinking that by 2001 we would have regular space travel and manned missions to Jupiter guided by AI. After all, on May 25, 1961, President Kennedy declared, "I believe that this nation should commit itself to achieving the goal, before this decade is out, of landing a man on the moon and returning him safely to the Earth."[14] By April 1968, Apollo 1 had completed its mission and on July 21, 1969—only a little more than a year after *2001: A Space Odyssey* was released—Neil Armstrong and Buzz Aldrin walked on the moon.

But we have actually come a long way since the first moon walk. Our handheld computers are far more powerful than the whole of Apollo 11's command module. Such devices are not reserved to the rich and famous; 81 percent of American adults own a smartphone.[15] The emergence and proliferation of smartphones have revolutionized our social lives for the better and have made innovative companies such as Uber possible. The internet—which allows billions of devices across the world to connect to one another—has prompted a degree of change in our economy, politics, and culture unparalleled since the invention of the movable-type printing press in the 15th century.

We are a long way from establishing Mars colonies; however, we shouldn't be too down on the "140 characters." Twitter and other social media giants may be on the receiving end of bipartisan criticism these days, but it is undeniable that on net these companies have provided us with new, cheap, and valuable ways to connect with one another.

Climbing Olympus Mons and walking on a mined asteroid may be achievements for the yet unborn, but the near future holds some exciting possibilities.

Driverless cars may well be regular fixtures in the coming decades. Fitness wearables such as those from Fitbit are increasingly popular. Both driverless cars and wearables are parts of the growing "internet of things," which also includes appliances like the Amazon Echo, "smart" refrigerators and thermostats, and energy monitors.

The internet of things promises to make our lives more comfortable and safer. Wouldn't it be great to have all the devices in your home communicate with one another? In the morning, your wearable devices and phone would communicate valuable information to your refrigerator and car, including how well you slept and your schedule.

In the afternoon as you travel home in your driverless car, your wearable would already be communicating to your home. Maybe your wearable device can sense that you had a rough day at the office and may feel more inclined to have a glass of wine than a Diet Coke. Perhaps your home entertainment system will be playing soothing music as you walk through the door. Unbeknownst to you, your daughter's soccer practice ended early (the coach had to deal with an unexpected family emergency). Consequently, your car drives a little faster than usual so that once it drops you off at home it can quickly make its way to the field to pick her up.

A world full of driverless cars and interconnected appliances might be convenient, but it is far from perfect. People still die too young of disease and suffer painful deaths, accidents, and disabilities. Fortunately, new and emerging technologies are contributing to the ongoing battles against cancer, diabetes, and other deadly and chronic conditions.

Researchers at China's National Center for Nanoscience and Technology and Arizona State University have built robots the size of dust mites, which, when injected into mice's bloodstreams, can shrink the size of tumors.[16] A San Diego–based company is developing bioprinting technology, which one day may result in our being able to create replacement organs from a handful of donor cells.[17] This technology is especially exciting, given that about 20 people die in the United States every day while awaiting a transplant.[18]

When unexpected accidents do occur, it would be great to have thousands of nanobots in your bloodstream communicating important details to medical professionals.[19] Those nanobots might also be able to send information to medical drones, which would deliver supplies to you that cater to your needs while streaming video to the EMTs en route.

Predicting the future is, of course, hazardous. Some predictions will eventually be realized; others will be viewed as absurd. Even science fiction writers, who constantly consider possible technologies, have major blind spots. In *Blade Runner*, the classic 1982 dystopian science fiction movie based on a Philip K. Dick novel, machines as intelligent as humans walk among us. And yet people are still reading newspapers. In *2001: A Space Odyssey*,

Dr. Heywood Floyd can fly to a space station in a Pan Am spacecraft as part of his trip to a moon base, but he has to enter a phone booth to video-chat with his daughter. *The Fifth Element* creator Luc Besson could envision the rise of flying vehicles for the 1997 movie, but he couldn't imagine a world where taxis have gone the way of the horse and buggy. Those of us who spend our time pondering what future technologies might look like should embrace humility and be aware that we could be wrong.

But government regulators and lawmakers should embrace humility too. Not every consequence of every new technology can be determined beforehand. The negative unintended consequences are, of course, possible, but we mustn't sacrifice innovation on the altar of safety.

Regulatory reform is a necessary but not sufficient condition for libertarian technology policy. If lawmakers dramatically changed the current regulatory environment governing technology, that would be a massive improvement. But more changes are required.

In a libertarian world, firms can hire whomever they want to work on their projects. Technological talent, like all talent, appears all over the world. Fortunately for the technology firms in Libertopia, firms don't have to worry about restrictions on immigration. They can hire whomever they want. Libertopia is also a much more open and transparent world than our current one. More access to government data would allow innovators to make better products. Once the U.S. National Oceanic and Atmospheric Administration made weather satellite data available to the public, the private sector could build a weather-forecasting industry worth billions of dollars.[20]

If we want to live in a world of efficient and innovative technologies, engineers will need access to high-quality data and a talented workforce. The government can contribute by making more data accessible and by abolishing practically all restrictions on migration.[21]

Conclusion

In Libertopia, inventors can pursue their interests and private companies are free to explore the numerous applications of new technologies. Technology firms can hire whomever they want without having to worry about a government agency grounding their projects. Entrepreneurs, inventors, and scientists are in the position of asking for forgiveness rather than permission.

We can't be confident about what technology in Libertopia looks like. Perhaps some people will sit on their porches overseeing marijuana farms, listening to the distant buzz of crop-dusting drones while waiting for a driverless vehicle to deliver a new robot nanny for their children. Perhaps others will spend most of their lives in virtual reality, with astronauts training for asteroid mining operations and doctors inspecting their patients' blood vessels and organs with footage from medical nanobots. This world will also have accidents and unintended consequences associated with new technologies, but the benefits will far outweigh the costs. Libertopia isn't perfect, but it's much better than the world we currently inhabit.

16

A History of Libertarian Utopianism

Anthony Comegna

*The earth, restive, confronts a new era, perhaps a general divine war,
No one knows what will happen next, such portents fill the days
and nights;*
*Years prophetical! The space ahead as I walk, as I vainly try to
pierce it, is full of phantoms,*
*Unborn deeds, things soon to be, project their shapes around me,
This incredible rush and heat, this strange ecstatic fever of dreams
O years!*
*Your dreams O years, how they penetrate through me! (I know not
whether I sleep or wake;)*
*The perform'd America and Europe grow dim, retiring in shadow
behind me,*
The unperform'd, more gigantic than ever, advance, advance upon me.

—Walt Whitman, "Years of the Modern"

History—while always the result of human actions—is never the product of human design. For at least four centuries, generation upon generation of individuals in search of greater personal liberty have encountered their world, revolted against its limitations, and charted countless paths to a better future. In some sense, we have *always* been there: everywhere, in all societies across time, *surely* at least one person has favored liberty over slavery, one individual who preferred to make it on his or her own rather than take sustenance from his or her neighbors. Surely every strongman has had his detractors; surely history is never truly devoid of people who despise tyranny and resist tyrants.

Nonetheless, many libertarians and historians alike will probably locate the origins of libertarianism in the English tradition of dissenting religion, specifically that country's intensely violent civil wars in the 1640s and 1650s. Much of modernity as we know it spawned during the 17th century as part of a long-unfolding set of processes. On the one end was the eroding basis of feudal kingship highlighted by a constant dearth of royal funds and a steady march toward bureaucracy, corporatism, and wider ruling classes. On the other end was the explosion of popular print culture, global commercialism, transoceanic travel, and a growing recognition among the populace that commoners, too, had great power. As kings raised taxes, armies, navies, and corporations the world over, awakened and rebellious minds responded with their own programs.

During two decades of cyclical warfare between elite factions, England's common people did all they could to avoid the conflict and live as freely as possible in the power vacuum. While Cavaliers and Cromwellians murdered each other on the battlefield, antinomians, Ranters, Seekers, Levelers, Diggers, Familists, Fifth Monarchists, Muggletonians, Quakers, and many, many more flooded the land with new ideas and new possibilities.

Some radicals tried to *rant* their way out of modernity's ugly side by shouting at all who would listen in endless, fiery torrents about the evils of the world. Some took a slightly softer approach, preferring to *seek* for honest souls among London's working poor. Others formed what some historians have considered the first proper political party, the Levelers, and tried to use political reform to even out those great iniquities history had produced. Perhaps the most radical of all were the "True Levelers," who tried to *dig* their way out of it all—if the great lords would not relinquish the common lands only recently fenced in by statute, then the True Levelers would simply *occupy it themselves* and put it to productive use. Neither king nor Cromwell could tolerate this kind of threat to constituted property rights, and a combination of military and judicial force crushed the Diggers, dispersing them to somewhat less action-oriented religious movements like the Society of Friends, called the Quakers. Between these main strands of dissent, English men and women wove dozens more, each tradition with its own distinctive philosophy and style.

Different as they could be, many dissenters shared a broad agreement with antinomianism. Most Christians consider antinomianism a heresy. From the Greek words for "against laws," antinomians took the Protestant doctrine of "salvation by faith alone" to its logical extreme. They believed that literally *the only thing* necessary for eternal salvation of the soul was a genuine faith connection to God; because only this connection mattered, anything with a tendency to distort, obscure, or contradict one's revelation of God should be rejected. Therefore, any human-made laws—including the basic laws of interpersonal ethics—can and should be ignored when they pose a challenge to one's personal experience of God's will. It made for an intensely radical set of beliefs, perhaps best illustrated in the life and trial of Anne Hutchinson in the Puritan Massachusetts Bay Colony.

Hutchinson hosted mixed-sex Bible study sessions in her home in the mid-1630s, driven by the conviction that God commanded women to instruct one another in religion. What's more, she preached in her meetings that the colony's young men did not *really* have to sign up for militia service to kill Indians and steal their land. Sure, the law said service was compulsory and the government pronounced the Indians enemies; but those were mere human legislations, no contest for the divine revelation present in every awakened soul. Governor John Winthrop knew the colony's manpower could not withstand Hutchinson's assault, so he cooked up a trial for violating the Ten Commandments, banished her from the colony, and prosecuted a miniature reign of terror to root out her followers. For the moment, at least, the most radical elements of modern English life were at least contained.

Then, the English Civil Wars turned the world upside down and twisted it inside out. And some of the earliest direct ancestors of modern libertarianism diligently worked to make them history's turning point toward a more antinomian future. The king was already dead, but they could also level the great estates, strip the lords of their powers and privileges, and smash the armies of corporate creatures who pioneered new forms of enslavement on the oceans and the American plantations. The war years had shown common people everywhere that they did not have to live this way—we human beings are not condemned to serve a powerful few at the expense of ourselves, our families, and our very souls.

Modern libertarianism—the full package of ideas as we know it—grew from this tradition of English antinomianism, or moral opposition to human-made laws, and a dozen different strands of fever-brained, radical, left-wing utopianisms.[1] During the civil wars in the 1640s and 1650s, but especially after the monarchy returned to England in the 1660s, antinomians dispersed all over the world. From the lines of Cromwell's New Model Army, they were dispatched to Ireland and West Africa, or banished by the king to be indentured servants in Virginia. From Ranting or Seeking in London's most troubled boroughs, dissenters filtered across the ocean to Philadelphia, New York, or Barbados. England was a frontier of possibilities during the wars, but to flourish under the Restoration, dissenters would have to build their own worlds *out there*, somewhere—*anywhere*—else.

On the New World frontiers, indentured servants joined hands with black slaves; "red" Indians accepted "white Indians" into their own societies and families; Quakers led the world's first movement to abolish slavery; and average people everywhere teased out innumerable new intellectual threads for themselves.[2] Over the next 200 years, people with liberated hearts and minds pioneered feminism, vegetarianism, abolitionism, Spiritualism, individualism, and ultimately the package of political and social ideals we call libertarianism.

At every step of the way, powerful people with personal stakes in maintaining the status quo thwarted reform, squelched challengers, co-opted movements, corrupted popular education, stifled dissent, quashed rebellions, smashed revolutions, systematically destroyed alternative lifestyles, and even exterminated whole peoples. If you were so inclined, it would be easy enough to read modern history as one gloomy triumph of power over liberty after another, with only relatively brief moments of libertarianism peeping through.

Viewed from above, modernity has been the rise of modern states, global empires, constituted governments, and the great and powerful statesmen who lead the rest of us into a designed and controlled future. Viewed from below, modernity has given us history's greatest murder machines, industrial exploitation, the most inhumane and abject forms of slavery ever devised, and death and destruction beyond reckoning. Yet always, people did their best to live freely under the worst of conditions; and no matter what the new megastates did, they could not stop new ideas and their agents from changing the world in spontaneous, unplanned, chaotic, and disruptive ways. Humanity has indeed enjoyed great material and intellectual progress in the past 200 years, but every scrap of it has been fought for, labored for, and made manifest through deliberate and determined action. To the extent that we have crept our way toward true utopia, we owe thanks to the nameless, faceless, and historically voiceless rogues and radicals who have kept liberty alive in an age of otherwise devastating statism.

The 19th century was the world's greatest era of reform.[3] Changes of all sorts tore through the world, shaping and remaking society in ways few at the time could understand and no one could predict. After two centuries of modernity in politics, production, and consumption, common people established a permanent place for themselves in decisionmaking and changemaking. When once a medieval chronicler could write the history of entire decades with a few lines about a single king, now countless millions made microscopic contributions to create the future. Governments did what they could to aggrandize power throughout the period, and many did so successfully. Successful states became more powerful than ever before, and empires like Great Britain reached their historical peaks after the 1884 Berlin Conference that partitioned Africa.

Steam engines, quinine, steel hulls, railroads, and especially the telegraph all opened new opportunities for empire, new frontiers for exploitation and slavery around the planet. But they also empowered average people in new and exciting ways. Transportation technology allowed people to move about the planet with increasing liberty and ease; it opened new markets while expanding and intensifying the extent of others. Communications advances like telegraphy revolutionized political ideas and figuratively shrank continents to the size of cities. And the unending stream of new scientific knowledge inspired countless new philosophies bubbling up from below like what happened long before in London gutters during the civil wars. The unimaginably brilliant burst of new technologies, new productive possibilities, and new methods of social organization all inspired novel thinking about average people's effects on their world and its future.

In America, at least, no futuristic visions surpassed the dazzling glimpses perceived by one of the nation's many new religious communities: the Spiritualists. They are a strange bunch to our present-day ears, but their somewhat brief and rather niche history deserves consideration, especially when embarking on a volume like this. Spiritualism has never been so clearly defined as its more ancient or dogmatic counterparts. But from its birth and in its very conception, it was a sort of *world* religion open to all peoples without regard to class, race, gender, or any other considerations of identity.

Broadly speaking, Spiritualists believed that souls or spirits existed as real parts of the material world and were, therefore, open to communication with living beings. They believed in a spiritual existence beyond one's instantiation in a physical body and drew upon the new Victorian science to reinforce and inspire their faith. Spiritualists observed experiments with electricity and corpses, concluding that if it was possible to induce animation of the body, it may be possible to reanimate the mind or soul. They witnessed the energizing powers of batteries and concluded that they could be used to charge one's aura—a concept imported from Asia—for communication with the dead. And they invested in the burgeoning field of telegraphy by purchasing their own machines, becoming expert in their use, and converting them for modern necromancy.

Spiritualists were practically addicted to reform movements. Most of their prominent figures were active in a wide variety of them, from the workingman's movement to feminism and abolitionism; and many drew inspiration directly from their supposed communications with the spirit world. Spiritualists were not necessarily antinomians. Many of them were not Christians of any description.

Like agnostics and atheists, Spiritualists were in a sense *beyond heretical*—to violate fundamental doctrine, they would first have to fit cleanly into a preexisting religious tradition. But this was the electrified, magnetized new faith of the industrial era, and it did not require submission even to the will or revelation of God. Spiritualists were less interested in "salvation by faith alone"; they were more concerned with just reviving the dead already. In fact, this was the core belief Spiritualists erected for themselves on 200 years of antinomian prehistory: when the powerful stand aside, human beings have limitless potential.[4]

And they were not without their reasons. Their era was America's first great "singularity," when so much technological change was crammed into so short a period with so many revolutionary implications and consequences that virtually everything about life changed from the beginning of the period to the end. Steam-driven presses, iron and steel ships, railroads, and innumerable other inventions transformed the way people related and linked to one another first across the country, then the entire planet, transforming societies in ways no one could possibly predict.

But the greatest of all 19th-century innovations was Samuel Morse's magnetic telegraph, which practically collapsed time and space with a few taps. Spiritualists imbibed the new Victorian science, the electrified and magnetized laws of nature unfolding all around them, and joined the never-ending chorus of reform movements intent on perfecting the world.

Technological change sparked new thinking across the intellectual board: shifts from pop homeopathy to more systematic nutritionism, from Christian cosmologies to occultist metaphysics, from laissez faire to "scientific management" of firms and bureau-cratic regulation, and from belief in a limited republic to mystical reverence for the great national state, bound together by telegraph wires, the electrified new "cords of Union."

At the very pinnacle of radical thought from the era was the Spiritualist's conviction that human knowledge *applied* in service of human needs could even conquer death itself. Proof positive: spirits spoke to them with electricity, and electricity reanimated corpses. If only we could find a way to unify the two processes, to sort of smush the soul back into the body, history would finally be over.

Perhaps they were wrong, and perhaps you see no reason to identify your own libertarianism with their inveterate reformism (or the English antinomians', for that matter). But these early strands of libertarian history have much to suggest to those of us charting the future today. Dissenters and Spiritualists alike knew that history was more than they had been told, more than the product of kings, queens, great battles, and great thinkers. They understood that history was *made* by deliberate and distrib-uted human action from below, that no one person controlled its course, but that all of us contribute to its flow. What's more, they saw that a liberated humanity *could actually accomplish* our grandest desires, fulfill our wildest visions, and create a world more like utopia than the one we were born into. They knew that if utopia ever *did* exist, we would have to build it ourselves, bit by bit, with humility, goodwill, and cheer.

17

The Presidency

Gene Healy

Imagine there's no president: it's not easy if you try. The chief executive officer of the U.S. federal government is omnipresent and inescapable: hijacking our social media feeds, hectoring us from the screens above every treadmill at the gym, and injecting himself into virtually every area of our lives, from grocery shopping to *Monday Night Football*.[1] You can't get him out of your head—or off your phone: in October 2018, every operational cellphone in the United States received a compulsory "presidential alert," in the first test of an emergency warning system originating in a 2006 executive order from President George W. Bush.[2] It's little wonder that doctors examining stroke or concussion victims often ask them to name the current president—someone who doesn't know *that* is clearly impaired.[3]

In its long march toward full-spectrum dominance of American life, the American presidency has become both absurd and menacing. Our political culture has invested the office with preposterously vast responsibilities and, as a result, the officeholder wields powers that no one fallible human being ought to have.

In his 1956 book *The American Presidency*, political scientist Clinton Rossiter outlined 10 roles that the modern president was expected to fulfill. Four of them are actually in the Constitution. Among other things, the president is the "Manager of Prosperity"—he sits up in the cockpit of the national economy twiddling knobs and dials to create jobs and spur economic growth. He's the "World Leader," responsible not just for American security but also for the spread of democracy abroad, and the "Voice of the People," as Rossiter describes it, "the moral spokesman for us all."[4]

Modern presidential candidates promise all those miracles and more. On the campaign trail in 2008, then-senator Barack Obama pledged, among other things, to provide "a cure for cancer in our time," to "slow the oceans' rise," to deliver "a complete transformation of the economy," and, perhaps most quixotically, to "fundamentally change the way Washington works." In 2016, candidate Donald J. Trump rhapsodized: "I will give you everything. I will give you what you've been looking for, for 50 years. I'm the only one."[5] In one of his less controversial tweets that year, Trump promised that, if he won, "all of the bad things happening in the U.S. will be rapidly reversed!"[6]

It all adds up to a remarkable vision of the presidency. No longer a limited constitutional officer charged with faithful execution of the laws, the president is now responsible for all things great and small: the state of the national soul, the price of a tank of gas, and freedom all around the world. He's our Guardian Angel, our

Shield against Harm, and America's Life Coach, as well as the Supreme Warlord of the Earth.

That vision is fundamentally incompatible with limited constitutional government. With great responsibility comes great power. When we demand that the president provide seamless protection from natural disasters, economic dislocation, and terrorist strikes, we shouldn't be surprised when presidents seek powers to match those daunting expectations.

On the home front, our presidents increasingly rule by executive order and administrative edict, deciding what your health insurance covers, who gets to enter the United States and who gets to stay, and what rules govern free speech disputes and sexual assault claims on every college campus in the country.

You may not be interested in the presidency, but the presidency is interested in you. After the terrorist attacks of September 11, 2001, presidents seized staggering new surveillance powers. The call-records program that Edward Snowden revealed in 2013 was just the tip of the iceberg. The National Security Agency is currently sweeping up vast amounts of Americans' private, domestic communications—email, texts, and phone calls—that happen to transit abroad. And the president's war powers have become practically uncheckable: he can add new groups and individuals to the Predator drone kill list—and even launch thermonuclear "fire and fury"—virtually at will.

In short, the modern presidency is a constitutional monstrosity and a libertarian nightmare. Given the enormous power the president has over American life and liberty, we'd forget him only at our peril.

The Way We Were

"It was not always so," George Reedy observed in his 1970 classic *The Twilight of the Presidency*. During his boyhood in Chicago five decades earlier, Reedy recalled, mayors, city councilmen, and even ward bosses had much greater name recognition than the occupant of 1600 Pennsylvania Avenue. That was because local officials "had a direct bearing on our daily lives; the president did not." A summer trip to Washington, DC, during the Coolidge administration made Reedy "the only child in the neighborhood who could identify the president—and few of my classmates really cared."[7]

Reedy's generation would witness "the emergence of the presidency as the center of national life." By midcentury, it had become routine for Americans to refer to the presidency as "the most powerful office in the world," and the president as the "leader of the free world." Our first president used a far more modest title: most often, George Washington referred to his post as that of "chief magistrate."

The Framers never envisioned the president as "the leader of the free world"; he wasn't even supposed to be *America's* national leader. The *Federalist Papers* understood the Constitution "to establish an 'anti-leadership system,'" constitutional scholar Peter Lawler observes, structured to resist the impositions of innovations proposed by leaders."[8] *The Federalist* opens and closes with warnings about the dangers of popular leadership: "Throughout history, those who have destroyed republics began by flattering the people," Publius cautions in the first essay, and he raises the specter of "the military despotism of a victorious demagogue" in the last.[9]

The men who designed the Constitution didn't believe in what Teddy Roosevelt would later call the "bully pulpit." The very idea of a president claiming a special mandate to speak for the people, pounding the podium and rallying the masses behind his agenda, was anathema to them. Part of the president's job, as they saw it, was to resist public pressure. Rather than comply with—or fan—"every sudden breeze of passion" or "transient impulse which the people may receive from the arts of men, who flatter their prejudices to betray their interests," the president was supposed to "withstand the temporary delusion, in order to give them time and opportunity for more cool and sedate reflection."[10]

Hard as it may seem for 21st-century Americans to imagine, in the early years of the republic, the prevailing norm was that the president was mostly supposed to keep his mouth shut. From Washington to Jackson, presidents gave about three public speeches a year on average and rarely presumed to dictate to Congress.[11]

The president had a limited public role—and limited powers. Congress was the prime mover on national policy; the president's responsibility was to take care that the laws were faithfully exe-cuted and to slap Congress back with the occasional veto when it slipped its constitutional bonds. In foreign affairs, the president had the power to "repel sudden attacks," but no authority to launch them.[12]

In the original design, the office could hardly be called imperial. In Federalist No. 69, Alexander Hamilton answered the charge that the presidency contained the seeds of monarchy by going through a side-by-side comparison between the powers and responsibilities of the British king and those of the American president.[13]

For example, the fact that the British king "not only appoints to all offices, but can create offices" revealed "a great inferiority in the power of the President," who cannot. Further, the king is head of the national church; the president has "no particle of spiritual jurisdiction." The king can start wars; the president cannot. Yes, the president has the role of "commander in chief," but as Hamilton explains, that just means he's the "first general and admiral" of U.S. military forces. And generals and admirals don't get to decide whether, when, and with whom we go to war.[14]

There were hints of the modern presidency to come in some of the 19th-century presidencies: Andrew Jackson showed that the president could be a popular leader, claiming the "mandate of the people" as a whole. James K. Polk showed that the president could use the army to start a war and then get Congress to go along. Abraham Lincoln exercised vast emergency powers during the Civil War.[15] But for most of the century, the constitutional center held, the tide receded, and we returned to forgettable presidents who lacked the power and ambition to inflict great harm.

In 1888, the British academic and member of Parliament James Bryce endeavored to explain "Why Great Men Are Not Chosen Presidents." In large part, it was the nature of the job. Englishmen assume that the American president "ought to be a dazzling orator, able to sway legislatures or multitudes," Bryce noted, but they forget that

> the president does not sit in Congress, that he ought not to address meetings, that he cannot submit bills nor otherwise influence the action of the legislature. His main

duties are to be prompt and firm in securing the due execution of the laws and maintaining the public peace . . . .
Four-fifths of his work is the same in kind as that which
devolves on the chairman of a commercial company or
the manager of a railway.[16]

The Presidency Transformed

The modern presidency isn't nearly so simple and unassuming. Over
the course of the 20th century, the president's powers and duties
expanded in ways that effaced nearly every distinction Hamilton
drew between the American chief executive and the British king.
Today, like monarchs of old, the president can "create offices"; in fact,
"since the end of World War II, presidents have unilaterally created
over half of all administrative agencies in the United States," using
the power of the pen to spawn new government bodies "that would
never have been created through legislative action" and designing
those agencies in ways that maximize presidential control.[17]

America lacks an established church, but contemporary public
intellectuals variously describe the president's role as "a center
of moral authority," the "high priest and chief unifier" of the
American civil religion—even our "theologian in chief."[18] And
"commander in chief" has become far more than a military
title; modern presidents have the power, if not the legal right, to
initiate war.

What brought this transformation about? There's no single
cause: our expanding presidency is depressingly overdetermined.
Presidential scholars have identified a host of factors, among them

increasing economic complexity coupled with a perceived need to "stabilize an industrializing society," technological changes that shrank the distance between the president and the people, and America's increasing role on the world stage.[19]

America's rise to superpower status played a key role in the presidency's transformation. "War is the health of the state," Randolph Bourne's famous aphorism has it, but Bourne could just as easily have written, "War is the health of the presidency." As America stepped out on the world stage, the "chief magistrate" increasingly became a domineering commander in chief.

Changes in broadcast technology also contributed to the presidency's growth. Through radio and then television, presidents acquired a sort of "electronic bully pulpit." It was easier for them to go "over the heads" of Congress and speak to the American people directly, the better to accumulate power. One of Franklin D. Roosevelt's early fireside chats urged Americans to "tell me your troubles"—and they did. A man named Ira Smith was head of the White House mail service for five decades, beginning in the McKinley administration. As late as President Taft's term, Smith ran the shop all by himself, getting maybe 200 letters a week. Early on in FDR's first term, he got more than 5,000, and soon found that he needed 50 people to answer all the requests for help.[20]

"Although no one realized it at the time," George Reedy observed, in the midst of the New Deal, "something else had happened. The American people were now conditioned to look to Washington for help when they were in trouble." FDR "made the presidency a living reality to Americans and began the period when the White House became the focal point of the nation's social, economic, and political life."[21]

But structural explanations can lead us to downplay the role of ideology. Ideas about the presidency's proper function changed radically throughout the 20th century and helped produce an office radically different from the one the Framers designed. The Progressives of the late 19th and early 20th century got the process started with a sustained critique of Madisonian checks and balances and the modest presidency envisioned in the Constitution. As they saw it, the president's job was to move the masses, uniting them behind reformist crusades at home and abroad. The *New Republic*'s Herbert Croly captured the Progressive vision of the presidency when he described Teddy Roosevelt as "a sledge-hammer in the cause of national righteousness."[22] And the Progressives took advantage of three great crises—World War I, the Great Depression, and World War II—to fundamentally reshape the office.

The Imperial Presidency is a bipartisan creation, however; the right would help complete the presidency's transformation. Midcentury conservatives had originally stood athwart the activist presidency, yelling "stop!" After FDR's 12-year reign, conservatives in Congress championed the Twenty-Second Amendment, limiting presidential terms. Most of the intellectuals who coalesced around William F. Buckley's *National Review* in 1955 associated powerful presidents with activist liberalism: with New Deals, New Frontiers, and the Great Society.

But by the early 1970s, the "emerging Republican majority" in the electoral college seemed to promise that conservatives would hold the presidency more often than not. And conservatives liked the sound of that. By Ronald Reagan's first term, they'd developed a legal rationale—unitary executive theory (UET)—designed to give the president broad unilateral powers. Initially, the idea was that he'd use those powers for good, to ride herd on overzealous regulators and rein in the bureaucracy. But by the second Bush administration, and in the wake of 9/11, UET became shorthand for claims that were far less defensible: that simply by waving the bloody flag of "national security," the president could override legal prohibitions on torture, the Foreign Intelligence Security Act, and other laws validly enacted by Congress.[23]

Then–vice president Dick Cheney used to describe the Bush administration's mission as "leaving the presidency stronger than we found it." Mission accomplished: the Bush administration dramatically expanded presidential power, and not just in areas like surveillance and foreign policy. In his last month in office, Bush unilaterally ordered a multibillion-dollar auto bailout just days after Congress voted the program down.

Barack Obama—who as a candidate pledged to "turn the page on the imperial presidency"—took those powers and expanded them still further. As president, Obama launched two undeclared wars—in Libya and against ISIS—and defied the limits imposed by the 1973 War Powers Resolution on the novel theory that you're not engaged in "hostilities" if the foreigners you're bombing can't hit you back. Bragging that "I've got a pen and I've got a phone," in his second term, Obama increasingly governed by executive order and even invented a presidential power of the purse, allowing him to spend billions of dollars Congress never appropriated.

Both presidents warped the authorization for use of military force that Congress passed three days after 9/11 into a sort of enabling act for permanent presidential war. Obama left office as the first two-term president in American history to have been at war every single day of his presidency. In his last year alone, U.S. forces dropped more than 26,000 bombs on seven different countries—a tally that President Trump blew past a mere nine months into his tenure.

Lessons from Abroad

It's probably the case that "utopia is not one of the options," as a Libertarian presidential candidate once put it.[24] Our task then isn't to imagine a world utterly transformed, but to imagine something *better*: a federal executive less overbearing, less ubiquitous and menacing, and better constrained by law—a world in which one can, for hours or even days at a time, afford to forget that the head of the national government exists.

Is such a thing possible? Writing in the wake of Watergate, political scientist Aaron Wildavsky posited, "The importance of Presidents is a function of the scope of government; the more it does, the more important they become."[25] Reducing the scope of government is a valuable project in its own right, one that would also help reduce executive power. But is it essential to the latter project?

If we look abroad, we may learn that other developed countries with large state sectors suffer somewhat less than does the United States from the problems of one-person rule. On that front, parliamentary systems seem to offer distinct advantages over presidential ones.

In a pioneering 1990 article, "The Perils of Presidentialism," Juan Linz argued that presidential systems, which encourage cults of personality and foster instability, are especially bad for developing countries.[26] Subsequent studies have bolstered Linz's insights, showing that presidential systems are more prone to corruption, more likely to suffer catastrophic breakdowns, and more likely to degenerate into autocracies than parliamentary ones.[27] Building on Linz's work, in 2014, George Mason University's F. H. Buckley found that, even in developed democracies, "presidentialism is significantly and strongly correlated with less political freedom."[28]

Political scientists Tom Ginsburg and Aziz Huq observe that parliamentary systems "seem to have more effective instruments for maintaining accountability and checking efforts at charismatic populism," among them, the parliamentary practice of Prime Minister's Questions, in which the chief executive is regularly and ruthlessly grilled by the opposition.[29]

Parliamentary regimes may also do a better job of restraining executives' proclivity for launching wars. That's a counterintuitive claim: after all, under British law, the prime minister has the prerogative to use military force without specific parliamentary approval. But in practice, it is "politically inconceivable that the government would proceed with the use of troops if Parliament actually disapproved."[30] After a Syrian chemical weapons attack in 2013, for example, when the United States and the United Kingdom contemplated punitive airstrikes against the Bashar al-Assad regime, then–secretary of state John Kerry kept insisting that "the president has the power" to wage war "no matter what

Congress does"; but when the House of Commons rejected military force, his counterpart across the pond, then–foreign secretary William Hague, simply said, "Parliament has spoken."[31]

Moreover, presidential regimes invite executive dominance by combining the roles of "head of state" and "head of government" in one figure, making the chief executive the living symbol of nationhood—the focal point of national hopes, dreams, and fears. That combination encourages presidents to imagine themselves the living embodiment of the popular will. The president "becomes the focus for whatever exaggerated expectations his supporters may harbor," Linz writes, and in turn may "conflate his supporters with 'the people' as a whole."[32]

If any developed country has enshrined the "right to ignore the president," however, it's Switzerland. The Swiss constitution rejects the unitary executive in favor of the Federal Council, seven members elected by the two legislative chambers jointly; the president, who serves for a single 12-month term, is selected from that seven-person body. He or she is not the head of state but merely "first among equals."[33] "In practice," as one scholar put it, "the Swiss President is the most inconspicuous chief of any republican state."[34] Ordinary Swiss citizens may not even be able to name the current officeholder—although, in 2014, a photo of then-president Didier Burkhalter waiting alone at a train station, without bodyguards, went viral on Twitter (sort of: 800 retweets).[35] Is it entirely a coincidence that Switzerland routinely places near the top in various rankings of greatest places to live?[36]

De-Imperializing the Presidency

Short of adopting a parliamentary system—or the Swiss constitution—what can be done to get the American presidency back to its proper constitutional size?

The most radical reform proposals in recent years challenge the very concept of the "unitary executive." University of Chicago professors Christopher Berry and Jacob Gersen have argued for a "partially unbundled executive," in which separately elected officers are given executive power over discrete policy areas. Most American states have "special-purpose executives"—treasurers, state auditors, and independent attorneys general, often separately elected, who help keep the chief executive in line. Perhaps a divided executive, containing several independent officers that the president can't easily remove, would do a better job of protecting individual liberty than a unified one.[37]

One way to break up the executive monolith is to free the attorney general from service at the president's pleasure. Writing in the *Yale Law Journal*, William P. Marshall makes the case for an independent federal attorney general, either elected or appointed, with a fixed term of service, shielded from removal except for cause. That actually reflects the American norm almost everywhere but the federal level: 43 states elect their attorneys general separately.[38]

Short of convincing the body politic to undertake radical constitutional surgery, can anything be done within our existing constitutional structure to relimit the presidency? In theory, yes: legal scholar Charles Black once commented, "My classes think I am trying to be funny when I say that . . . Congress could reduce the president's staff to one secretary . . . [and] put the White House up at auction. . . . [But] these things are literally true."[39]

If Congress has the legal power to sell the White House, it certainly has the ability to defund unauthorized wars, rein in unauthorized spying, stop unauthorized spending, and reclaim the power to make the laws Americans have to follow. Any number of worthy "framework" statutes, with strained acronyms, have been proposed toward those ends: the REINS Act (Regulations from the Executive in Need of Scrutiny) requires a vote on major regulations before they become law; the SCRUB Act (Searching for and Cutting Unnecessarily Burdensome Regulations) applies a base-closing commission approach to repealing swaths of the *Federal Register*. In the *Cato Handbook for Policymakers*, I've provided further suggestions for strengthening the War Powers Resolution and reining in presidential adventurism abroad. But even the best-designed reforms depend on the political will to make them happen: a Congress that doesn't flee from responsibility, a voting public that won't let them get away with it.

We're not there yet; but external pressures may, in the coming years, make it easier to rein in some of the national security powers the executive branch has accrued. America's increasing global role in the 20th century and its unrivaled supremacy after the collapse of the Soviet Union helped drive the Imperial Presidency's growth. The 21st century will likely see the reversal of that process, and, as John Glaser points out in this volume, retrenchment is a common response to relative decline. The emergence of new powers could encourage the United States to behave more like a normal country in the international sphere. That in turn could help enable a shift to a more "normal" presidency.

Moreover, the mystique of the presidency has taken a well-deserved hit in recent years. Americans today are finding it increasingly difficult to look upon the presidency with anything but revulsion. In 2016, we suffered through an electoral contest between the two most widely reviled and distrusted major-party candidates in American political history.

Say what you will about the winner of that contest, but he's done impressive work undermining the notion that the presidency is a center of "moral leadership." No president in living memory has been nearly as vocal about his contempt for legal limits, publicly broadcasting his desire to throw them off to millions of followers on a Twitter feed that's like the Watergate tapes unspooling in real time.

It took a couple of repulsive, abusive, power-hungry presidents—Lyndon Johnson and Richard Nixon—to generate the support for post-Watergate reforms that began to rein in the Imperial Presidency. If there's ever going to be a "teachable moment" on the dangers of concentrating too much power in the executive branch, we seem to be living through it right now.

The State in the Gaps

Jason Kuznicki

One sometimes gets the impression that libertarians' reach exceeds their grasp. We share little with utopian socialists, but we often share their utopianism. This utopian streak has helped ensure that both groups remain marginal, but both remain committed to their respective radicalisms for reasons that aren't likely to disappear. Radicalism and utopianism seem to co-occur.

Appreciate the irony, however: libertarian social thought has offered the clearest warning about the danger of an unconstrained vision. To the extent that the American mainstream has appreciated any insight of ours, it has appreciated this one. Utopia is dangerous. Utopian social planning is a delusion, a delusion that humans are peculiarly prone to. When we embrace it, terrible things happen. Utopias are not to be trusted, nor are their peddlers.

Americans seem to understand all this, more or less, as do libertarians . . . more or less. Yet both have all too often crept back to comprehensive social planning. Politicians of most other stripes like to imagine that *they are in charge*—and so things will be as they determine. Libertarians, meanwhile, like to imagine that in their own idealized society, *impersonal market forces are in charge*—and so things will be as market forces determine.

In its own way the latter claim is as ambitious as the former: not even libertarians could know the precise outcomes of the market process at some future time, not when their whole ideology declares that no one can ever have such knowledge. Being more than usually appreciative of markets does not give any greater-than-usual insight into how markets will behave. By the same token, being more than usually aware that the future is hard to predict does not endow anyone with the ability to predict the future.

But what, then, is the *use* of vision? If envisioning a utopia is dangerous—and if we bear firmly in mind that tens of millions have died in vain for this or that vision of a perfected society—then what on earth are we doing here? How dare we offer our visions at all?

* * * * *

As I have observed elsewhere, one strong and potentially motivating reason to imagine social arrangements radically other than our own is simply that it is entertaining to imagine the disappearance of various severe social problems and to imagine them replaced by intellectually satisfying solutions. We read about utopias, libertarian and otherwise, because we enjoy them, and not, crucially, because utopian visions track a reasonable future course of events. There remains an appeal to seeing all the loose ends tied up, even if it can never be so in the realm of everyday life. Perhaps we can retreat to books for inspiration and solace.

Yet philosophers since the time of Plato have warned that entertaining falsehoods are to be avoided, whereas ugly truths should be confronted and even shouted from the rooftops when the occasion demands. The task of philosophy is in part to sort the entertaining falsehoods from the hard truths, and to deal with each as its nature requires. Confusing the two would be bad form, and at some point, confusing them would be an assent to a lie.

One approach to this philosopher's task—although admittedly an imperfect one—is simply to make certain that whenever we consider a view, it isn't dressed up in such a way that it unduly entertains. Let truth and falsehood both be boring, and virtue may just settle the contest. This, though, requires that the knowing purveyors of falsehoods likewise constrain themselves, although they will probably not comply. Even in our solitary contemplation, we may still dress up the side that we favor, and we may even do so without realizing what we have done. Bias runs deep.

Another approach is to think about the future in ways that are consciously less than utopian. The contributors to this volume are notably less than starry-eyed about the prospects for comprehensive or radical social change. One seldom gets the impression, on completing the essays of this volume, that one has glimpsed the world transfigured. Rather, in one area after another, our authors simply imagine things running on a more voluntary basis than they currently are. As our contributors are all libertarian, they generally find that this more voluntary basis has better consequences than, and is preferable to, the status quo.

That modesty is probably for the best, and there are some clear reasons for it. Most of us are policy wonks of one kind or another, and we have mostly stuck to our respective areas of expertise. Experts generally struggle like the rest of us when they stray beyond their specialization. Away from their home territory, they struggle not only to predict the future accurately—which is generally the case within their home territory—but also simply to predict the future plausibly, that is, to predict in such a way that experts from other fields find their predictions worthy of sustained consideration.

Faced with this plausibility deficit, utopian thinkers generally reach for beauty. After all, it's entertaining. And one might add that beautiful stories inspire more popular action than do plausible expert predictions. In its capacity as an inspiring story, and not as an expert prediction, Marxism conquered half of Europe. Long before Marxism was making the world tremble, the experts in Marx's own field, economics, had generally rejected his theoretical framework and knew it to be unsound. The masses—and more important, the specific members of the Russian intelligentsia who formed the core of the first successful Marxist revolution—were unfazed. Their story was beautiful; the good guys would win in the end, and the bad guys would be defeated forever. Then, all would be peace and plenty forever.

This volume has taken a less lovely approach. Untrue to libertarian form, it has assembled a planning committee. In the real world, the indictment against such committees is both long and grim. But our committee can do no more than suggest. It cannot command. Although I know and trust many of the people who wrote for this volume, depriving them of the power to command is still probably for the best.

A committee may and probably should improve on the knowledge that one person can bring to a task; but against this advantage, a committee always acquires the disadvantage of incoherence. This disadvantage means that implementing simultaneously all policy proposals offered herein would likely not be such a great idea. Conflicts would arise, the likes of which individual authors could not have foreseen even if they had tried.

As F. A. Hayek observed, the utility gain that utilitarians claim might be had from a particular policy change or a particular economic intervention always presumes a great deal about the rest of the economy. Specifically, Hayek argued persuasively that an accurate prediction in any one area of the economy requires, in effect, countless accurate predictions about other areas of the economy as well. "The effects of any rule," he wrote, "will depend not only on its being always observed but also on the other rules observed by the acting persons and on the rules being followed by all the other members of the society. To judge the utility of any one rule would therefore always presuppose that some other rules were taken as given and generally observed . . . so that among the determinants of the utility of any one rule there would always be other rules which could not be justified by their utility."[1]

In simpler terms, it can be hard to assess the usefulness of changes to the rules by which individuals conduct themselves. The reason for this difficulty is that rules exist in an ecosystem full of other rules, only some of which we are capable of knowing or articulating. It is plausible to think that too many changes to the rules, pursued too quickly, will result in a situation in which no rules are felt to be binding by individuals; they may see no purpose in any particular rule, in light of the general disorder all around them. Rules owe much of their persuasive force, and their intelligibility, to the existence of other rules.

This limitation has consequences for social planning. Any intervention depends for its success on at least two background conditions: (a) the planners who conceived of the change must have accurately assessed the economic conditions surrounding their intervention and (b) these conditions must not change in unforeseen ways once the intervention has been attempted. If conditions change outside the scope of the proposed course of action, those changes could make the action harmful or even nonsensical.

In a sense, each essay in this volume takes for granted, implicitly, that a stable social ordering will remain in the background, and that the changes to this ordering will be few. Yet collectively, this volume also proposes some fairly sweeping change. So what gives?

* * * * *

We live in a world where nearly everyone takes the state wholly for granted, and where many are convinced that, were it not for the state, modern life would be utterly impossible. Modern people have tasked the state with so much, and the state actually does so much for us, that it is hard to imagine a life without it, libertarian qualms about inefficiency and coercion notwithstanding. Maybe we just have to put up with the state's negative qualities? Bad as coercion may be, some things are still worse than coercion, one might be tempted to answer, and the state protects us from exactly those things. Or so the argument goes.

If one were to assert that the state does essential work for us, such that we must brave the state's admitted ethical drawbacks, the person making this claim ought to back it up with a demonstration of the necessity of the state. This argument would be one for statists to make—and for libertarians to falsify.

The statists' view may be completely correct, and if so, then libertarianism is busted. How, though, could we be sure of it? The obvious answer is that we should test the hypothesis. Testing a hypothesis requires that it be stated clearly and that a clear agreement exist on what the hypothesis implies observationally. It also requires that we fairly undertake experiments in doing without the state, to see what happens in a variety of stateless conditions, not merely those stateless conditions prompted (for example) by wars, rioting, or natural disasters.

We should bear in mind that the failure of any particular experiment does not mean that the state itself is necessarily justified. Many modes of life exist without a state, and some are doubtless preferable to others. Statelessness is not a unitary condition, and the failure of a given instance of statelessness does not mean that no form of statelessness can ever succeed.

Yet should a stateless state of affairs prevail—in just one issue area, or in many—the defenders of the state would have a lot of explaining to do. Were they not the ones who assured us that all this coercion was absolutely necessary? And if we can do without the coercion while retaining the advantages of modernity under a more voluntary set of institutions, why not go that way instead?

If the necessity of the state is falsified in one issue area, how sure are we about the others?

Here, one possible hypothesis that we might want to test would look as follows:

> X is a problem that is best (or only) solved in a manner that requires a state.

Does education require a state? Does welfare require a state? Does money? If it does, then the question is simple: Is education or welfare or money worth the coercion inherent in having a state? But if sufficiently attaining those goals doesn't require a state, then presumably the state should shrink. We have thus far only been accepting its existence as a necessary evil, as a stopgap that gets us to a place that we want to be, albeit while incurring a serious drawback.

I must stress that describing the state in this way—as a doubtfully necessary evil to be chipped away at—does not imply that the state is justified. Being unable to envision a satisfactory nonstate solution to a given social problem does not mean that no nonstate solution exists. It could just mean that we've experienced a failure of the imagination.

This volume is best understood, then, as a piecemeal attempt to imagine a more voluntary social order. Just as it is unsatisfactory to say, in the face of natural phenomena whose explanations we cannot imagine, that "God did it," so too it is unsatisfactory to say, when we can think of no nonstate solution to a social problem, that the state must exist in order to solve it.

Perhaps we do need a state for this type of problem, but let's make the advocates of statism prove their case. Where is the necessity of the state? Have we really eliminated all possible challengers? If the best that advocates of a state solution can say is, "Well, I can't *imagine* anything better," then let them consider the inadequacy of this argument. After all, it is only an argument from ignorance.

Notes

Foreword

1. F. A. Hayek, "The Intellectuals and Socialism," *University of Chicago Law Review* 16, no. 3 (Spring 1949): 417-33, https://doi.org/10.2307/1597903.

Chapter 1

1. Michael D. Tanner, "The American Welfare State: How We Spend Nearly $1 Trillion a Year Fighting Poverty—And Fail," Cato Institute Policy Analysis no. 694, April 11, 2012.

2. Rachel Sheffield and Robert Rector, "The War on Poverty after 50 Years," Heritage Foundation Backgrounder no. 2955, September 15, 2014.

3. Tyler Cowen, "Does the Welfare State Help the Poor?" *Social Philosophy and Policy* 19, no. 1 (2002): 39, https://doi.org/10.1017/S0265052502191035.

4. S. M., "Are We Helping the Poor?" *The Economist*, December 18, 2013, http://www.economist.com/blogs/democracyinamerica/2013/12/anti-poverty-programmes.

5. Council of Economic Advisors, "Economic Perspectives on Incarceration and the Criminal Justice System," April 2016, p. 45.

6. Council of Economic Advisors, p. 5.

7. See, for example, Michael Greenstone et al., "Thirteen Economic Facts about Social Mobility and the Role of Education," The Hamilton Project policy memo, June 2013.

8. U.S. Census Bureau, "Income and Poverty in the United States: 2016," Table 3, https://www2.census.gov/programs-surveys/demo/tables/p60/259/pov_table3.xls.

9. See, for example, Reyn van Ewijik and Peter Sleegers, "The Effect of Peer Socioeconomic Status on Student Achievement," *Education Research Review* 5, no. 1

(June 2011): 134–50, https://doi.org/10.1016/j.edurev.2010.02.001; Robert Putnam, *Our Kids: The American Dream in Crisis* (New York: Simon and Schuster, 2015), p. 165.

10. Ryan Bourne, "Government and the Cost of Living: Income-Based vs. Cost-Based Approaches to Alleviating Poverty," Cato Institute Policy Analysis no. 847, September 4, 2018.

11. Edward L. Glaeser and Joseph Gyourko, "The Impact of Building Restrictions on Housing Affordability," *Economic Policy Review* 9, no. 2 (June 2003): 21–39, https://www.newyorkfed.org/medialibrary/media/research/epr/03v09n2/0306glae.pdf.

12. Robert deFina and Lance Hannon, "The Impact of Mass Incarceration on Poverty," *Journal of Crime and Delinquency* 59, no. 4 (June 2013): 562–86, https://doi.org/10.1177/0011128708328864.

13. Council of Economic Advisers, "Occupational Licensing: A Framework for Policymakers," July 2015, https://obamawhitehouse.archives.gov/sites/default/files/docs/licensing_report_final_nonembargo.pdf.

14. See, for example, Marvin Olasky, *The Tragedy of American Compassion* (New York: Free Press, 1986).

15. Robert Ellis Thompson, *Divine Order of Human Society: Being the L. P. Stone Lectures for 1891, Delivered in Princeton Theological Seminary* (Philadelphia: J. D. Wattles, 1891), p. 246.

16. "Giving USA 2016: The Annual Report on Philanthropy for the Year 2015," Giving USA, Chicago.

17. "Most Americans Practice Charitable Giving, Volunteerism," Gallup Inc., Washington, December 13, 2013, http://www.gallup.com/poll/166250/americans-practice-charitable-giving-volunteerism.aspx.

18. Tanner, "American Welfare State."

19. See, for example, Russell Roberts, "A Positive Model for Private Charity and Public Transfers," *Journal of Political Economy* 92, no. 1 (February 1984): 2136–48.

20. Charles Murray, *In Pursuit: Of Happiness and Good Government* (New York: Simon and Schuster, 1988), pp. 275–76.

21. Jonathan Meer, David Miller, and Elisa Wulfsberg, "The Great Recession and Charitable Giving," National Bureau of Economic Research Working Paper no. 22902, December 2016, https://doi.org/10.3386/w22902.

22. Meer, Miller, and Wulfsberg, "Charitable Giving."

23. Megan McArdle, "How Utah Keeps the American Dream Alive," Bloomberg Opinion, March 28, 2017, https://www.bloomberg.com/view/articles/2017-03-28/how-utah-keeps-the-american-dream-alive.

24. "One Hundred Seventh Semi-Annual Conference of the Church of Jesus Christ of Latter-Day Saints," October 1936, p. 3, https://archive.org/details/conferencereport 1936sa.

25. David Beito, *From Mutual Aid to the Welfare State: Fraternal Societies and Social Services, 1890–1967* (Chapel Hill: University of North Carolina Press, 2000).

26. See, for example, "Feeding Intolerance: Prohibitions on Sharing Food with People Experiencing Homelessness," National Law Center on Homelessness and Poverty and National Coalition on Homelessness, November 2007, http://nationalhomeless .org/publications/foodsharing/Food_Sharing.pdf.

27. John K. Ross, "Missouri Still Forbids Free Health Care from Outside State," *Reason*, August 6, 2013, https://reason.com/archives/2013/08/06/mo-still-forbids -free-health-care-from-o.

28. Jeff Reicert, "Dear New York Uninsured: Screw You, Love Governor Cuomo," *Huffington Post*, January 19, 2015.

29. Richard R. Hammer, "Zoning Laws and Homeless Shelters," *Church Law & Tax Report*, March/April 1995.

Chapter 2

1. Benjamin Rush, "Thoughts upon the Mode of Education Proper in a Republic," in *Essays on Education in the Early Republic*, ed. Frederick Rudolph (Cambridge, MA: Belknap Press of Harvard University Press, 1965), p. 9.

2. Rush, "Thoughts upon the Mode of Education," pp. 13–14.

3. Noah Webster, "On the Education of Youth in America," in *Essays on Education in the Early Republic*, ed. Frederick Rudolph (Cambridge, MA: Belknap Press of Harvard University Press, 1965), p. 77.

4. See, for example, Horace Mann, "Lecture IV: What God Does, and What He Leaves for Man to Do, in the Work of Education," *Life and Works of Horace Mann*, vol. 2 (Boston: Horace B. Fuller, 1868), pp. 212–15.

5. Horace Mann, "Report for 1848," in *Life and Works of Horace Mann*, vol. 3 (Boston: Horace B. Fuller, 1868), pp. 691–93.

6. Mann, "Report for 1848," p. 695.

7. Quoted in John W. Meyer et al., "Public Education as Nation-Building in America: Enrollments and Bureaucratization in the American States, 1870–1930," *American Journal of Sociology* 85, no. 3 (November 1979): 601.

8. David B. Tyack, *The One Best System: A History of American Urban Education* (Cambridge, MA: Harvard University Press, 1974), p. 178.

9. Ellwood P. Cubberley, *Changing Conceptions of Education* (Boston, MA: Houghton Mifflin, 1909), pp. 15–16.

10. *Zelman v. Simmons-Harris*, 536 U.S. 639 (2002).

11. Cubberley, *Changing Conceptions of Education*, p. 57.

12. Cubberley, *Changing Conceptions of Education*, p. 10.

13. U.S. Department of Education, "A Nation at Risk," April 1983, https://www2.ed.gov/pubs/NatAtRisk/risk.html.

14. National Center for Education Statistics, *Digest of Education Statistics*, 2016, table 205.50, https://nces.ed.gov/programs/digest/d16/tables/dt16_205.50.asp?current=yes.

15. Anna Fifield, "In Education-Crazy South Korea, Top Teachers Become Multi-millionaires," *Washington Post*, December 30, 2014, https://www.washingtonpost.com/world/asia_pacific/in-education-crazy-south-korea-top-teachers-become-multimillionaires/2014/12/29/1bf7e7ae-849b-11e4-abcf-5a3d7b3b20b8_story.html?utm_term=.6674b9209101.

16. See, for instance, James K. Rilling and Larry J. Young, "The Biology of Mammalian Parenting and Its Effect on Offspring Social Development," *Science* 345, no. 6198 (August 15, 2014): 771–776, https://doi.org/10.1126/science.1252723.

17. Abby Jackson and Andy Kiersz, "The Latest Ranking of Top Countries in Math, Reading, and Science Is Out—and the US Didn't Crack the Top 10," *Business Insider*, December 6, 2016, https://www.businessinsider.com/pisa-worldwide-ranking-of-math-science-reading-skills-2016-12.

18. Patrick J. Wolf and Stephen Macedo, eds., *Educating Citizens: International Perspectives on Civic Values and School Choice* (Washington: Brookings Institution Press, 2004).

19. Devon Haynie, "The Great Game for International Students," *US News and World Report*, January 23, 2018.

20. James Tooley, *The Beautiful Tree: A Personal Journey into How the World's Poorest People Are Educating Themselves* (Washington: Cato Institute, 2009).

21. Albert Fishlow, "Levels of Nineteenth-Century American Investment in Education," *Journal of Economic History* 26, no. 4 (December 1966): 418–36, https://doi.org/10.1017/S0022050700077470.

22. Edward George Hartmann, *The Movement to Americanize the Immigrant* (New York: Columbia University Press, 1948).

23. Patrick J. Wolf, "Civics Exam: Schools of Choice Boost Civic Values," *Education Next* 7, no. 3 (2007): 67–72.

Chapter 3

1. See Kevin D. Williamson, *The End Is Near and It's Going to Be Awesome: How Going Broke Will Leave America Richer, Happier, and More Secure* (New York: HarperCollins, 2013).

2. See "21st Century Healthcare Symposium: Can We Harmonize Access, Quality & Cost?" Willamette University College of Law, Salem, OR, February 27, 2015, http://willamette.edu/law/events/library/2015/healthcare/index.html. See also Michael F. Cannon, "Health Care's Future Is So Bright, I Gotta Wear Shades," *Willamette Law Review* 51, no. 4 (2015): 559–71.

3. "Were it not for today's tangled web of subsidies, administered prices, and regulations that constrain competition, today's general hospitals would not be economically or competitively viable. . . . The Coxa Hospital for Joint Replacement in Tampere, Finland, achieves similarly better costs than general hospitals. The 64 general hospitals in Finland that perform similar surgeries average unanticipated complication rates of 10 to 12 percent; the rate at Coxa is 0.1 percent. . . . The high cost of hospitalization isn't driven by the excess profits of general hospitals. . . . The costs are simply inherent to the one-size-fits-all value proposition they offer." Clayton M. Christensen, Jerome H. Grossman, and Jason Hwang, *The Innovator's Prescription: A Disruptive Solution for Health Care* (New York: McGraw-Hill, 2009), pp. 76, 82, 237.

4. "The Canadian-born Bieber never plans on becoming an American citizen. 'You guys are evil,' he jokes. 'Canada's the best country in the world.' He adds, 'We go to the doctor and we don't need to worry about paying him, but here, your whole life, you're broke because of medical bills. My bodyguard's baby was premature, and now he has to pay for it. In Canada, if your baby's premature, he stays in the hospital as long as he needs to, and then you go home.'" "Justin Bieber Talks Sex, Politics, Music and Puberty," *Rolling Stone*, February 16, 2011, http://www.rollingstone.com/music/news/justin-bieber-talks-sex-politics-music-and-puberty-in-new-rolling-stone-cover-story-20110216.

5. Contrary to *Terminator 2: Judgment Day*, directed by James Cameron (Los Angeles: Orion Pictures 1991):

> T-800 TERMINATOR: The Skynet Funding bill is passed. The system goes online August 4th, 1997. Human decisions are removed from strategic defense. Skynet begins to learn at a geometric rate. It becomes self-aware at 2:14 a.m. Eastern time, August 29th. In a panic, they try to pull the plug.
> SARAH CONNOR: Skynet fights back.
> T-800 TERMINATOR: Yes. It launches its missiles against the targets in Russia.

JOHN CONNOR: Why attack Russia? Aren't they our friends now?

T-800 TERMINATOR: Because Skynet knows the Russian counter-attack will eliminate its enemies over here.

6. "Let us realize that the arc of the moral universe is long, but it bends toward justice." Clayborne Carson and Kris Shepard, eds., *A Call to Conscience: The Landmark Speeches of Dr. Martin Luther King, Jr.* (New York: Intellectual Properties Management, 2001), p. 199. See generally Theodore Parker, *Ten Sermons of Religion* (Boston: Crosby Nichols; New York: C. S. Francis, 1853), pp. 84–85. Steven Pinker argues that this is the most peaceful era yet. Steven Pinker, *The Better Angels of Our Nature: Why Violence Has Declined* (New York: Viking, 2011).

7. Pinker, *Better Angels*, p. 304.

8. "Commerce, entrepreneurial capitalism takes more people out of poverty than aid, of course, we know that." Bono, address at Georgetown University, Washington, November 12, 2012, http://www.theguardian.com/social-enterprise-network/2012 /nov/14/social-enterpise-bono-georgetown. According to Brookings Institution researchers Laurence Chandy and Geoffrey Gertz, "Poverty reduction of this magnitude is unparalleled in history: never before have so many people been lifted out of poverty over such a brief period of time." Chandy and Gertz, "Poverty in Numbers: The Changing State of Global Poverty from 2005 to 2015," Brookings Institution Report, January 2011, p. 3. See also Marian L. Tupy, "Bono: Only Capitalism Can End Poverty," *Cato at Liberty* (blog), July 31, 2013.

9. "Hi, welcome to the future. San Dimas, California, 2688. And I'm telling you it's great here. The air is clean. The water's clean. Even the dirt—it's clean! Bowling averages are way up. Mini-golf scores are way down. And we have more excellent water slides than any other planet we communicate with. I'm telling you, this place is great!" *Bill & Ted's Excellent Adventure*, directed by Stephen Herek (Los Angeles: Orion Pictures, 1989).

10. See Shirley V. Svorny, "Liberating Telemedicine: Options to Eliminate the State-Licensing Roadblock," Cato Institute Policy Analysis no. 826, November 15, 2017.

11. Peter Van Doren, "Uber Provides Case against Occupational Licensing," *Cato at Liberty* (blog), January 28, 2015.

12. For example: "Pager, in New York City, dispatches doctors or nurse practitioners via Uber, for $200. Heal, in Los Angeles, San Francisco and Orange County, Calif., promises to 'get a doctor to your sofa in under an hour' for $99. (A medical assistant goes along to do the driving and parking.) RetraceHealth, in Minneapolis, has a nurse practitioner consult with patients via video (for $50), and only comes to their homes if hands-on care like a throat swab or blood draw is necessary (for $150). Atlanta-based MedZed sends a nurse to a patient's home to do a preliminary exam. Then the nurse

connects via laptop with a doctor who provides a treatment plan remotely. . . . And thanks to the boom in mobile-medical technology, providers can carry key equipment with them, from portable blood analyzers to hand-held ultrasounds. . . . 'Health checks,' in which a nurse does cholesterol, blood pressure, blood sugar and other tests for $75, are also popular—even in office settings." Melinda Beck, "Startups Vie to Build an Uber for Health Care," *Wall Street Journal*, August 11, 2015, http://www.wsj.com/articles /startups-vie-to-build-an-uber-for-health-care-1439265847.

13. See Kaveh G. Shojania et al., "Changes in Rates of Autopsy-Detected Diagnostic Errors over Time: A Systematic Review," *Journal of the American Medical Association* 289, no. 21 (June 4, 2003): 2849-2856, https://doi.org/10.1001/jama.289.21.2849. The analysis of 53 distinct autopsy series over a 40-year period showed a significant decrease over time for major diagnostic errors detected at autopsy.

14. See generally Christensen, Grossman, and Hwang, *The Innovator's Prescription*.

15. "Ordinary health insurance provides a tangible benefit only when you need health care. Tontine insurance pays a cash benefit when you *don't* use it, as well as covering your medical expenses when you do. As such, tontine insurance is structured to be maximally attractive to those who have an overly optimistic assessment of risk. . . . Tontine health insurance should be especially enticing to people who do not purchase coverage because they think they would 'lose' the ordinary health insurance bet by being healthy—the invincibles." Tom Baker and Peter Siegelman, "Tontines for the Young Invincibles," *Regulation* 32, no. 4 (Winter 2009/2010): 4, 20. See generally Jeff Guo, "It's Sleazy, It's Totally Illegal, and Yet It Could Become the Future of Retirement," *Washington Post*, September 28, 2015, http://www.washingtonpost.com/news/wonkblog/wp/2015/09/28 /this-sleazy-and-totally-illegal-savings-scheme-may-be-the-future-of-retirement/.

16. Reed Abelson, "UnitedHealth to Insure the Right to Insurance," *New York Times*, December 2, 2008.

See also Michael F. Cannon, "ObamaCare Is Now Optional," *Washington Examiner*, August 1, 2018, https://www.washingtonexaminer.com/opinion/obamacare-is-now -optional. On health insurance innovation, see generally John H. Cochrane, "Health-Status Insurance: How Markets Can Provide Health Security," Cato Institute Policy Analysis no. 633, February 18, 2009.

17. "The PPACA's 'community rating' price controls will destroy innovations that make health insurance better and more secure. They have already caused the markets for child-only health insurance to collapse in 17 states and caused insurers to flee the child-only market in a further 18 states. When implemented elsewhere, these price controls have forced health insurance companies to compete to avoid and mistreat the sick.

Millions of Americans will suffer those consequences if these price controls take full effect in 2014. When informed that these price controls will reduce the quality of care their families receive, consumers overwhelmingly oppose these supposedly popular provisions." Michael F. Cannon, director of health policy studies, Cato Institute, "The PPACA's Health Insurance Exchanges and Medicaid Expansion," Testimony before the Florida House Select Committee on Patient Protection and Affordable Care Act, January 22, 2013, http://www.cato.org/publications/congressional-testimony/ppacas -health-insurance-exchanges-medicaid-expansion.

18. "Republicans are nervous about repealing ObamaCare's supposed ban on discrimination against patients with pre-existing conditions. But a new study by Harvard and the University of Texas-Austin finds those rules penalize high-quality coverage for the sick, reward insurers who slash coverage for the sick, and leave patients unable to obtain adequate insurance." Michael F. Cannon, "How ObamaCare Punishes the Sick," *Wall Street Journal*, February 28, 2017, https://www.wsj.com/articles/how-obamacare -punishes-the-sick-1488327340.

According to economist John C. Goodman: "Many of the country's top hospitals are off limits to patients covered by ObamaCare's current plans. Take Houston's MD Anderson Cancer Center, which was named America's best cancer-care hospital by *U.S. News & World Report* in 13 of the past 16 years. The hospital's website suggests that it takes even Medicaid, but it doesn't accept a single private health-insurance plan sold on the individual market in Texas. Since Blue Cross of Minnesota withdrew from the individual market in 2016, the state's Mayo Clinic—once cited by President Obama as a model for the nation—has been off limits to Minnesotans covered by ObamaCare exchange plans. Memorial Sloan Kettering appears out of bounds for every exchange plan in New York. Both of these hospitals are open to some Medicaid patients, though Mayo's chief executive has predicted publicly that Medicaid patients may eventually have to queue behind their privately insured peers." Goodman, "ObamaCare Can Be Worse than Medicaid," *Wall Street Journal*, June 26, 2018, https://www.wsj.com /articles/obamacare-can-be-worse-than-medicaid-1530052891.

See also Michael F. Cannon, "Is ObamaCare Harming Quality? (Part 1)," *Health Affairs* (blog), January 4, 2018, https://www.healthaffairs.org/do/10.1377 /hblog20180103.261091/full/; and Michael F. Cannon, "How to Ensure Quality Health Coverage (Part 2)," *Health Affairs* (blog), January 5, 2018, https://www.healthaffairs .org/action/showDoPubSecure?doi=10.1377/hblog20180103.932096&format=full. See generally Jeffrey Young, "How Your Health Insurance Company Can Still Screw You, Despite Obamacare," *Huffington Post*, July 21, 2014, http://www.huffingtonpost .com/2014/07/21/health-insurance-obamacare_n_5599544.html.

19. "The individual health insurance market is already moving in the direction of [a total-satisfaction guarantee]. To let [such] insurance emerge fully, we must remove the legal and regulatory pressure to provide employer-based group insurance over individual insurance and remove regulations limiting risk-based pricing and competition among health insurers." Cochrane, "Health-Status Insurance," p. 1.

20. See generally Elisabeth Kübler-Ross, *On Death and Dying* (New York: Macmillan, 1969).

21. "Critics therefore call [the Independent Payment Advisory Board] a 'death panel,' but one could just as defensibly call it a 'life panel.'" Michael F. Cannon, "More Reasons Why IPAB, ObamaCare's 'Death Panel,' Is Relevant to Sylvia Burwell's Nomination," *Forbes*, April 15, 2014, http://www.forbes.com/sites/michaelcannon/2014/04/15/more -reasons-why-ipab-obamacares-death-panel-is-relevant-to-sylvia-burwells-nomination/.

22. "Caren Misky, a nurse practitioner with True North Health Navigation in Denver, says she recently responded to a call where an Alzheimer's patient had fallen and cut his head. She was able to staple his wound at the kitchen table while he had breakfast. 'His wife said the last time that happened, they spent eight hours in the ER and had a $10,000 bill,' Ms. Misky says. . . . [T]he True North mobile unit goes to the scene along with the fire department's paramedics. Once the paramedics confirm the situation isn't life-threatening, the caller can choose between being treated by a nurse practitioner on the spot, for $200 to $300 (which is covered by most Colorado insurance plans), or going by ambulance to the ER, which typically costs $3,000 or more." Beck, "Startups Vie to Build an Uber."

23. "We may be wasting perhaps 30% of U.S. health care spending on medical care that does not appear to improve our health." Elliott S. Fisher, "More Care Is Not Better Care," National Institute for Health Care Management Foundation, *Expert Voices* 7 (January 2005): 2.

24. See, for example, Charles Lane, "Medicare Reform's Slow Progress," *Washington Post*, March 4, 2013, https://www.washingtonpost.com/opinions/charles-lane-medicare -reforms-slow-progress/2013/03/04/9624c4c4-84f8-11e2-999e-5f8e0410cb9d_story .html. Lane describes industry resistance to a proposal to use competitive bidding to reduce the prices that Medicare pays for medical equipment: "One man's absurd waste of taxpayer funds, however, is another man's rice bowl. Organized into an effective lobby, medical equipment manufacturers and distributors resisted change."

25. "A powerful physician lobby can block changes to the scopes of practice of mid-level practitioners that would impinge on its members' turf." Shirley V. Svorny, "Medical Licensing: An Obstacle to Affordable, Quality Care," Cato Policy Analysis no. 621, September 17, 2008, p. 2.

26. See, for example, Margot Sanger-Katz, "Why Doctors Dictate How Much the Government Pays Them," *National Journal*, May 18, 2013. Medicare accepts most recommendations proposed by the Relative Value Scale Update Committee, an advisory panel of 31 doctors from different specialties.

27. Cf. Thomas Jefferson's letter of January 16, 1787, to Edward Carrington, in which he said, "And were it left to me to decide whether we should have a government without newspapers, or newspapers without a government, I should not hesitate a moment to prefer the latter." Jefferson, in *The Founders' Constitution*, vol. 5, eds. Philip B. Kurland and Ralph Lerner (Chicago: University of Chicago Press, 1987), pp. 121–22.

28. See Patient Protection and Affordable Care Act, Pub. L. No. 111-148, 124 Stat. 119 (2010).

29. See generally Michael F. Cannon, "Yes, Mr. President: A Free Market Can Fix Health Care," Cato Policy Analysis no. 650, October 21, 2009, which offers an agenda for liberalizing health care.

30. "Quality assurance in today's medical marketplace doesn't come from state medical [licensing] boards but from the fear of medical malpractice liability and from market mechanisms such as malpractice insurers; independent certification agencies like the Joint Commission, specialty boards, and credentials verification organizations; consumer guides such as *Consumer Reports*, HealthGrades, and Angie's List; and insurers' and providers' interest in protecting their reputations and brand names." Svorny, "Medical Licensing," p. 12.

31. Morris M. Kleiner and Kyoung Won Park estimate that "greater autonomy by legally allowing hygienists to work independently of dentists is associated with an approximately 10 percent higher wage and a 6 percent increase in the employment growth of dental hygienists. In contrast, these state provisions are associated with approximately a 16 percent reduction in dental hourly earnings and a 26 percent reduction in dental employment growth in the states." Kleiner and Park, "Battles among Licensed Occupations: Analyzing Government Regulations on Labor Market Outcomes for Dentists and Hygienists, National Bureau of Economic Research Working Paper no. 16560, November 2010, pp. 19–20, https://doi.org/10.3386/w16560.

32. See Kleiner and Park, "Battles among Licensed Occupations," noting that states lose approximately 1 percent of output of dental services by not allowing hygienists to practice on their own.

33. See generally "Should Ohio Expand Medicaid?," Michael F. Cannon, director of health policy studies, Cato Institute, Testimony before the Ohio House Subcommittee on Health and Human Services, March 13, 2013, http://www.cato.org/publications /testimony/should-ohio-expand-medicaid. Volunteer groups engage doctors and other

clinicians from around the country to treat indigent patients in rural and inner-city areas. Because they are not licensed to practice medicine in the states they are visiting, those clinicians are prevented from providing free medical care to the poor. See also Jeff Reichert and Farihah Zaman, "Dear New York City's Uninsured: Screw You, Love Governor Cuomo," *Huffington Post*, November 19, 2014, http://www.huffingtonpost.com/jeff -reichert/dear-new-york-citys-unins_b_6184470.html, criticizing New York governor Andrew Cuomo for not allowing a Remote Area Medical free clinic in New York City.

34. "Missouri now joins states like Tennessee, Illinois, and Connecticut that have enacted similar Good Samaritan laws." Michael F. Cannon, "Missouri Lawmakers Override Veto to Enact Good Samaritan Law," *Cato at Liberty* (blog), September 12, 2013.

35. "Medicare reforms that allow individuals to control their health care dollars would eliminate wasteful spending, would provide enrollees better choices and better medical care, and would do so at a lower cost to taxpayers. Congress should move retiree health care from today's dysfunctional system of central planning to an innovative system based on personal savings, individual choice, and competition." Michael F. Cannon and Chris Edwards, "Medicare Reforms," *Downsizing the Federal Government*, September 1, 2010, http://www.downsizinggovernment.org/hhs/medicare-reforms.

36. "The creation of tax-free health savings accounts presents a new opportunity to reduce the distortions created by federal tax preferences for health-related expenditures that ultimately could help eliminate those distortions." Michael F. Cannon, "Large Health Savings Accounts: A Step toward Tax Neutrality for Health Care," *Forum for Health Economics and Policy* 11, no. 2 (2008): 1080, https://doi.org/10.2202/1558 -9544.1080. See also Michael F. Cannon, "On Health Care, Walker and Rubio Offer Obamacare Lite," *Manchester Union-Leader*, August 27, 2015.

37. Gigi A. Cuckler et al., "National Health Expenditure Projections, 2017–26: Despite Uncertainty, Fundamentals Primarily Drive Spending Growth," *Health Affairs* 37, no. 3 (March 2018): 482–83, https://doi.org/10.1377/hlthaff.2017.1655. The figure is the projected U.S. national health expenditures for 2020.

38. "At long last, the Trump administration has created a 'freedom option' for people suffering under Obamacare. A final rulemaking issued Wednesday reverses an Obama-era regulation that exposed the sick to medical underwriting. The new rule will expand consumer protections for the sick, cover up to two million uninsured people, reduce premiums for millions more, protect conscience rights, and make Obamacare's costs more transparent. And unlike President Barack Obama's implementation of his signature healthcare legislation, it works within the confines of the law." Cannon, "ObamaCare Is Now Optional."

39. See generally Christy Ford Chapin, *Ensuring America's Health: The Public Creation of the Corporate Health Care System* (New York: Cambridge University Press, 2015); Alain C. Enthoven and Laura A. Tollen, eds., *Toward a 21st Century Health System: The Contributions and Promise of Prepaid Group Practice* (San Francisco: Jossey-Bass, 2004); and Shannon Brownlee, *Overtreated: Why Too Much Medicine Is Making Us Sicker and Poorer* (New York: Bloomsbury, 2008).

40. "A better way to generate comparative-effectiveness information would be for Congress to eliminate government activities that suppress private production. . . . That laissez-faire approach would both increase comparative-effectiveness research and increase the likelihood that patients and providers would use it." Michael F. Cannon, "A Better Way to Generate and Use Comparative-Effectiveness Research," Cato Institute Policy Analysis no. 632, February 2, 2009, p. 1.

41. See Darcy Olsen, *The Right to Try: How the Federal Government Prevents Americans from Getting the Lifesaving Treatments They Need* (New York: Harper, 2015).

42. Timbuk 3, "The Future's So Bright, I Gotta Wear Shades," on *Greetings from Timbuk 3*, I.R.S. Records, released 1986.

43. "I'm sure that in 1985, plutonium is available in every corner drugstore, but in 1955, it's a little hard to come by." *Back to the Future*, directed by Robert Zemeckis (Universal City, CA: Universal Pictures, 1985).

44. *Back to the Future: Part II*, directed by Robert Zemeckis (Universal City, CA: Universal Pictures, 1989).

> Doc Brown: The shock of coming face to face with oneself 30 years older . . . would create a time paradox, which would unravel the very fabric of the space-time continuum and destroy the entire universe. Granted, that's a worst-case scenario. The destruction might in fact be very localized, limited to merely our own galaxy.
> Marty McFly: Oh, hey, well, that's a relief.

Chapter 4

1. In 2017, the most recent year for which we have numbers, the overdose crisis claimed about 72,000 lives per year. Approximately 30,000 of those deaths were from fentanyl, up 540 percent in three years. This extrapolation to an unknown future assumes that the number will continue to climb, which is likely if prohibitionist policies are still pursued. See "Overdose Death Rates" webpage, National Institute for Drug Abuse, https://bit.ly /1RxOFVr; Josh Katz, "The First Count of Fentanyl Deaths in 2016: Up 540% in Three Years," *New York Times*, September 2, 2017, https://nyti.ms/2iPuc3B.

2. Glen Greenwald, "Drug Decriminalization in Portugal: Lessons for Creating Fair and Successful Drug Policies," Cato Institute White Paper, April 2, 2009.

3. Christopher Ingraham, "Why Hardly Anyone Dies of a Drug Overdose in Portugal," *Washington Post*, June 15, 2015, https://wapo.st/2QCngqc.

4. Ingraham, "Drug Overdose in Portugal."

5. As will be discussed later, decriminalization differs from legalization, and in fully legalized drug markets, drug use is likely to rise.

6. "Drug Decriminalisation in Portugal: Setting the Record Straight," Transform Drug Policy Foundation, Bristol, UK, June 11, 2014, https://transformdrugs.org/drug-decriminalisation-in-portugal-setting-the-record-straight/.

7. The term "opioid" has been used to describe synthetic opiates, whereas "opiates" describes natural products derived from the opium poppy. Increasingly, "opioid" is becoming the preferred term for both, and that is how it will be used in this chapter. "Opium" is the more natural form of the drug that was popular in the 19th century.

8. Jacob Sullum, "America's War on Pain Pills Is Killing Addicts and Leaving Patients in Agony," *Reason*, April 2018, https://reason.com/archives/2018/03/08/americas-war-on-pain-pills-is.

9. Kristina Davis and Sandra Dibble, "Fentanyl Has Taken Over America's Drug Market: Where Is It Coming From?" *San Diego Tribune*, June 17, 2018, https://www.sandiegouniontribune.com/news/public-safety/sd-me-fentanyl-pipeline-20180617-story.html.

10. "Fentanyl: What Is a Lethal Dosage?" Oxford Treatment Center, Oxford, MS, August 18, 2017, https://www.oxfordtreatment.com/fentanyl/lethal-dose/.

11. Madeline Holcombe, "Distraught Husband Says Wife of 30 Years Was Given a Lethal Dose of Fentanyl. He Wants To Know Why," CNN, January 17, 2019, https://cnn.it/2CtVwen.

12. "Arsenic Toxicity Clinical Assessment," Agency for Toxic Substances and Disease Registry, Atlanta, 2010, https://www.atsdr.cdc.gov/csem/csem.asp?csem=1&po=12.

13. The mixture of cocaine and heroin has traditionally been known as a "speedball" and has long been popular.

14. German Lopez, "Why America's Cocaine Problem Is Now a Fentanyl Problem Too," *Vox*, May 4, 2018, https://www.vox.com/science-and-health/2018/5/4/17307296/cocaine-opioid-crisis-fentanyl-overdose.

15. Utsha G. Khatri, Kendra Viner, and Jeanmarie Perrone, "Lethal Fentanyl and Cocaine Intoxication," *New England Journal of Medicine* 379, no. 18 (2018): 1782, http://doi.org/10.1056/NEJMc1809521.

16. Jennifer J. Carroll et al., "Exposure to Fentanyl-Contaminated Heroin and Overdose Risk among Illicit Opioid Users in Rhode Island: A Mixed Methods Study," *International Journal of Drug Policy* 46 (August 2017): 136–45, https://doi.org/10.1016/j.drugpo.2017.05.023.

17. Carroll et al., "Heroin and Overdose Risk."

18. According to the FBI, 11,004 gun homicides occurred in 2016. "Crime in the United States 2016" webpage, Federal Bureau of Investigation, https://ucr.fbi.gov/crime-in-the-u.s/2016/crime-in-the-u.s.-2016/tables/expanded-homicide-data-table-4.xls.

19. Jacob Sullum, *Saying Yes: In Defense of Drug Use* (New York: TarcherPerigee, 2004), Kindle edition, location 3304.

20. William J. Bennett, "Introduction," *National Drug Control Strategy* (Washington: Office of National Drug Control Policy, 1989), p. 11.

21. "Speaking Out against Drug Legalization," Drug Enforcement Administration, Washington, 1994, p. 11. https://www.druglibrary.net/schaffer/dea/pubs/legaliz/claim1.htm.

22. Carl Hart, *High Price: A Neuroscientist's Journey of Self-Discovery That Challenges Everything You Know about Drugs and Society* (New York: Harper, 2013), p. 306.

23. James C. Anthony, Lynn A. Warner, and Ronald C. Kessler, "Comparative Epidemiology of Dependence on Tobacco, Alcohol, Controlled Substances, and Inhalants: Basic Findings from the National Comorbidity Survey," *Experimental and Clinical Psychopharmacology* 2, no. 3 (August 1994): 244–68, https://doi.org/10.1037/1064-1297.2.3.244 and https://pdfs.semanticscholar.org/60cd/d49b5ed6a84423762a366727ae4880c6f255.pdf.

24. Lloyd D. Johnston, Patrick M. O'Malley, and Jerald G. Backman, *National Survey Results on Drug Use from the Monitoring the Future Study, 1975–1994*, vol. 2 (Washington: Government Printing Office, 1996), pp. 83–85.

25. Leo Beletsky and Corey S. Davis, "Today's Fentanyl Crisis: Prohibition's Iron Law, Revisited," *International Journal of Drug Policy* 46 (August 2017): 156–59, https://doi.org/10.1016/j.drugpo.2017.05.050.

26. Beletsky and Davis, "Today's Fentanyl Crisis."

27. Beletsky and Davis, "Today's Fentanyl Crisis."

28. David T. Courtwright, *Dark Paradise: A History of Opiate Addiction* (Cambridge: Harvard University Press, 2001), Kindle edition, location 1026.

29. Courtwright, *Dark Paradise*, 1088.

30. Courtwright, *Dark Paradise*.

31. Courtwright, *Dark Paradise*, 1099.

32. Courtwright, *Dark Paradise*, 1435.

33. Courtwright, *Dark Paradise*.

34. Courtwright, *Dark Paradise*, 1444.

35. From 2016 to 2017 in Colorado, daily or near-daily use of marijuana slightly increased for adults from 6.4 percent to 7.6 percent. For kids, it has stayed the same since before legalization, at 20 percent, which is the national average. Colorado Department of Public Health and Environment, "Marijuana Use in Colorado Rises for Adults, Stays the Same for Kids," news release, July 18, 2018, https://www.colorado.gov/pacific/cdphe/marijuana-use-2017.

36. Johann Hari, *Chasing the Scream: The First and Last Days of the War on Drugs* (New York: Bloomsbury USA, 2015), Kindle edition, locations 3316–95.

37. Hart, *High Price*, pp. 309–10.

38. "Mass Incarceration and Criminalization" webpage, Drug Policy Alliance, 2018, http://www.drugpolicy.org/issues/mass-criminalization.

39. John Pfaff, *Locked In: The True Causes of Mass Incarceration and How to Achieve Real Reform* (New York: Basic Books, 2017), pp. 7–15.

40. Radley Balko, *Rise of the Warrior Cop: The Militarization of America's Police Forces* (New York: PublicAffairs, 2013), pp. 160–80.

41. Dick M. Carpenter II et al., "Policing for Profit: The Abuse of Civil Asset Forfeiture," Institute for Justice Report, November 2015, https://ij.org/report/policing-for-profit/.

42. German Lopez, "There's Nearly a 40 Percent Chance You'll Get Away with Murder in America," *Vox*, September 24, 2018, https://www.vox.com/2018/9/24/17896034/murder-crime-clearance-fbi-report.

43. Lopez, "You'll Get Away with Murder in America."

44. "War Comes Home: The Excessive Militarization of American Policing," American Civil Liberties Union Report, June 2014, https://www.aclu.org/report/war-comes-home-excessive-militarization-american-police.

45. E. Ann Carson, "Prisoners in 2016," Bureau of Justice Statistics *Bulletin* (Prisoners Series), January 2018, p. 19, https://www.bjs.gov/index.cfm?ty=pbdetail&iid=6187.

46. Carson, "Prisoners in 2016," p. 20.

47. "Drug War Statistics" webpage, Drug Policy Alliance, 2018, http://www.drugpolicy.org/issues/drug-war-statistics.

48. Christopher Ingraham, "More People Were Arrested Last Year over Pot Than for Murder, Rape, Aggravated Assault and Robbery—Combined," *Washington Post*, September 16, 2017, https://wapo.st/2Ql8Yec.

49. Ingraham, "More People Were Arrested Last Year."

Chapter 5

1. Adam Smith, *An Inquiry into the Nature and Causes of the Wealth of Nations*, Bk. 1, Chap. 1 (London, 1776).

2. Walter Eltis, "The Contrasting Theories of Industrialization of François Quesnay and Adam Smith," *Oxford Economic Papers* 40, no. 2 (June 1988): 269–88, https://doi.org/10.1093/oxfordjournals.oep.a041851.

3. Maddison Project Database 2018, 1990 benchmark; Jutta Bolt et al., "Rebasing 'Maddison': New Income Comparisons and the Shape of Long-Run Economic Development," Maddison Project Working Paper no. 10, January 2018, https://www.rug.nl/ggdc/historicaldevelopment/maddison/research.

4. The Smithsonian Institution, *Our History*, https://www.si.edu/about/history, p. 1. Accessed April 2019.

5. Marlana Portalana, *The Passionate Empiricist: The Eloquence of John Quincy Adams in the Service of Science State* (University of New York Press: Albany, 2009) p. 109.

6. The Smithsonian Institution, "2017 Annual Report," https://www.si.edu/sites/default/files/about/smithsonianannualreport2017.pdf.

7. Eric Jones, *The European Miracle: Environments, Economies and Geopolitics in Europe and Asia*, 3rd ed. (Cambridge, UK: Cambridge University Press, 2003), p. 218.

8. James Buchanan, "Veto Message Regarding Land-Grant Colleges," Miller Center, University of Virginia, Charlottesville, February 24, 1859, https://millercenter.org/the-presidency/presidential-speeches/february-24-1859-veto-message-regarding-land-grant-colleges.

9. Advisory Council on Science and Technology, *Developments in Biotechnology* (London: HMSO, 1990).

10. Cited in United States Congress House Committee on Science and Technology Task Force on Science, "A History of Science Policy in the United States, 1940-1985," Science Policy Study Background Report No. 1 (1986), p. 30, https://archive.org/details/historyofscience00unit.

11. Paula Stephan, "The Endless Frontier: Reaping What Bush Sowed," in *The Changing Frontier: Rethinking Science and Innovation Policy*, ed. Adam B. Jaffe and Benjamin F. Jones (Chicago: University of Chicago Press, 2015), pp. 321–66, http://www.nber.org/chapters/c13034.pdf.

12. Dwight D. Eisenhower, "Farewell Radio and Television Address to the American People," January 17, 1961, https://www.eisenhowerlibrary.gov/sites/default/files/file/farewell_address.pdf.

13. Joseph Schumpeter, *Capitalism, Socialism and Democracy* (1942; repr., London: Routledge, 1994), p. 83 (emphasis in original).

14. David Hounshell, "The Cold War, RAND, and the Generation of Knowledge, 1946–1962," *Historical Studies in the Physical and Biological Sciences* 27, no. 2 (1997): 237–67, repr. RAND Corporation, 1998, pp. 27–58, https://www.rand.org/pubs /reprints/RP729.html.

15. Richard R. Nelson, "The Simple Economics of Basic Scientific Research," *Journal of Political Economy* 67, no. 3 (June 1959): 297–306, https://doi.org/10.1086/258177; Kenneth J. Arrow, "Economic Welfare and the Allocation of Resources for Invention," in *The Rate and Direction of Inventive Activity: Economic and Social Factors* (Princeton, NJ: Princeton University Press, 1962), pp. 609–26.

16. Paul A. Samuelson, "A Pure Theory of Public Expenditure," *Review of Economics and Statistics* 36, no. 4 (November 1954): 387–89, https://doi.org/10.2307/1925895.

17. Terence Kealey and Martin Ricketts, "Modelling Science as a Contribution Good," *Research Policy* 43, no. 6 (July 2014): 1014–24, https://doi.org/10.1016/j.respol.2014.01.009.

18. Edwin Mansfield, Mark Schwartz, and Samuel Wagner, "Imitation Costs and Patents: An Empirical Study," *Economic Journal* 91, no. 364 (December 1981): 907–18, https://doi.org/10.2307/2232499.

19. Richard C. Levin et al., "Appropriating the Returns from Industrial Research and Development," *Brookings Papers on Economic Activity* 18, no. 3 (1987): 783–820.

20. Nathan Rosenberg, "Why Do Firms Do Basic Research (with Their Own Money)?" *Research Policy* 19, no. 2 (April 1990): 165–74, https://doi.org/10.1016/0048 -7333(90)90046-9.

21. Wesley M. Cohen and Daniel A. Levinthal, "Innovation and Learning: The Two Faces of R&D," *Economic Journal* 99, no. 397 (1989): 569–96.

22. Z. Griliches, "Productivity, R&D and Basic Research at Firm Level in the 1970s," *American Economic Review* 76, no. 1 (1986): 141–54.

23. Edwin Mansfield, "Basic Research and Productivity Increase in Manufacturing," *American Economic Review* 70, no. 5 (1980): 863–73.

24. George J. Stigler, "The Economics of Information," *Journal of Political Economy* 69, no. 3 (June 1961): 213–25.

25. Leo Sveikauskas, "R&D and Productivity Growth: A Review of the Literature," Bureau of Labor Statistics Working Paper no. 408, September 2007, pp. 1, 32, https:// www.bls.gov/osmr/pdf/ec070070.pdf (emphasis in original).

26. OECD, *The Sources of Economic Growth in OECD Countries* (Paris: OECD, 2003), pp. 84-85: https://doi.org/10.1787/9789264199460-en.

27. Walter Park, "International R&D Spillovers and OECD Economic Growth," *Economic Inquiry* 33, no. 4 (October 1995): 571–90, https://doi.org/10.1111/j.1465-7295

.1995.tb01882.x; Terence Kealey, "The Economic Laws of Research," *Science and Technology Policy* 7 (1994): 21–27.

28. United States Congress House Committee on Science and Technology Task Force on Science, p. 54.

29. Daniele Archibugi and Andrea Filippetti, "The Retreat of Public Research and Its Adverse Consequences on Innovation," *Technological Forecasting and Social Change* 127 (February 2018): 97–111, https://doi.org/10.1016/j.techfore.2017.05.022.

30. Archibugi and Filippetti, "The Retreat of Public Research."

31. David Edgerton, "The 'Linear Model' Did Not Exist: Reflections on the History and Historiography of Science and Research in Industry in the Twentieth Century," in *The Science-Industry Nexus: History, Policy, Implications*, ed. Karl Grandin and Nina Wormbs (New York: Watson, 2004), pp. 1–36.

32. Robert N. Proctor, "The History of the Discovery of the Cigarette–Lung Cancer Link: Evidentiary Traditions, Corporate Denial, Global Toll," *Tobacco Control* 21, no. 2 (2012): 87–91, http://doi.org/10.1136/tobaccocontrol-2011-050338.

33. Quoted in David Dickson, "Charities Taking the Strain," *Nature* 364 (1993): 742–44, https://doi.org/10.1038/364742a0.

34. Kealey, "Economic Laws of Research," 245–46.

35. Paul David, "From Market Magic to Calypso Science Policy: A Review of Terence Kealey's *Economic Laws of Scientific Research*," *Research Policy* 26, no. 2 (1997): 229–55.

36. Archibugi and Filippetti, "The Retreat of Public Research."

37. Eric Lander, "The Heroes of CRISPR," *Cell* 164, no. 1 (January 2016): 18–28, https://doi.org/10.1016/j.cell.2015.12.041.

38. Rani Molla, "Amazon Spent Nearly $23 Billion on R&D Last Year—More than Any Other U.S. Company," *Recode*, April 9, 2018, https://www.recode.net/2018/4/9/17204004/amazon-research-development-rd.

39. Smith, *Wealth of Nations*. Bk. 5, Chap. 1.

Chapter 6

1. Patrick J. Michaels and Terence Kealey, eds., *Scientocracy: The Tangled Web of Public Science and Public Policy* (Washington: Cato Institute, 2019), pp. 185–186.

2. Edward J. Calabrese, "Key Studies Used to Support Cancer Risk Assessment Questioned," *Environmental and Molecular Mutagenesis* 52, no. 8 (2011): 595–606, https://doi.org/10.1002/em.20662; Edward J. Calabrese, "How the US National Academy of Sciences Misled the World Community on Cancer Risk Assessment: New Findings Challenge Historical Foundations of the Linear Dose Response,"

Archives of Toxicology 87, no. 12 (2013): 2063–81, https://doi.org/10.1007/s00204
-013-1105-6.

3. The National Academy of Sciences established the Biological Effects of Atomic Radiation panel in 1956.

4. Edward J. Calabrese, "On the Origins of the Linear No-Threshold (LNT) Dogma by Means of Untruths, Artful Dodges and Blind Faith," *Environmental Research* 142 (2015): 432–42, https://doi.org/10.1016/j.envres.2015.07.011; Edward J. Calabrese, "LNTgate: How Scientific Misconduct by the U.S. NAS Led to Governments Adopting LNT for Cancer Risk Assessment," *Environmental Research* 148 (2016): 535–46, https://doi.org/10.1016/j.envres.2016.03.040.

5. Calabrese, "On the Origins of LNT Dogma"; Calabrese, "LNTgate."

6. Theo Emery, "Uranium Mining Debate in Virginia Takes a Step," *New York Times*, December 19, 2011, https://www.nytimes.com/2011/12/20/us/virginia-warned -of-hurdles-on-uranium-mining.html.

7. National Research Council, *Uranium Mining in Virginia: Scientific, Technical, Environmental, Human Health and Safety, and Regulatory Aspects of Uranium Mining and Processing in Virginia* (Washington: National Academies Press, 2012), p. 9.

8. Although the reference is dated 2001, the article was written in 1981. The only change in 2001 was to update the 30-year climate "normals" to 1971–2000. Bruce P. Hayden and Patrick J. Michaels, "Virginia's Climate," *University of Virginia News Letter* 57, no. 5 (1981): 17–20.

9. National Research Council, *Uranium Mining in Virginia*, p. 41.

10. Historical maps of North Atlantic tropical cyclones are available at the "Unisys Weather" webpage, http://weather.unisys.com/hurricane/atlantic/index.php.

11. Virginia Energy Resources was serially unable to get Virginia's moratorium on uranium mining reversed. Ultimately it appealed to the courts that the ban was unconstitutional and that regulation of uranium mining was the sole province of the U.S. Department of Energy. The former Atomic Energy Commission was folded into that department, which was created by President Jimmy Carter.

District and appellate courts rejected Coles's claims, but, remarkably, the Supreme Court granted certiorari on the question of Virginia's authority for its 2018–2019 session.

12. Daniel McGroarty, principal, Carmot Strategic Group, Testimony on "EPA's Bristol Bay Watershed Assessment: A Factual Review of a Hypothetical Scenario" before the Subcommittee on Oversight of the Committee on Science, Space, and Technology, U.S. House of Representatives, 113th Cong., 1st sess., August 1, 2013, http:// americanresources.org/epas-bristol-bay-watershed-assessment-a-factual-review-of-a -hypothetical-scenario/.

13. Paul Voosen, "Climate Scientists Open Up Their Black Boxes to Scrutiny," *Science* 354, no. 6311 (2016): 401–2, https://doi.org/10.1126/science.354.6311.401.

14. Ross McKitrick and John Christy, "A Test of the Tropical 200- to 300-hPa Warming Rate in Climate Models," *Earth and Space Science* 5, no. 9 (2018): 529–36, https://doi.org/10.1029/2018EA000401.

15. Gaven A. Schmidt et al., "Practice and Philosophy of Climate Model Tuning across Six US Modeling Centers," *Geoscientific Model Development* 10, no. 9 (2017): 3207–23, https://doi.org/10.5194/gmd-10-3207-2017.

16. Schmidt et al. "Practice and Philosophy of Climate Model Tuning."

17. Frédéric Hourdin et al., "The Art and Science of Model Tuning," *Bulletin of the American Meteorological Society* 98, no. 3 (2017): 589–602, https://doi.org/10.1175/BAMS-D-15-00135.1.

18. John R. Christy, professor, University of Alabama at Huntsville, and director, Earth System Science Center, Testimony before the House Committee on Science, Space, and Technology, 115th Cong., 1st sess. Figure 2, Tropical Mid-Tropospheric Temperature Changes, Models vs. Observations, 1979–2016. March 29, 2017, https://object.cato.org/sites/cato.org/files/testimony/michaels-kealey-house-testimony-march-29-2017.pdf. Note: The one model that tracks the observations is the Russian model INM-CM4. The data are also summarized in tabular form in the American Meteorological Society's "State of the Climate" report for 2016. Jessica Blunden and Derek S. Arndt, eds., "State of the Climate in 2016," Special Supplement, *Bulletin of the American Meteorological Society* 98, no. 8 (2017), https://doi.org/10.1175/2017BAMSStateoftheClimate.1. Further Note: Christy's testimony, linked above, is as devastating an indictment of the distortions in climate science that are driving global policies. The author cannot more strongly recommend downloading and reading it.

19. Daniele Fanelli, "Negative Results Are Disappearing from Most Disciplines and Countries," *Scientometrics* 90, no. 3 (2012): 891–904, https://doi.org/10.1007/s11192-011-0494-7.

20. Daniele Fanelli and John P. A. Ioannidis, "U.S. Studies May Overestimate Effect Sizes in Softer Research," *Proceedings of the National Academy of Sciences* 110, no. 37 (2013): 15031–36, https://doi.org/10.1073/pnas.1302997110.

21. If you don't, your proposal may be defunded at annual review time.

22. See the op-ed by Randy Schekman, "How Journals Like Nature, Cell and Science Are Damaging Science," *Guardian*, December 9, 2013. Two days earlier, he was awarded the Nobel Prize in Physiology or Medicine.

23. World Wildlife Fund, "Financial Info" webpage, https://www.worldwildlife.org/about/financials.

24. Robert E. Davis et al., "Changing Heat-Related Mortality in the United States," *Environmental Health Perspectives* 111, no. 14 (2003): 1712–18, https://doi.org/10.1289/ehp.6336.

25. In May 2017, the Trump administration allowed Pebble to apply for a permit to mine, which will include its environmental impact statement. Then on January 26, 2018, according to an EPA official news release, "EPA is suspending its process to withdraw those proposed restrictions, leaving them in place while the Agency receives more information on the potential mine's impact on the region's world-class fisheries and natural resources." See U.S. Environmental Protection Agency, "EPA Administrator Scott Pruitt Suspends Withdrawal of Proposed Determination in Bristol Bay Watershed, Will Solicit Additional Comments," news release, January 26, 2018, https://www.epa.gov/newsreleases /epa-administrator-scott-pruitt-suspends-withdrawal-proposed-determination-bristol-bay.

Chapter 7

1. John Stuart Mill, *On Liberty* (New Haven, CT: Yale University Press, 2003), p. 80.

2. See, for example, Paul J. Larkin, "Public Choice Theory and Overcriminalization," *Harvard Journal of Law and Public Policy* 36, no. 2 (2013): 715–93.

3. For example, the federal mandatory minimum sentence for cultivating 1,000 or more marijuana plants—even in a state that has legalized marijuana—is 10 years.

4. Alexander Hamilton, *The Federalist Papers*, No. 83, in *The Federalist*, ed. George Carey and James McClellan (Indianapolis: Liberty Fund, 2001).

5. H. A. Washington, ed., *Writings of Thomas Jefferson*, vol. 3 (Washington: Taylor & Maury, 1853), p. 71.

6. See, for example, William R. Kelly with Robert Pitman, *Confronting Underground Justice: Reinventing Plea Bargaining for Effective Criminal Justice Reform* (Lanham, MD: Rowman & Littlefield, 2018); and Stephanos Bibas, *The Machinery of Criminal Justice* (Oxford, UK, and New York: Oxford University Press, 2012). See also Jed S. Rakoff, "Why Innocent People Plead Guilty," *New York Review of Books*, November 20, 2014; and H. Mitchell Caldwell, "Coercive Plea Bargaining: The Unrecognized Scourge of the Justice System," *Catholic University Law Review* 61, no. 1 (2011): 63.

7. See "The Trial Penalty: The Sixth Amendment Right to Trial on the Verge of Extinction and How to Save It," National Association of Criminal Defense Lawyers, 2018.

8. See, for example, Richard A. Oppel Jr. and Jugal K. Patel, "One Lawyer, 194 Felony Cases, and No Time," *New York Times*, January 31, 2019.

9. See Albert Alschuler, "The Defense Attorney's Role in Plea Bargaining," *Yale Law Journal* 84, no. 6 (1975): 1179, 1210, 1222, https://doi.org/10.2307/795498. "With a grinding, overwhelming caseload, a public defender may 'play for the average' and fail to

represent individual clients with the vigor demanded by . . . professional responsibility. . . . The practical consequences of 'mutual trust' between a prosecutor and a defender . . . may become indistinguishable from those of a massive trade-out. An advantage to one client arises because the defender does not make the same effort for the others. Although never expressed in terms of explicit bargaining, this implicit trade-out may supply a basic governing principle in most negotiations between public defenders and prosecutors."

10. Clay Conrad, *Jury Nullification: The Evolution of a Doctrine* (Durham, NC: Carolina Academic Press, 1998).

11. Aliza Plener Cover, "Supermajoritarian Criminal Justice," *George Washington Law Review* 87, no. 4 (July 2019).

12. See Rakoff, "Why Innocent People Plead Guilty."

13. 18 U.S.C. § 201(c)(2).

14. For example, *United States v. Singleton*, 165 F.3d 1297 (10th Cir. 1999).

15. See, for example, *Lozman v. City of Riviera Beach, Fla.*, 138 S. Ct. 1945 (2018) (refusing to dismiss claim for retaliatory arrest of protester at city council meeting).

16. *Sparf v. United States*, 156 U.S. 51 (1895).

17. *Reed v. Town of Gilbert*, 135 S. Ct. 2218 (2015).

18. *Monell v. New York City Dept. of Soc. Svcs.*, 436 U.S. 658 (1978).

19. "More Arrests in the US for Marijuana Possession Than Violent Crimes, 2020 Hopeful Cory Booker Says," *Politifact*, July 11, 2019.

Chapter 8

1. See N.J.E. Austin and N.B. Rankov, *Exploratio: Miltary and Political Intelligence in the Roman World from the Second Punic War to the Battle of Adiranople* (London: Routledge, 1995).

2. See Edwin C. Fishel, *The Secret War for the Union: The Untold Story of Military Intelligence in the Civil War* (New York: Houghton Mifflin Company, 1996).

3. See Capt. Wyman H. Packard, USN (Ret.), "A Century of U.S. Naval Intelligence," published jointly in 1996 by ONI and the Naval Historical Center and available online at http://ibiblio.org/pha/A%20CENTURY%20OF%20US%20NAVAL%20 INTELLIGENCE.pdf.

4. The records pertaining to the Secret Services' exploits during the Spanish-American War can be found in Record Group 87, A1/Entry 16 – Letters and Reports Relating to Spy Suspects during the Spanish-American War, National Archives and Records Administration, College Park, MD.

5. See Record Group 87, A1/Entry 39 – Lists of Suspected Anarchists, 1901–02, National Archives and Records Administration, College Park, MD.

6. H.R. 21260, Public No. 141, May 27, 1908 via United States Statutes At Large, 60th Congress (First Session).

7. See American Big Brother: A Century of Political Surveillance and Repression via the Cato Institute.

8. See Roy Talbert Jr., *Negative Intelligence: The Army and the American Left, 1917–1941* (Jackson: University Press of Mississippi, 1991), p. 19.

9. 18 U.S.C. Chapter 37.

10. Ch. 106, 40 Stat. 411.

11. Public Law 65-41, August 10, 1917.

12. See *United States ex rel. Milwaukee Social Democratic Pub. Co. v. Burleson, Postmaster General.*

13. Talbert, *Negative Intelligence*, pp. 208–66.

14. "Investigation of Communist Propaganda," Report No. 2290, United States House of Representatives, 71st Congress (Third Session), p. 56.

15. A brief description of the files and activities of the McCormack-Dickstein Committee can be found on the National Archives website at https://www.archives .gov/legislative/guide/house/chapter-22-select-propaganda.html.

16. The inventory of Dies Committee records maintained by the National Archives can be viewed at the following: https://www.google.com/url?sa=t&rct=j&q=&esrc =s&source=web&cd=12&ved=2ahUKEwip17K7v8_eAhUR84MKHctcDykQ FjALegQIChAC&url=https%3A%2F%2Fhistory.house.gov%2FRecords-and -Research%2FFinding-Aids%2FSpecial-PIs%2FRecords-of-the-Special-Committee -on-Un-American-Activities%2C-1938-1944-(The-Dies-Committee)%2F&usg=AO vVaw1dyFaIhXWn1kViRViLFmtN.

17. August Raymond Ogden, *The Dies Committee: A Study of the Special House Committee for the Investigation of Un-American Activities, 1938–1944* (Washington: Catholic University Press, 1945), p. 296.

18. See "Historical Highlights: The Permanent Standing House Committee on Un-American Activities," viewable at https://history.house.gov/Historical-Highlights /1901-1950/The-permanent-standing-House-Committee-on-Un-American-Activities/.

19. *Weeks v. United States* can be viewed at https://supreme.justia.com/cases/federal /us/232/383/.

20. National Archives Record Group 87, Daily Reports of Agents, 1876–1936 reel 364. Daily Report of Agent for April 11, 1917.

21. *Debs v. United States* can be viewed at https://supreme.justia.com/cases/federal /us/249/211/.

22. *Olmstead v United States* can be viewed at https://supreme.justia.com/cases /federal/us/277/438/.

23. Details on *Korematsu v. United States* can be found on the United States Courts website at http://www.uscourts.gov/educational-resources/educational-activities/facts -and-case-summary-korematsu-v-us.

24. See "Katz v. United States: The Fourth Amendment adapts to new technology," via the National Constitution Center.

25. The brief official history of the Church Committee can be viewed on the Senate website at https://www.senate.gov/artandhistory/history/common/investigations /ChurchCommittee.htm.

26. The findings of the Church Committee can be found on the Senate Select Committee on Intelligence website at https://www.intelligence.senate.gov/resources /intelligence-related-commissions.

27. A very brief description of the FISC can be found on its official website at http:// www.fisc.uscourts.gov/about-foreign-intelligence-surveillance-court.

28. The text and basic legislative history of the PATRIOT Act can be viewed on Congress.gov at https://www.congress.gov/bill/107th-congress/house-bill/3162.

29. Glenn Greenwald and Spencer Ackerman, "NSA collected US email records in bulk for more than two years under Obama," *The Guardian*, June 27, 2013.

30. James Risen and Eric Lichtblau, "Bush Lets U.S. Spy on Callers Without Courts," *New York Times*, December 16, 2005.

31. The text and basic legislative history of the Protect America Act can be found on Congress.gov at https://www.congress.gov/bill/110th-congress/senate-bill/1927.

32. The text and basic legislative history of the FISA Amendments Act can be found on Congress.gov at https://www.congress.gov/bill/110th-congress/house-bill /6304.

33. Glenn Greenwald, "NSA collecting phone records of millions of Verizon custom-ers daily," *The Guardian*, June 6, 2013.

34. Patrick G. Eddington, "The Patriot Act Is Not Fit for Purpose. Nor Is Its Replacement," *Newsweek*, June 1, 2015.

35. For details, see section 5 of *the FBI Domestic Investigations and Operations Guide*, https://fas.org/irp/agency/doj/fbi/diog.pdf.

Chapter 9

1. Douglas A. Irwin, *Clashing over Commerce: A History of US Trade Policy* (Chicago: University of Chicago Press, 2017).

2. Gary Clyde Hufbauer and Zhiyao (Lucy) Lu, "The Payoff to America from Globalization: A Fresh Look with a Focus on Costs to Workers," Peterson Institute for International Economics Policy Brief 16–17, May 2017.

3. Frédéric Bastiat, *Economic Sophisms*, trans. Patrick James Stirling (New York: G. P. Putnam's Sons, 1922), pp. 69–70, as quoted in Leland B. Yeager, *Free Trade: America's Opportunity* (New York: Robert Schalkenbach Foundation, 1954), p. 13.

4. U.S. International Trade Commission (USITC) DataWeb (website).

5. USITC DataWeb (website).

6. For more details on "Buy American" restrictions, see Daniel Ikenson, "The False Promise of 'Buy American,'" *Cato at Liberty* (blog) January 20, 2017, https://www.cato.org/blog/false-promise-buy-american.

7. For more details on commercial airline restrictions, see Kenneth J. Button, "Opening the Skies: Put Free Trade in Airline Services on the Transatlantic Trade Agenda," Cato Institute Policy Analysis no. 757, September 15, 2014.

8. For more details on maritime shipping restrictions, see Colin Grabow, Inu Manak, and Daniel Ikenson, "The Jones Act: A Burden America Can No Longer Bear," Cato Institute Policy Analysis no. 845, June 28, 2018.

9. For more details on protectionism masquerading as a national security imperative, see Daniel Ikenson, "The Danger of Invoking National Security to Rationalize Protectionism," *China-US Focus*, May 15, 2017.

10. For more details on restrictions on trade in health care and education services, see Simon Lester, "Expanding Trade in Medical Care through Telemedicine," Cato Institute Policy Analysis no. 769, March 24, 2015; and Simon Lester, "Liberalizing Cross-Border Trade in Higher Education: The Coming Revolution of Online Universities," Cato Institute Policy Analysis no. 720, February 5, 2013.

11. For more details on occupational licensing, see Angela C. Erickson, "The Tangled Mess of Occupational Licensing," Cato Policy Report, September–October 2018.

12. Bureau of Economic Analysis, National Income and Product Accounts, Employment by Industry, Table 6.5D: Full-Time Equivalent Employees by Industry, https://www.bea.gov/data/employment/employment-by-industry.

13. Bureau of Economic Analysis, Gross Domestic Product by Industry, Table 5: Value Added by Industry Group.

14. Bureau of Economic Analysis.

15. Bureau of Economic Analysis.

16. Bradley Sawyer and Cynthia Cox, "How Does Health Spending in the U.S. Compare to Other Countries?" Peterson-Kaiser Health System Tracker, February 13, 2018.

17. "Education Expenditures by Country," National Center for Education Statistics (website), https://nces.ed.gov/programs/coe/indicator_cmd.asp.

18. Beth Braverman, "1.4 Million Americans Will Go Abroad for Medical Care This Year. Should You?" *Fiscal Times*, August 17, 2016.

19. "Trends in U.S. Study Abroad," NAFSA (website), https://www.nafsa.org/policy -and-advocacy/policy-resources/trends-us-study-abroad.

20. Lester, "Expanding Trade in Medical Care."

21. Lester, "Liberalizing Cross-Border Trade in Higher Education."

Chapter 10

1. James A. R. Nafziger, "The General Admission of Aliens under International Law," *American Journal of International Law* 77, no. 4 (1983): 804–47, https://doi.org /10.2307/2202535; Ilya Somin, "Immigration, Freedom, and the Constitution," *Harvard Journal of Law and Public Policy* 40, no. 1 (2017): 1–7.

2. Claudia Goldin, "The Political Economy of Immigration Restriction in the United States, 1890 to 1921," in *The Regulated Economy: A Historical Approach to Political Economy*, ed. Claudia Goldin and Gary D. Libecap (Chicago: University of Chicago Press, 1994).

3. "1869: Frederick Douglass Describes the 'Composite Nation,'" BlackPast, January 28, 2007, http://www.blackpast.org/1869-frederick-douglass-describes-composite-nation.

4. Tanvi Misra, "The Long, Strange History of Non-Citizen Voting," CityLab, November 7, 2016, https://www.citylab.com/equity/2016/11/the-long-strange-history -of-non-citizen-voting/504974/.

5. Alex Nowrasteh, "The Failure of the Americanization Movement," *Cato at Liberty* (blog), December 18, 2014, https://www.cato.org/blog/failure-americanization-movement/.

6. Nowrasteh, "Failure of the Americanization Movement."

7. Nowrasteh, "Failure of the Americanization Movement"; Vasiliki Fouka, "Backlash: The Unintended Effects of Language Prohibition in U.S. Schools after World War I," Stanford Center for International Development Working Paper no. 591, December 2016.

8. About half of the number who actually migrated between 1916 and 1970. Wikipedia's "Great Migration (African-American)," entry, https://en.wikipedia.org/wiki /Great_Migration_(African_American).

9. The real-world U.S. population at this time was only about 100 million.

10. Seymour Martin Lipset and Gary Marks, *It Didn't Happen Here: Why Socialism Failed in the United States* (New York: W. W. Norton, 2000).

11. This law is modeled on the policy positions of the Know-Nothing Party in the 1850s. *Encyclopaedia Britannica Online*, https://www.britannica.com/topic/Know -Nothing-party.

12. Milton Friedman and Anna Jacobson Schwartz, *A Monetary History of the United States, 1897–1960* (Princeton, NJ: Princeton University Press, 1963).

13. Wikipedia's "Wall Street Crash of 1929" entry, https://en.wikipedia.org/wiki/Wall_Street_Crash_of_1929.

14. Tom Nicholas and Anna Scherbina, "Real Estate Prices during the Roaring Twenties and the Great Depression," *Real Estate Economics* 41, no. 2 (2012): 278–309, https://doi.org/10.1111/j.1540-6229.2012.00346.x.

15. Joseph Bishop-Henchman, "How Taxes Enabled Alcohol Prohibition and Also Led to Its Repeal," Tax Foundation, October 5, 2011, https://taxfoundation.org/how-taxes-enabled-alcohol-prohibition-and-also-led-its-repeal/.

16. Wikipedia's "Smoot-Hawley Tariff Act" entry, https://en.wikipedia.org/wiki/Smoot%E2%80%93Hawley_Tariff_Act.

17. Wikipedia's "James Wolcott Wadsworth, Jr." entry, https://en.wikipedia.org/wiki/James_Wolcott_Wadsworth,_Jr.

18. Michelangelo Landgrave and Alex Nowrasteh, "Voice, Exit, and Liberty: The Effect of Emigration on Origin Country Institutions," *Economic Development Bulletin*, no. 25, May 26, 2016.

19. Mihir Zaveri, "Anne Frank's Family Was Thwarted by U.S. Immigration Rules, Research Shows," *New York Times*, July 6, 2018, https://www.nytimes.com/2018/07/06/us/anne-frank-family-escape-usa.html.

20. "Scientist Refugees and the Manhattan Project," Atomic Heritage Foundation, January 27, 2019, https://www.atomicheritage.org/article/scientist-refugees-and-manhattan-project.

21. Wikipedia's "Charles Lindbergh" entry, https://en.wikipedia.org/wiki/Charles_Lindbergh.

22. Allan Carlson, "The Family Factors: Lessons from History about the Future of Marriage and Family in the United States," *Touchstone*, January–February 2006, https://www.touchstonemag.com/archives/article.php?id=19-01-023-f.

23. Wikipedia's "General Agreement on Tariffs and Trade" entry, https://en.wikipedia.org/wiki/General_Agreement_on_Tariffs_and_Trade.

24. Landgrave and Nowrasteh, "Voice, Exit, and Liberty."

Chapter 11

1. Kenneth N. Waltz, "The Emerging Structure of International Politics," *International Security* 18 (1993): 44–79, https://doi.org/10.2307/2539097.

2. Dov H. Levin, "When the Great Power Gets a Vote: The Effects of Great Power Electoral Interventions on Election Results," *International Studies Quarterly* 60, no. 2 (2016): 189–202, https://doi.org/10.1093/isq/sqv016.

3. Stephen Watts et al., *A More Peaceful World? Regional Conflict Trends and U.S. Defense Planning* (Santa Monica, CA: RAND Corporation, 2017), p. xxii, https://doi.org/10.7249/RR1177.

4. Barbara Salazar Torreon, "Instances of Use of United States Armed Forces Abroad, 1798–2017," Congressional Research Service, Washington, October 12, 2017, https://fas.org/sgp/crs/natsec/R42738.pdf.

5. Nick Turse, "Donald Trump's First Year Set a Record for Use of Special Operations Forces," *Nation*, December 14, 2017.

6. John Glaser, "Withdrawing from Overseas Bases: Why a Forward-Deployed Military Posture Is Unnecessary, Outdated, and Dangerous," Cato Institute Policy Analysis no. 816, July 18, 2017.

7. Caroline Dorminey and Trevor Thrall, "Risky Business: The Role of Arms Sales in U.S. Foreign Policy," Cato Institute Policy Analysis no. 836, March 13, 2018.

8. Office of Management and Budget, "Historical Table 8.2—Outlays by Budget Enforcement Act Category in Constant (FY2009) Dollars: 1962–2022." From FY1990 to FY2017, the U.S. government incurred $14.3673 trillion worth of outlays for the national defense. This estimate is in constant FY2009 dollars.

9. Randolph Bourne, *The State*, ca. 1918. Published posthumously.

10. John Chester Miller, *Crisis in Freedom: The Alien and Sedition Acts* (Boston: Little, Brown, 1951).

11. Woodrow Wilson, Third Annual Message to Congress, December 7, 1915, http://www.presidency.ucsb.edu/ws/index.php?pid=29556.

12. Bruce D. Porter, *War and the Rise of the State: The Military Foundations of Modern Politics* (New York: Free Press, 1994), p. 273.

13. Porter, *War and the Rise of the State*, p. 273.

14. Susan A. Brewer, *Why America Fights: Patriotism and War Propaganda from the Philippines to Iraq* (Oxford and New York: Oxford University Press, 2009), p. 69.

15. Charlie Savage, "Judge Questions Legality of N.S.A. Phone Records," *New York Times*, December 16, 2013.

16. Matthew Weed, "Presidential References to the 2001 Authorization for Use of Military Force in Publicly Available Executive Actions and Reports to Congress," memorandum, Congressional Research Service, May 11, 2016, https://fas.org/sgp/crs/natsec/pres-aumf.pdf.

17. Dara Lind, "Cops Do 20,000 No-Knock Raids a Year. Civilians Often Pay the Price When They Go Wrong," *Vox*, May 15, 2015, https://www.vox.com/2014/10/29/7083371/swat-no-knock-raids-police-killed-civilians-dangerous-work-drugs.

18. Blaine Harden, "The U.S. War Crime North Korea Won't Forget," *Washington Post*, March 24, 2015, https://www.washingtonpost.com/opinions/the-us-war-crime-north-korea-wont-forget/2015/03/20/fb525694-ce80-11e4-8c54-ffb5ba6f2f69_story.html.

19. Mai Elliott, *RAND in Southeast Asia: A History of the Vietnam War Era* (Santa Monica, CA: RAND Corporation, 2010), p. 75; "Draft Memorandum from John McNaughton to Robert McNamara, 'Proposed Course of Action Re: Vietnam,'" March 24, 1965, in *The Pentagon Papers*, Gravel edition, vol. 3, ed. Mike Gravel (Boston: Beacon Press, 1971), pp. 694–702.

20. Nick Turse, *Kill Anything That Moves: The Real American War in Vietnam* (New York: Metropolitan Books, 2013), p. 79.

21. United Nations, "Afghanistan: Protection of Civilians in Armed Conflict Annual Report 2017," Kabul, February 2018, https://unama.unmissions.org/sites/default/files/afghanistan_protection_of_civilians_annual_report_2017_final_6_march.pdf.

22. Arthur Schlesinger Jr., "Good Foreign Policy a Casualty of War," *Los Angeles Times*, March 23, 2003, http://articles.latimes.com/2003/mar/23/news/war-opschlesinger23.

23. Michael Huemer, *The Problem of Political Authority: An Examination of the Right to Coerce and the Duty to Obey* (New York: Palgrave MacMillan, 2013), pp. 288–320.

24. John Mueller, "Embracing Threatlessness: US Military Spending, Newt Gingrich, and the Costa Rica Option," in *U.S. Grand Strategy in the 21st Century: The Case for Restraint*, ed. A. Trevor Thrall and Benjamin H. Friedman (New York: Routledge, 2018), pp. 198–219.

25. Benjamin H. Friedman and Christopher A. Preble, "Budgetary Savings from Military Restraint," Cato Policy Analysis no. 667, September 23, 2010.

26. A. Trevor Thrall, "U.S. Foreign Policy and the Switzerland Test," *Cato at Liberty* (blog), November 4, 2016, https://www.cato.org/blog/us-foreign-policy-switzerland-test.

27. John Quincy Adams, Speech to the U.S. House of Representatives, July 4, 1821, https://millercenter.org/the-presidency/presidential-speeches/july-4-1821-speech-us-house-representatives-foreign-policy.

28. Niall McCarthy, "The World's Biggest Employers," *Forbes*, June 23, 2015, https://www.forbes.com/sites/niallmccarthy/2015/06/23/the-worlds-biggest-employers-infographic/#19d7fa34686b.

29. Dana Priest and William M. Arkin, "Top Secret America: A Hidden World, Growing Beyond Control," *Washington Post*, July 19, 2010, http://projects.washingtonpost.com/top-secret-america/articles/a-hidden-world-growing-beyond-control/.

30. T. X. Hammes, "Technologies Converge and Power Diffuses: The Evolution of Small, Smart, and Cheap Weapons," Cato Institute Policy Analysis no. 786, January 27, 2016.

31. Paul K. MacDonald and Joseph M. Parent, *Twilight of the Titans: Great Power Decline and Retrenchment* (Ithaca, NY: Cornell University Press, 2018).

Chapter 12

1. Herbert Spencer, *Social Statics: or, The Conditions Essential to Happiness Specified, and the First of Them Developed* (London: John Chapman, 1851), p. 396.

2. See Lawrence H. White, *Free Banking in Britain: Theory, Experience, and Debate, 1800–1845.* 2nd ed. (London: Institute of Economic Affairs, 1995).

3. Spencer, *Social Statics*, p. 402.

4. See George Selgin, *Good Money: Birmingham Buttonmakers, The Royal Mint, and the Beginnings of Modern Coinage, 1775–1821.* (Michigan: University of Michigan Press, 2008).

5. See Deniz Anginer and Asli Demirguc-Kunt, "Bank Runs and Moral Hazard: A Review of Deposit Insurance." World Bank Policy Research Working Paper WPS 8589, September 2018.

6. Lawrence H. White, "Making the Transition to the Gold Standard," in *Monetary Alternatives: Rethinking Government Fiat Money*, ed. James A. Dorn (Washington: Cato Institute, 2017), p. 217.

7. A gradually increasing purchasing power—commensurate with improvements in productivity and a consequent decline in gold's average unit cost of production—may also be acceptable. See George Selgin, *Less Than Zero: The Case for a Falling Price Level in a Growing Economy* (Washington: Cato Institute, 2018).

8. Allan H. Meltzer, *Why Capitalism?* (Oxford, UK, and New York: Oxford University Press, 2012), p. 22.

9. In brief, that law said that loose coins "deposited" with a moneychanger or banker automatically became the banker's property, which the banker might use as he or she pleased, whereas persons wanting to retain ownership of coins placed on deposit had to placed them in a sealed container. See George Selgin, "The "Bagging Rule" – Or Why We Shouldn't Arrest (All) the Bankers." *Alt-M* (blog), September 6, 2017.

10. Eric Grover, "Banks Can Succeed without the Fed," *BankThink* (blog), *American Banker*, August 15, 2017.

Chapter 13

1. Satoshi Nakamoto, "Bitcoin: A Peer-to-Peer Electronic Cash System," white paper, 2008, https://bitcoin.org/bitcoin.pdf.

2. The emerging convention seems to be to capitalize Bitcoin when referring to the network and to use small caps for individual tokens (bitcoins).

3. Vitalik Buterin, "What Is Ethereum?" Coin Center, Washington, March 9, 2016.

4. "Why Are Venezuelans Mining So Much Bitcoin?" *The Economist*, April 3, 2018.

5. John Stuart Mill, *On Liberty* (London: Penguin, 1974), p. 63.

6. Thomas Philippon, "Has the U.S. Finance Industry Become Less Efficient? On the Theory and Measurement of Financial Intermediation," *American Economic Review* 105, no. 4 (2015): 1412, https://doi.org/10.1257/aer.20120578.

7. Alex de Vries, "Bitcoin's Growing Energy Problem," *Joule* 2, no. 5 (2018): 801–5, https://doi.org/10.1016/j.joule.2018.04.016.

8. Recent data on Bitcoin's electricity needs are available from Digiconomist, https://digiconomist.net/bitcoin-energy-consumption.

9. The average transaction on the Bitcoin network (as of January 2019) is about $10,000. On the Visa network, it is $90.

10. Data on Bitcoin volume are from CoinMarketCap, https://coinmarketcap.com. For Visa, see the company's 2018 annual report, https://s1.q4cdn.com/050606653/files/doc_financials/annual/2018/Visa-2018-Annual-Report-FINAL.pdf.

11. Diego Zuluaga, "Why Bitcoin Is Not an Environmental Catastrophe," *Alt-M* (blog), September 4, 2018.

12. Monica Long, "Ripple and XRP Can Cut Banks' Global Settlement Costs Up to 60 Percent," Ripple Insights, February 23, 2016, https://ripple.com/insights/ripple-and-xrp-can-cut-banks-global-settlement-costs-up-to-60-percent/.

13. Phil Gramm and Hernando de Soto, "How Blockchain Can End Poverty," *Wall Street Journal*, January 25, 2018.

14. John Perry Barlow, "A Declaration of the Independence of Cyberspace," February 8, 1996.

Chapter 14

1. Steven Johnson, "Inside Cloudflare's Decision to Let an Extremist Stronghold Burn," *Wired*, January 16, 2018, https://www.wired.com/story/free-speech-issue-cloudflare/.

2. Rebecca Ratcliffe and Samuel Okiror, "Millions of Ugandans Quit Internet Services as Social Media Tax Takes Effect," *Guardian*, February 27, 2019, https://www.theguardian.com/global-development/2019/feb/27/millions-of-ugandans-quit-internet-after-introduction-of-social-media-tax-free-speech.

3. "Overview of the NetzDG Network Enforcement Law," Center for Democracy and Technology, July 17, 2017, https://cdt.org/insight/overview-of-the-netzdg-network-enforcement-law/.

4. Daphne Keller, "Who Do You Sue? State and Platform Hybrid Power over Online Speech," Hoover Institution Aegis Series Paper no. 1902, January 29, 2019, https://www.hoover.org/research/who-do-you-sue.

5. Wayne Ma, "Marriott Employee Roy Jones Hit 'Like.' Then China Got Mad," *Wall Street Journal*, March 3, 2018, https://www.wsj.com/articles/marriott-employee -roy-jones-hit-like-then-china-got-mad-1520094910.

6. Change the Terms—a recent anti-hate speech campaign—targeted domain registrars and payment processors as well as traditional publishing platforms. "Change the Terms FAQs," https://www.changetheterms.org/faqs.

7. VRChat users work to support a fellow chat participant having a seizure. His avatar's spasms alert them to his emergency, after which they attempt to comfort him and have medical help sent to his physical location. Rogue Shadow, "Seizure in Virtual Reality with Full Body Tracking [VRChat]," YouTube, January 17, 2018, https://www .youtube.com/watch?v=D3V0aw-ljEg.

8. Michael Fischer, T. J. Purtell, and Monica S. Lam, "Email Clients as Decentralized Social Apps in Mr. Privacy," paper presented at the 4th Hot Topics in Privacy Enhancing Technologies Symposium, Waterloo, Ontario, Canada, July 2011, https:// petsymposium.org/2011/papers/hotpets11-final1Fischer.pdf.

9. Marco Iansiti and Karim R. Lakhani, "The Truth about Blockchain," *Harvard Business Review*, January 1, 2017, pp. 118–27, https://hbr.org/2017/01/the-truth-about -blockchain.

10. Steven Johnson, "Beyond the Bitcoin Bubble," *New York Times*, January 16, 2018, https://www.nytimes.com/2018/01/16/magazine/beyond-the-bitcoin-bubble.html.

11. Brady Dale, "Turkey Can't Block This Copy of Wikipedia," *Observer*, May 10, 2017, https://observer.com/2017/05/turkey-wikipedia-ipfs/.

12. Megan Farokhmanesh, "The Anti-Sex Trafficking Crackdown Is Pushing Sex Workers to Mastodon," *The Verge*, April 11, 2018, https://www.theverge.com/2018 /4/11/17188772/trump-sesta-fosta-bill-switter-sex-workers-mastodon.

13. Jeffrey Lee, "How Mesh Networking Will Make IoT Real," Hacker Noon, May 8, 2018, https://hackernoon.com/how-mesh-networking-will-make-iot-real-b5b88baab63b.

14. Chris Cook and Ben Teitelbaum, "On Air: Lightning-Powered Data Broadcasts from Space," Blockstream, January 16, 2019, https://blockstream.com/2019/01/16 /satellite_api_beta_live/.

15. Victoria Turk, "The DIY Tool to Silence Twitter Harassment," Motherboard, December 9, 2014, https://motherboard.vice.com/en_us/article/qkvepm/the-diy-tool -to-silence-harassment-on-twitter.

Chapter 15

1. Derek Thompson, "The 100-Year March of Technology in 1 Graph," *Atlantic*, April 7, 2012, https://www.theatlantic.com/technology/archive/2012/04/the-100-year-march-of-technology-in-1-graph/255573/.

2. Alex Hern, "Amazon Claims First Successful Prime Air Drone Delivery," *Guardian*, December 14, 2016, https://www.theguardian.com/technology/2016/dec/14/amazon-claims-first-successful-prime-air-drone-delivery.

3. Frederic Lardinois, "Flytenow Shuts Down after Court Rules against Flightsharing Startups," TechCrunch, December 22, 2015, https://techcrunch.com/2015/12/22/flytenow-shuts-down-after-court-rules-against-flightsharing-startups/.

4. Anna Vlasits, "How 23andMe Won Back the Right to Foretell Your Diseases," *Wired*, April 8, 2017, https://www.wired.com/2017/04/23andme-won-back-right-foretell-diseases/. See also Ron Bailey, "Let My Genes Go! And Leave 23andMe Alone," *Reason*, November 29, 2013, http://reason.com/archives/2013/11/29/why-the-fda-should-leave-23andme-alone.

5. Adam Thierer, "Evasive Entrepreneurs and Permissionless Innovation," interview by Chad Reese, *Bridge*, September 11, 2018, https://www.mercatus.org/bridge/commentary/evasive-entrepreneurs-and-permissionless-innovation.

6. Satoshi Nakamoto, "Bitcoin: A Peer-to-Peer Electronic Cash System," white paper, 2008, https://bitcoin.org/bitcoin.pdf.

7. National Academies of Sciences, Engineering, and Medicine, *Assessing the Risks of Integrating Unmanned Aircraft Systems into the National Airspace System* (Washington: National Academies Press, 2018), https://doi.org/10.17226/25143.

8. *The Suicide Club*, exhibit, Smithsonian National Postal Museum, Washington, https://postalmuseum.si.edu/exhibits/current/airmail-in-america/some-early-pilots/the-suicide-club.html.

9. *Suicide Club* exhibit.

10. "Hours-Based Fatal Injury Rates by Industry, Occupation, and Selected Demographic Characteristics," Census of Fatal Occupational Injuries, Current and Revised Data, Bureau of Labor Statistics, https://www.bls.gov/iif/oshcfoi1.htm#rates.

11. "Hours-Based Fatal Injury Rates."

12. David Boaz, "What If Newspapers Reported the Real News about Human Progress?" *Cato at Liberty* (blog), March 8, 2018, https://www.cato.org/blog/what-newspapers-reported-real-news-about-human-progress.

13. Christopher Mims, "What's the Next Big Thing in Tech? It's Up to Us," *Wall Street Journal*, November 16, 2018, https://www.wsj.com/articles/whats-the-next-big-thing-in-tech-its-up-to-us-1542376800.

14. John F. Kennedy, "Special Message to the Congress on Urgent National Needs," May 25, 1961.

15. "Mobile Fact Sheet" webpage, Pew Research Center, February 5, 2018, http://www.pewinternet.org/fact-sheet/mobile/.

16. Edd Gent, "These Tiny Robots Could Be Disease-Fighting Machines inside the Body: Nanobots Could Provide Cancer Treatment Free from Side Effects," *NBC News*, March 30, 2018, https://www.nbcnews.com/mach/science/these-tiny-robots-could-be-disease-fighting-machines-inside-body-ncna861451.

17. Hasan Chowdhury, "Liver Success Holds Promise of 3D Organ Printing," *Financial Times*, March 5, 2018, https://www.ft.com/content/67e3ab88-f56f-11e7-a4c9-bbdefa4f210b.

18. "Organ Donation Statistics" webpage, HRSA Division of Transplantation, https://www.organdonor.gov/statistics-stories/statistics.html.

19. Trevor English, "Nanobots Will Be Flowing through Your Body by 2030," *Interesting Engineering*, April 25, 2017, https://interestingengineering.com/nanobots-will-flowing-body-2030.

20. Christina Rogawski, Stefaan Verhulst, and Andrew Young, "NOAA Open Data Portal: Creating a New Industry through Access to Weather Data," Open Data's Impact, January 2016, http://odimpact.org/files/case-studies-noaa.pdf.

21. These recommendations are based on proposals outlined by Caleb Watney: Caleb Watney, "Reducing entry barriers in the development and application of AI," R Street Institute Policy Study no. 153, October 9, 2018. https://www.rstreet.org/2018/10/09/reducing-entry-barriers-in-the-development-and-application-of-ai/.

Chapter 16

1. Christopher Hill, *The World Turned Upside Down: Radical Ideas during the English Revolution* (New York: Viking Press, 1972).

2. John Frantz, ed., *Bacon's Rebellion: Prologue to the Revolution?* (Lexington, MA: D. C. Heath, 1969); Joseph Kelly, *Marooned: Jamestown, Shipwreck, and a New History of America's Origin* (New York and London: Bloomsbury Publishing, 2018); Sidney Lens, *Radicalism in America: Great Rebels and the Causes for Which They Fought from 1620 to the Present* (New York: Thomas Crowell, 1969); Staughton Lynd, *Intellectual Origins of American Radicalism* (New York: Pantheon Books, 1968); Gary Nash, *Red, White, and Black: The People of Early North America*, 5th ed. (Upper Saddle River, NJ: Prentice-Hall, 2006); Peter Linebaugh and Marcus Rediker, *Many-Headed Hydra: The Hidden History of the Revolutionary Atlantic* (Boston: Beacon Press, 2000); Alan Taylor, *American Colonies: The Settling of North America* (New York: Penguin Books, 2001).

3. C. A. Bayly, *The Birth of the Modern World, 1780–1914: Global Connections and Comparisons* (Malden, MA: Blackwell Publishing, 2004); Craig Calhoun, *The Roots of Radicalism: Tradition, the Public Sphere, and Early Nineteenth-Century Social Movements* (Chicago: University of Chicago Press, 2012); Daniel Walker Howe, *What Hath God Wrought: The Transformation of America, 1815–1848* (New York: Oxford University Press, 2007); Lewis Perry, *Radical Abolitionism: Anarchy and the Government of God in Antislavery Thought* (Ithaca, NY: Cornell University Press, 1973).

4. Sarah C. O'Dowd, *A Rhode Island Original: Frances Harriet Whipple Green McDougall* (Hanover, NH: University Press of New England, 2004).

Chapter 17

1. Brad Tuttle, "Lots of Your Favorite Things Could Cost More if Trump Adds a 20% Mexican Import Tax," *Money*, January 27, 2017, http://money.com/money/4651919/trump-import-tax-mexico-build-wall/; Kevin Baker, "The Politicization of Everything," *Politico*, January 31, 2017, https://www.politico.com/magazine/story/2017/01/the-politicization-of-everything-214714.

2. Robert N. Charette, "The Long Journey to FEMA's Presidential Alert Test," *IEEE Spectrum*, October 5, 2018, https://spectrum.ieee.org/riskfactor/computing/networks/the-long-journey-to-femas-presidential-alert-test; "The IPAWS National Test," fact sheet, October 3, 2018, https://www.fema.gov/emergency-alert-test.

3. H. L. Roediger III and K. A. DeSoto, "Forgetting the Presidents," *Science* 346, no. 6213 (November 28, 2014): 1106, https://doi.org10.1126/science.1259627.

4. Clinton Rossiter, *The American Presidency* (New York: Harcourt, Brace, 1956; Baltimore: Johns Hopkins University Press, 1987), pp. 2–3.

5. Jenna Johnson, "'I Will Give You Everything.' Here Are 282 of Donald Trump's Campaign Promises," *Washington Post*, November 28, 2016, https://www.washingtonpost.com/politics/i-will-give-you-everything-here-are-282-of-donald-trumps-campaign-promises/2016/11/24/01160678-b0f9-11e6-8616-52b15787add0_story.html?utm_term=.0e70ed463d3d.

6. Donald J. Trump (@realDonaldTrump), "Wisconsin has suffered a great loss of jobs and trade, but if I win, all of the bad things happening in the U.S. will be rapidly reversed!" Twitter, April 2, 2016, https://twitter.com/realdonaldtrump/status/716222480738869248?lang=en.

7. George E. Reedy, *The Twilight of the Presidency* (New York: Mentor Press, 1970; New York: New American Library, 1987), pp. 1, 4.

8. Peter Augustine Lawler, "The Federalist's Hostility to Leadership and the Crisis of the Contemporary Presidency," *Presidential Studies Quarterly* 17, no. 4 (1987): 712.

9. Alexander Hamilton, *The Federalist Papers*, Nos. 1 and 85, in *The Federalist*, ed. George Carey and James McClellan (Indianapolis: Liberty Fund, 2001), pp. 2, 457.

10. Hamilton, *Federalist Papers*, No. 71, in *The Federalist*, ed. Carey and McClellan, p. 371.

11. Jeffrey Tulis, *The Rhetorical Presidency* (Princeton, NJ: Princeton University Press, 1987), p. 64.

12. Max Farrand, ed., *The Records of the Federal Convention of 1787*, vol. 2 (New Haven, CT: Yale University Press, 1911), https://oll.libertyfund.org/titles/farrand-the-records -of-the-federal-convention-of-1787-vol-2#Farrand_0544-02_2016.

13. James T. Patterson, "Rise of Presidential Power before World War II," *Law and Contemporary Problems* 40, no. 2 (1976): 54.

14. Hamilton, *Federalist Papers*, No. 69, in *The Federalist*, ed. Carey and McClellan, p. 357.

15. See, for example, David K. Nichols, *The Myth of the Modern Presidency* (University Park: Pennsylvania State University Press, 1994).

16. James Bryce, "Why Great Men Are Not Chosen Presidents," *The American Commonwealth* (London and New York: Macmillan and Co., 1891), p. 104–5.

17. William G. Howell and David E. Lewis, "Agencies by Presidential Design," *Journal of Politics* 64, no. 4 (2002): 1096, https://doi.org/10.1111/1468-2508.00164. "Presidents also were less likely [than Congress] to create agencies governed by independent boards or commissions. . . . [A]gencies created through executive action almost always reported directly to the president" p. 1099.

18. Gene Healy, "Take Me to Our 'Moral Leader'!" *Cato at Liberty* (blog), August 23, 2017, https://www.cato.org/blog/take-me-our-moral-leader.

19. Patterson, "Rise of Presidential Power," p. 39.

20. Patterson, "Rise of Presidential Power," p. 54.

21. Reedy, *Twilight of the Presidency*, p. 9.

22. Herbert Croly, *The Promise of American Life* (New York: MacMillan Company, 1909), p. 174.

23. See Stephen Skowronek, "The Conservative Insurgency and Presidential Power: A Developmental Perspective on the Unitary Executive," *Harvard Law Review* 122, no. 8 (2009): 2070–2103.

24. David Bergland, *Libertarianism in One Lesson* (Costa Mesa, CA: Orpheus Publications, 1984).

25. Aaron Wildavsky, "The Past and Future of the Presidency," *Public Interest* (Fall 1975): 56–76, https://www.nationalaffairs.com/public_interest/detail/the-past -and-future-presidency.

26. Juan J. Linz, "The Perils of Presidentialism," *Journal of Democracy* 1, no. 1 (1990): 51–69.

27. Although see Tom Ginsburg and Aziz Z. Huq, *How to Save a Constitutional Democracy* (Chicago: University of Chicago Press, 2019), pp. 179–80, suggesting that "unstable countries tend to choose presidentialism."

28. F. H. Buckley, *The Once and Future King: The Rise of Crown Government in America* (New York: Encounter Books, 2014), p. 177.

29. Ginsburg and Huq, *How to Save a Constitutional Democracy*, p. 183.

30. Jenny S. Martinez, "Inherent Executive Power: A Comparative Perspective," *Yale Law Journal* 115, no. 9 (2006): 2491–92, https://doi.org/10.2307/20455703.

31. Spencer Ackerman and Nicholas Watt, "Syria Crisis: Obama 'Has the Right' to Strike Regardless of Vote, Says Kerry," *Guardian*, September 2, 2013, https://www.theguardian.com/world/2013/sep/01/obama-strike-syria-congress-kerry.

32. Linz, "Perils of Presidentialism," p. 61.

33. "Tasks of the Federal Presidency," Swiss Government website, https://www.admin.ch/gov/en/start/federal-presidency/tasks-federal-presidency.html.

34. Karl Lowenstein, "The Presidency Outside the United States: A Study in Comparative Political Institutions," *Journal of Politics* 11, no. 3 (1949): 475, https://doi.org/10.2307/2126136.

35. Caroline Bishop, "Swiss Leader's Commute Turns Twitter Sensation," The Local (Switzerland), September 4, 2014, https://www.thelocal.ch/20140904/burkhalters-solo-train-journey-goes-viral.

36. Liam Stack, "The Best Country in the World? Survey Says It's Switzerland," *New York Times*, March 7, 2017, https://www.nytimes.com/2017/03/07/world/best-countries-world-switzerland-canada-britain-germany.html.

37. Christopher R. Berry and Jacob E. Gersen, "The Unbundled Executive," Public Law and Legal Theory Working Paper no. 214, University of Chicago Law School, March 2008.

38. William P. Marshall, "Break Up the Presidency? Governors, State Attorneys General, and Lessons from the Divided Executive," *Yale Law Journal* 115, no. 9 (2006): 2446, https://doi.org/10.2307/20455702.

39. Charles L. Black Jr., "The Working Balance of the American Political Departments," Faculty Scholarship Series no. 2601, 1974, http://digitalcommons.law.yale.edu/fss_papers/2601.

Chapter 18

1. F. A. Hayek, *Law, Legislation and Liberty*, vol. 2: *The Mirage of Social Justice* (Chicago: University of Chicago Press, 1967), p. 20.

Index

Note: Page numbers followed by f or t indicate figures and tables, respectively. Page numbers with "n" or "nn" indicate notes.

About the Editors

Aaron Ross Powell is director and editor of Libertarianism.org, which presents introductory material as well as new scholarship related to libertarian philosophy, theory, and history. He is also the cohost of the podcast *Free Thoughts*. His writing has appeared in the *Washington Post*, *Liberty*, and the *Cato Journal*. He earned a JD from the University of Denver.

Paul Matzko is the assistant editor for tech and innovation at Libertarianism.org. He received a PhD in history from Pennsylvania State University with a dissertation on the John F. Kennedy administration's successful efforts to censor right-wing radio broadcasters in the 1960s. He has published articles in *Presidential Studies Quarterly* and *Fides et Historia*.

About the Contributors

David Boaz is the executive vice president of the Cato Institute and has played a key role in the development of the Cato Institute and the libertarian movement. He is the author of *The Libertarian Mind: A Manifesto for Freedom* (Simon & Schuster, 2015) and the editor of *The Libertarian Reader: Classic & Contemporary Writings from Lao-Tzu to Milton Friedman* (Simon & Schuster, 2015).

Trevor Burrus is a research fellow in the Cato Institute's Robert A. Levy Center for Constitutional Studies, editor in chief of the *Cato Supreme Court Review*, and cohost of "Free Thoughts," a podcast from Libertarianism.org.

Michael F. Cannon is the Cato Institute's director of health policy studies. Cannon has been described as "an influential health-care wonk" (*Washington Post*), "ObamaCare's single most relentless antagonist" (*New Republic*), and "ObamaCare's fiercest critic" (*The Week*). Cannon is the coeditor of *Replacing Obamacare: The Cato Institute on Health Care Reform* (Cato Institute, 2012) and coauthor of *Healthy Competition: What's Holding Back Health Care and How to Free It* (Cato Institute, 2007).

Anthony Comegna received his PhD studying early American, Atlantic, and intellectual history at the University of Pittsburgh. He is the world's expert on the Locofoco movement and advocates "thick" libertarian futurism. He is currently the programs manager for internal discussion colloquia and advanced topics seminars at the Institute for Humane Studies. Comegna has been a frequent guest on the *Cato Daily Podcast*, and he often writes for *Reason* magazine.

Will Duffield is a research associate with the Cato Institute's Center for Representative Government, where he studies internet governance. He holds a BA from Sarah Lawrence College and an MSc in political theory from the London School of Economics.

Patrick G. Eddington is a research fellow in homeland security and civil liberties at the Cato Institute. From 2004 to 2014, he served as communications director and later as senior policy advisor to Rep. Rush Holt (D-NJ). Eddington's legislative portfolio included the full range of security-related issues, with an emphasis on intelligence policy reform in the areas of surveillance, detainee interrogation, and the use of drones, in both overseas and domestic contexts. He is also adjunct assistant professor at Georgetown University's Center for Security Studies. From 1988 to 1996, Eddington was a military imagery analyst at the CIA's National Photographic Interpretation Center.

Matthew Feeney is the director of the Cato Institute's Project on Emerging Technologies, where he works on issues concerning the intersection of new technologies and civil liberties. Before joining Cato, Feeney worked at *Reason* magazine as assistant editor of Reason.com. He has also worked at the *American Conservative*, the Liberal Democrats, and the Institute of Economic Affairs. Feeney received both his BA and MA in philosophy from the University of Reading.

John Glaser is director of foreign policy studies at the Cato Institute. He is a coauthor, with Christopher A. Preble and A. Trevor Thrall, of *Fuel to the Fire: How Trump Made America's Broken Foreign Policy Even Worse (and How We Can Recover)* (Cato Institute, 2019). Glaser earned an MA in international security at the Schar School of Policy and Government at George Mason University and a BA in political science from the University of Massachusetts Amherst.

Gene Healy is a vice president at the Cato Institute. His research interests include executive power and the role of the presidency as well as federalism and overcriminalization. He is the author of *False Idol: Barack Obama and the Continuing Cult of the Presidency* (Cato Institute, 2012) and *The Cult of the Presidency: America's Dangerous Devotion to Executive Power* (Cato Institute, 2008), and he is editor of *Go Directly to Jail: The Criminalization of Almost Everything* (Cato Institute, 2004). Healy holds a BA from Georgetown University and a JD from the University of Chicago Law School.

Daniel J. Ikenson is director of the Cato Institute's Herbert A. Stiefel Center for Trade Policy Studies, where he coordinates and conducts research on all manner of international trade and investment policy. Since joining Cato in 2000, Ikenson has written and spoken extensively about numerous aspects of trade policy, including U.S.-China trade relations; bilateral and multilateral trade agreements and institutions; globalization; U.S. manufacturing issues; trade politics; and trade protectionism.

Terence Kealey trained as an MD at London University and earned a PhD in biochemistry at Oxford University before lecturing for many years in clinical biochemistry at Cambridge University. In 2000, he became vice chancellor (president) of the University of Buckingham, Britain's first independent university. Since 2014, he has been a researcher at the Cato Institute.

Jason Kuznicki is the editor of Cato Books and of *Cato Unbound*, the Cato Institute's online journal of debate. His first book, *Technology and the End of Authority: What Is Government For?* (Palgrave Macmillan, 2017), surveys western political theory from a libertarian perspective. His second book, now in progress, will look at the role of imprisonment in political theory. Kuznicki was an assistant editor of the *Encyclopedia of Libertarianism*. He earned a PhD in history from Johns Hopkins University in 2005, where his work was offered both a Fulbright Fellowship and a Chateaubriand Prize.

Neal P. McCluskey is the director of the Cato Institute's Center for Educational Freedom. He is the author of the book *Feds in* *the Classroom: How Big Government Corrupts, Cripples, and Compromises American Education* (Rowman & Littlefield, 2007) and is coeditor of *Educational Freedom: Remembering Andrew Coulson, Debating His Ideas* and *Unprofitable Schooling: Examining Causes of, and Fixes for, America's Broken Ivory Tower* (Cato Institute, 2019). McCluskey holds a PhD in public policy from George Mason University.

Patrick J. Michaels is a senior fellow with the Competitive Enterprise Institute and former director of the Center for the Study of Science at the Cato Institute. He is the coauthor of several books, including *Lukewarming: The New Climate Science That Changes Everything* and *Climate of Extremes: Global Warming Science They Don't Want You to Know*, and he is the coeditor of *Scientocracy: The Tangled Web of Public Science and Public Policy*. Michaels holds AB and SM degrees in biological sciences and plant ecology from the University of Chicago, and he received a PhD in ecological climatology from the University of Wisconsin at Madison.

Clark Neily is vice president for criminal justice at the Cato Institute. Prior to joining Cato, he was a constitutional litigator at the Institute for Justice, and he served as cocounsel in *District of Columbia v. Heller*. He is the author of *Terms of Engagement: How Our Courts Should Enforce the Constitution's Promise of Limited Government* (Encounter Books, 2013).

Alex Nowrasteh is the director of immigration studies at the Cato Institute. His peer-reviewed academic publications have appeared in the *World Bank Economic Review*, the *Journal of Economic Behavior and Organization*, *Economic Affairs*, the *Fletcher Security Review*, the *Journal of Bioeconomics*, and *Public Choice*. He is a coauthor of the booklet *Open Immigration: Yea and Nay* (Encounter Broadsides, 2014) and of a forthcoming book for Cambridge University Press. Nowrasteh is a native of southern California, and he received a BA in economics from George Mason University and an MS in economic history from the London School of Economics.

George Selgin is a senior fellow and director of the Center for Monetary and Financial Alternatives at the Cato Institute and a professor emeritus of economics at the University of Georgia. He is the author of *The Theory of Free Banking* (Rowman & Littlefield, 1988); *Bank Deregulation and Monetary Order* (Routledge, 1996); *Less Than Zero: The Case for a Falling Price Level in a Growing Economy* (The Institute of Economic Affairs, 1997); *Good Money: Birmingham Button Makers, the Royal Mint, and the Beginnings of Modern Coinage* (University of Michigan Press, 2008); and, most recently, *Floored!: How a Misguided Fed Experiment Deepened and Prolonged the Great Recession* (Cato Institute, 2018). Selgin is one of the founders, along with Kevin Dowd and Lawrence H. White, of the Modern Free Banking School. He holds a BA in economics and zoology from Drew University and a PhD in economics from New York University.

Michael D. Tanner is a senior fellow with the Cato Institute, where he leads research on a variety of domestic policy issues, including social welfare, poverty, heath care, retirement, and entitlements. His most recent book, *The Inclusive Economy: How to Bring Wealth to America's Poor* (Cato Institute, 2018), looks at the ways government contributes to poverty in the United States and suggests reforms that will enable the poor to more fully participate in a growing economy.

Diego Zuluaga is a policy analyst at the Cato Institute's Center for Monetary and Financial Alternatives, where he covers financial technology and regulation. He frequently writes and speaks on cryptocurrencies and blockchain technology from a regulatory perspective. Prior to joining Cato, Zuluaga was head of financial services and tech policy at the Institute of Economic Affairs. Originally from Bilbao in northern Spain, Zuluaga holds a BA in economics and history from McGill University and an MSc in financial economics from the University of Oxford.

Libertarianism.org

Liberty. It's a simple idea and the linchpin of a complex system of values and practices: justice, prosperity, responsibility, toleration, cooperation, and peace. Many people believe that liberty is the core political value of modern civilization itself, the one that gives substance and form to all the other values of social life. They're called libertarians.

Libertarianism.org is the Cato Institute's treasury of resources about the theory and history of liberty. The book you're holding is a small part of what Libertarianism.org has to offer. In addition to hosting classic texts by historical libertarian figures and original articles from modern-day thinkers, Libertarianism.org publishes podcasts, videos, online introductory courses, and books on a variety of topics within the libertarian tradition.

Cato Institute

Founded in 1977, the Cato Institute is a public policy research foundation dedicated to broadening the parameters of policy debate to allow consideration of more options that are consistent with the principles of limited government, individual liberty, and peace. To that end, the Institute strives to achieve greater involvement of the intelligent, concerned lay public in questions of policy and the proper role of government.

The Institute is named for *Cato's Letters*, libertarian pamphlets that were widely read in the American Colonies in the early 18th century and played a major role in laying the philosophical foundation for the American Revolution.

Despite the achievement of the nation's Founders, today virtually no aspect of life is free from government encroachment. A pervasive intolerance for individual rights is shown by government's arbitrary intrusions into private economic transactions and its disregard for civil liberties. And while freedom around the globe has notably increased in the past several decades, many countries have moved in the opposite direction, and most governments still do not respect or safeguard the wide range of civil and economic liberties.

To address those issues, the Cato Institute undertakes an extensive publications program on the complete spectrum of policy issues. Books, monographs, and shorter studies are commissioned to examine the federal budget, Social Security, regulation, military spending, international trade, and myriad other issues. Major policy conferences are held throughout the year, from which papers are published thrice yearly in the *Cato Journal*. The Institute also publishes the quarterly magazine *Regulation*.

In order to maintain its independence, the Cato Institute accepts no government funding. Contributions are received from foundations, corporations, and individuals, and other revenue is generated from the sale of publications. The Institute is a nonprofit, tax-exempt, educational foundation under Section 501(c)3 of the Internal Revenue Code.

CATO INSTITUTE
1000 Massachusetts Avenue NW
Washington, DC 20001
www.cato.org